Buddhist Monastic Discipline

Buddhist Monastic Discipline:

The Sanskrit Prātimokṣa Sūtras of the Mahāsāṃghikas and Mūlasarvāstivādins

Charles S. Prebish

The Pennsylvania State University Press
University Park and London

Published in cooperation with
The Institute for Advanced Studies of World Religions
New York, N.Y.

Library of Congress Cataloging in Publication Data

Pātimokkha. English.
Buddhist monastic discipline.

"The Mahāsāṃghika and Mūlasarvāstivādin Prātimokṣa sūtras presented face to face for easy comparison."
Bibliography: p.151
1. Monasticism and religious orders, Buddhist—Rules. 2. Sarvāstivādins. 3. Mahāsāṅghikas.
I. Prebish, Charles S., ed. II. Title.
BQ2272.E5P73 294.3'822 74-10743
ISBN 0-271-01171-8

Preface

At the outset, this book was intended to be constituted of translations, with a brief introductory exposition, of the Sanskrit Prātimokṣa Sūtras of the Mahāsāṃghika and Mūlasarvāstivādin schools of Buddhism, deemed worthy of attention primarily because they superseded reliance on the Chinese translations of the texts (and in the case of the latter school, also the Tibetan) but also because they added considerably to both our linguistic understanding of Sanskrit Buddhist texts and a careful delineation of the meaning of Prātimokṣa in Buddhist monastic discipline. As the preparation of the translations proceeded, two supervenient problems became ostensible. First, and with but few exceptions, scholars writing on Buddhism have manifestly avoided presenting anything more than a bare, rudimentary explanation of the structure and contents of the Prātimokṣa. Second, the two texts under consideration were discovered to be, in fact, considerably heterogeneous with regard to several motifs. Toward a resolution of these problems, Chapter I attempts to define the structure and contents of the Prātimokṣa in the overall context of the rise of Buddhist monasticism. Since the Prātimokṣa, as we have it today, reflects the ritual format in which it was applied, the ritualization process is also examined, with the hope of uncovering the usefulness of the Prātimokṣa as a means for implementing ethical conduct on the part of Buddhist monks (and nuns). The notes to the translations attempt to uncover bits of diversity in the two texts and, wherever possible, offer explanations or conclusions. Also included in the study is a brief chapter noting the particulars of the two texts (such as how the manuscripts were obtained, edited, and translated), a concordance table comparing the two texts translated with other Prātimokṣa texts preserved in Indic languages, and a sorely needed bibliography. Thus my original intention remains firm, and with the addition of the Mahāsāṃghika and Mūlasarvāstivādin Prātimokṣa Sūtras, presented face to face for easy comparison, we can now read the Prātimokṣa texts of the Theravādin, Sarvāstivādin, Mahāsāṃghika, and Mūlasarvāstivādin schools in their original languages. It is hoped that by a careful reading of the Prātimokṣa, augmented by an understanding of the role of monastic discipline in Buddhist life, we can further our picture of the early Buddhist situation.

The research for this book was carried out under the auspices of a Ford

Foundation Fellowship, administered by The University of Wisconsin. Initial thanks must go to Professor Stephan V. Beyer of the Department of South Asian Studies at The University of Wisconsin, who patiently read the manuscript, making many valuable suggestions and criticisms. For this important task, and for the many hours spent engaging in furious Buddhological nit-picking, I can only express my profound gratitude and warmest affections. For my wife, who patiently endured the last several years being united both to her husband and the slew of Vinaya texts strewn all over our home, and who, amidst excruciating outside pressures, provided the necessary balance to my life, I express not only my love, but also an unyielding respect. Finally, I am most deeply indebted to Professor Richard H. Robinson, who, although not surviving to share in the joy of its completion, was the motivating factor in this study. Richard infused into our academic and personal relationship, in addition to his monumental genius, the proper proportions of encouragement, reproval, and counsel, combined with a greater individual commitment than any fledgling Buddhologist had the right to expect from his learned master. Acknowledging Richard's contribution to both this study and Buddhology, I humbly dedicate my work to his memory.

University Park, Pennsylvania
April 1974

Charles S. Prebish

Contents

I

The Rise of Buddhist Monasticism: An Overview

Historical Background

Shortly following Gautama's direct experience of bodhi or "awakening," after being persuaded by Brahmā Sahampati to go forth in the world and preach his doctrine or Dharma, Buddha's first sermon was delivered in the Deer Park near Benares to his five old ascetic friends with whom he had practiced austerities for six years. In hearing Buddha's abrogation of the two extremes of pleasure seeking and strict asceticism, as well as his cardinal doctrine of the Four Noble Truths [ārya satyas], one of the ascetics, Kauṇḍinya, experienced enlightenment. Following his attainment of enlightenment, Ājñāta Kauṇḍinya (as he was now called) requested the preliminary ordination into monkhood, called "going forth" or pravrajyā, and the full ordination or upasaṃpadā. This was accomplished by Buddha's simple exhortation of "Come, O monk" [ehi bhikṣu], and thus the Saṃgha or Buddhist community was founded. In rapid succession the other four ascetics, Aśvajit, Vāṣpa, Mahānāman, and Bhadrika, attained enlightenment and were ordained as monks or "bhikṣus" by the same formula. So, in short order, the Saṃgha was expanded to six members. Buddhist literature describes in detail the rapid growth of the community in the months and years that followed, replete with a shift in both the ordination formula and those sanctioned to confer it. A passage from the Pāli Mahāvagga clearly illustrates this shift:

> At that time the monks brought to the Blessed One, from various directions and areas, those who wished to receive the pravrajyā [novitiate] ordination and those who wished to receive the upasaṃpadā [full] ordination, thinking: "The Blessed One will confer the pravrajyā and upasaṃpadā ordinations on them." Thus both the monks and those wishing to receive the pravrajyā and upasaṃpadā ordinations grew weary. Then, when the Blessed One was alone, plunged in meditation, a thought arose in his mind: "At present, the monks bring people to me from the various directions and areas wishing to receive the pravrajyā

and upasaṃpadā ordinations, thinking, 'The Blessed One will confer the pravrajyā and upasaṃadā ordinations on them,' and consequently, both the monks and those wishing to receive the pravrajyā and upasaṃpadā ordinations grow weary. What if I were to give permission to the monks, saying: 'You, O monks, may now confer pravrajyā and upasaṃpadā in the various directions and areas?'"

Then the Blessed One, emerging from meditation in the evening, on this occasion, in this connection, having preached a Dharma-discourse, said to the monks: "When I was alone, O monks, plunged in meditation, the following thought occurred to me: At that time the monks bring to the Blessed One, from various directions and areas, those who wish to receive the pravrajyā and upasaṃpadā ordinations, thinking, 'The Blessed One will confer the pravrajyā and upasaṃpadā ordinations on them.' Thus both the monks and those wishing to receive the pravrajyā and upasaṃpadā ordinations grow weary. What if I were to give permission to the monks, saying, 'You, O monks, may now confer pravrajyā and upasaṃpadā in the various directions and areas?'"

"I permit you, O monks, to confer pravrajyā and upasaṃpadā in the various directions and areas. And thus, O monks, you should confer pravrajyā and upasaṃpadā in the following way: First, having made him cut off his hair and beard, having made him put on yellow robes, having made him place the upper robe over one shoulder, having made him honor the monks' feet, having made him sit in a squatting position, and having made him perform respectful salutation with his hands, he should be told to say:

> I go to the Buddha for refuge,
> I go to the Dharma for refuge,
> I go to the Saṃgha for refuge.

Also a second time:

> I go to the Buddha for refuge,
> I go to the Dharma for refuge,
> I go to the Saṃgha for refuge.

And also a third time:

> I go to the Buddha for refuge,
> I go to the Dharma for refuge,
> I go to the Saṃgha for refuge.

I permit, O monks, the pravrajyā and upasaṃpadā ordinations by these three goings for refuge."[1]

A note of caution must be voiced here regarding the arbitrary use of the term Saṃgha in that we find in the new ordination formula the religious aspirant takes refuge in not only the Buddha and Dharma, but also in the recently established Saṃgha. Does this phrase (i.e., "I go to the Saṃgha for refuge") mean that the future bhikṣu places his confidence in the monastic order he is seeking to join? Apparently not, for we discover that the word saṃgha, literally meaning simply "group," has several applications. The primary meaning designates the saṃgha or, more properly, the ārya-saṃgha as a group of those "spiritual élite" (as Bhikshu Sangharakshita renders it)[2] who have realized the path [mārga] and fruit [phala] of one or another of the following four stages:[3]

1. Stream-winner [srotāpanna]
2. Once-returner [sakṛdāgāmin]
3. Nonreturner [anāgāmin]
4. Perfected Saint [arhant]

Thus four pairs of noble personages [ārya pudgalas] are posited, and the rest of humanity is referred to by the generic term pṛthagjana or "common people." Now there is some dispute regarding the point at which one passes from the domain of the common worldling into the domain of the ārya-saṃgha,[4] but one point is remarkably clear: membership in the saṃgha in its second important aspect as an ecclesiastical unit is not coterminous with membership in the ārya-saṃgha. In other words, because attaining membership in the group of spiritually élite is such an arduous task, not all monks and nuns, although formally being members of the ecclesiastical or monastic saṃgha [saṃvṛti-saṃgha], are necessarily members of the former group. There is an important corollary here. In its third and broadest sense, saṃgha includes not only monks [bhikṣus] and nuns [bhikṣuṇīs], but also laymen [upāsakas] and laywomen [upāsikās]. Thus, as H. Saddhatissa points out in *Buddhist Ethics*,[5] it is possible that a member of the laity may indeed have "entered the stream" and accordingly become a member of the ārya-saṃgha without ever officially becoming a part of the conventional monastic group. The point of all this careful and perhaps confusing delineation of the meaning of the term saṃgha in its Buddhist context should be clear. Writing a history of the ārya-saṃgha, for obvious reasons, is a nearly impossible task, and given our scanty information on the position of the laity in early Buddhism, we would meet with little success here either. However, we do possess enough data about the saṃgha as a monastic order, gleaned from the monastic literature itself, to at least sketch some salient details concerning its early history and, more important, try to analyze the key monastic texts with a view toward understanding the monastic order as a viable social instrument, largely responsible for the perpetuation of the religion. The main point of concern in this first chapter, then, must be to try to understand the means by which the Buddhist monks abandoned their eremetical ideal, settled down to sedentary life, and began to differentiate themselves from other groups within the general wanderers' [parivrājaka] community, as well as establishing a modicum of individuality even within their own ranks.

In his exhortation to the monks to wander around teaching Dharma, Buddha charges his disciples to all go in separate directions,[6] i.e., to wander about in as many different places as the existing manpower allowed. This emphasis on solitary wandering finds expression not only in the monastic literature but also in many of what are considered to be the earliest strata of Buddhist texts: e.g., the Sutta-nipāta and Dhammapada, to cite two sources. In the Dhammapada, for example, we read (verse 404):[7]

> He who does not associate either with householders or homeless ones,
> Who is homeless and desires nothing,
> Him I call a Brāhmaṇa.

For his personal requisites, apart from the traditional possessions (three robes, begging bowl, razor, needle, girding for the robes, and water strainer), the monk is advised to depend only on four things: (1) begging food [piṇḍyālopabhojanaṃ], (2) using rags for robes [paṃsukūlacīvaraṃ], (3) dwelling at the foot of a tree [vṛkṣamūlaśayanāsanaṃ], and (4) using urine as medicine [pūtimuktabhaiṣajyaṃ]. These are traditionally referred to as the four niśrayas.[8] The only pause to the mendicant's wandering came during the rainy season or varṣā. This custom was certainly not distinct to the Buddhists, but rather was observed by many sects within the parivrājaka community, two examples being the Jains and Brāhmaṇical Sannyāsins. Of course travel during the monsoon season was made thoroughly impractical by the severity of the rains, and damage to the crops, which would certainly result from attempts at travel, would prove most harmful. By this time too the Jain notion of ahiṃsā or noninjury compounded the problem, for many small forms of life would fall prey, even inadvertently, to man's crude efforts at rainy season travel. All these factors led to Buddha's injunction to pass the rainy season in settled dwellings. Thus the monks found it most successful to carry out intensified study and meditation in temporary residence. Also blossoming from the foregoing enterprise was an opportunity for the laity to have a brief but sustained interaction with the monkhood, obviously resulting in mutual benefit. During varṣā, the monks were also able to engage in scholarly debate, sūtra discussion, and similar activities, fully utilizing their close proximity for intellectual (as well as spiritual) advancement. The desirability of such inter-monkhood relations, we shall soon see, resulted to a large extent in a conclusion necessarily contradictory to the Buddha's teaching.

The bhikṣus were advised to enter the rainy season dwelling, as recounted in the Mahāparinibbāna Suttanta, "according to the place where his friends, acquaintances, and intimates may live."[9] Since the Buddhist monks begged for their food, rain retreat settlements had to be made in a vicinity where alms-food would be available without extensive travel, so they usually settled near towns or villages. The requisites for a rain retreat settlement are clearly outlined in a passage from the Mahāvagga:

> Now where could the Lord stay that would be neither too far from a village nor too near, suitable for coming and going, accessible for people whenever they want, not crowded by day, having little noise at night, little sound, without folk's breath, haunts of privacy, suitable for seclusion?[10]

Rain retreat settlements were generally of two types: āvāsas and ārāmas. The āvāsas were monastic dwelling places staked out, constructed, and cared for by the monks themselves. A whole chapter in the Mahāvagga (Chapter III), or for that matter in the varṣāvastus of all the various Vinayas of the individual Buddhist sects, explains, with regard to the āvāsa, "its construction, maintenance, regulations for communal living within it, and also manners and points of etiquette to be observed."[11] A necessary part of āvāsa construction would, of course, be the demarcation of boundaries [sīmā]. Often these limits coincided with natural boundaries[12] such as a mountain, rock, tree, or body of water,[13] and great care was taken to insure that the boundaries of no two āvāsas coincided and that no one colony infringed upon another.[14] The house in which each monk resided was called a vihāra and amounted to little more than a small hut. Occasionally, however, several monks shared the same vihāra, in which case each monk's "cell" was called a pariveṇa.[15] Furniture too was kept to a bare minimum, each monk's allotment consisting only of a bed and seat [śayanāsana], little wooden bed [alpaśayanaphalaka], seat [pīṭha], and a spittoon [kheṭamallaka].[16] The other kind of dwelling place, ārāma, presents an almost total contrast to the āvāsa. Sukumar Dutt notes:

> The name, ārāma, denotes a pleasure-ground, usually the property within a town or city or in the suburb of a well to do citizen laid out as an orchard or flower-garden. When it was given to the monks by the owner, not for temporary use but permanently, it was named a Saṅghārāma. The term, meaning originally an ārāma owned by the Saṅgha, came later to shed its implication of a donated pleasure-ground and meant simply a campus, and later still a large monastery occupied by a company of monks. The donor of an ārāma would not lose interest in it even when it had been converted from private property into Saṅgha property. It seems that he would of his own accord continue to look after the property—raise fresh buildings upon it according to the monks' needs and keep it trim and in habitable condition.[17]

Several donations of this sort are mentioned in the legends, one notable example being King Bimbisāra's offer of Veḷuvana, representing the first gift of an ārāma to the Saṃgha.[18] Some ārāmas seem to have persisted for long durations, as with Jetavanārāma, which still existed at the time of Fa-hien's journey to India (from China) in AD 399–414.[19] In summarizing his work on āvāsas and ārāmas, Dr. Dutt remarks:

> The monk-built āvāsa was after all a temporary set-up, liable to be deserted, robbed and dismantled after its evacuation by monks at the end of the vassa [Skt. varṣā] period. An ārāma was more durable and worthwhile. It stood within an enclosure, obviating the laborious necessity for sīmā-fixation. Perhaps there were also some ready-made structures within. Besides, the charge of looking after and preserving it was the voluntary responsibility of the donor. Even a more important consideration perhaps was that an ārāma, by its permanent situation, favored the continuance from one vassa-period to another of those features of collective life that had already emerged in the Saṅgha. While in the legends we find many references by name to those ārāmas which became famous Saṅgha centres, none of the āvāsas bears a name. The ārāma to all seeming was the superior kind of habitat for vassāvāsa [Skt. varṣāvāsa].[20]

With the institutionalization of the rainy season retreat, many communal needs became evident, the most apparent perhaps being a common meeting hall [upasthāna-śālā]. This common meeting hall is provided for and allowed, at least, in the Pāli sources.[21] Sukumar Dutt points out one example when a Brāhmaṇa named Ghoṭamukha,[22] being eager to make a donation to the Saṃgha, is advised by a monk named Udena to build a meeting hall for the Saṃgha at Pāṭaliputra.[23] Other buildings soon begin to appear, strewn over the grounds of the settlement:[24]

1. Storeroom
2. Kitchen (literally "fire-room")
3. Warehouse
4. Privy
5. Place for walking about
6. Hall in the place for walking about
7. Bathroom
8. Hall in the bathroom
9. Temporary shed for special or festive occasions
10. Well
11. Hall at the well

All of these structures were the collective property of the Saṃgha. From this description we can conclude that the management and administration of the monastic settlement was no meager task. Sukumar Dutt, in working with Pāli sources, prepared a chart which outlines the monastic hierarchy that developed in the course of time. I have condensed it here to indicate just how the division of labor was apportioned:[25]

I. Permanent officers
   A. Connected with the commissariat
      1. Bhaṇḍāgārika—storeroom keeper
      2. Kappiya-kāraka—officer assigned to determine what is and is not allowable; he converted gifts of money into "goods"
      3. Bhattuddesaka—apportioner of food
      4. Yāgu-bhājaka—distributor of congee
      5. Phala-bhājaka—distributor of fruit
      6. Khajjaka-bhājaka—distributor of solid food
   B. Connected with chambers, wardrobe
      1. Senāsana-paññāpaka—assigner of lodgings
      2. Cīvara-paṭiggāhaka—receiver of robes
      3. Cīvara-bhājaka—distributor of robes
      4. Sāṭiya-gāhāpaka—receiver of bathing clothes
      5. Patta-gāhāpaka—receiver of alms bowls
      6. Appamattaka-vissajjaka—disposer of trifles

C. Superintendents
1. Ārāmika-pesaka—superintendent of workers
•2. Sāmaṇera-pesaka—superintendent of novices

II. Temporary officers
A. Navakammika—superintendent of buildings (including repairs)
B. Kaṭhina-vatthāraka—distributor of robes
C. Salāka-gāhāpaka—receiver of voting tickets

III. Miscellaneous officers[26]
A. Pānīya-vārika—officer in charge of drinks
B. Bhājana-vārika—officer in charge of vessels
C. Upadhivāra—steward
D. Parisaṇḍa-vārika—officer in charge of groves
E. Muṇḍasenāsana-vārika—officer of lodgings not in use

Given the physical structure of the monastic dwelling, with its growing number of buildings, and the expanding number of monastic officers, one begins to get the feeling that what is being described is not a temporary dwelling for the rainy season but rather a permanent residing place (i.e., monastery) for the monks; and most definitely, this is exactly what happened. The three-month rainy season residence generally begins on the full moon of Āṣāḍha (June-July). At this time śayanāsana or "dwelling" (literally beds and seats) were assigned to each monk. A second time of assigning dwellings, however, is also mentioned.[27] This second time occurs one month following the full moon of Āṣāḍha. In other words, some monks entered the rain retreat one month later on the full moon of Śrāvaṇa (July-August). These late arriving monks were accommodated by the later time of assignment. The two periods for assigning dwellings should more than adequately suffice to meet the monks' needs, since the rainy season dwellings were to be for one year only and surrendered at the end of the rainy season on the full moon of Kārttika (October-November). Now, however, we meet a most curious event. Following the Pravāraṇā or Invitation ceremony at the conclusion of the rainy season, we find a third assignment of dwelling places. The Cullavagga (VI.11.4) of the Pāli Vinaya describes this third assignment as antaramuttaka or intervening, with reference to the *next rainy season*. Since assignments for the next rainy season could easily be accommodated at that time, this third assignment is functionally superfluous. The third assignment exists simply because monks did not wander randomly, settling down with their friends and companions with the onset of the rains, wherever they might be at the time, but rather returned to the dwelling place of the previous year(s). With reservations already made one year in advance, they were assured of a satisfactory dwelling for the next year's rains. Once year to year assignments were established, it was only a short step for the monks to abolish there eremetical ideal altogether and cease their wanderings even during the dry season. In this fashion the collective monastic life developed, a life requiring permanent physical structures and administrative officers, as described above. As the permanent individual monastic dwellings arise and proliferate, we begin to hear of individual saṃghas, such as the "Saṃgha of Śrāvastī" or the "Saṃgha of Vaiśālī," and the original "Saṃgha of the Four Quarters" seems to exist no longer. Apart from the obvious implications of the above for the sectarian movement in early Buddhism, to call an āvāsa or ārāma a place of rain retreat is now a fiction. Āvāsas and ārāmas now take on a new, collective name: "vihāra," reinterpreted to no longer mean a single hut but a complete monastery. It is likely that the process of the emergence of the monastery took perhaps 100 years, a period which we shall later try to corollate with the rise of Buddhist monastic literature. However, within a relatively short period of time, we find yet another transition in Buddhist monastic life. The vihāras gave way to a new kind of collective term for monastic dwellings, referred to in the Pāli legends as a leṇa (of which there are five kinds with the vihāra simply being one).[28] Sukumar Dutt describes the leṇa in the following way:

> A leṇa was not a monks' colony open to all comers; it was a compact unitary establishment for a settled body of monks, enabling it to function without disturbance as a corporate body—as a Saṅgha by itself.[29]

Of the five types of leṇa which seem to have originally existed, the term later comes to be specifically identified with "cave" monasteries, cut into the hills by man rather than being natural structures.[30] The cave monasteries, coupled with monasteries growing up around famed stūpas or reliquary mounds, such as that at Amarāvatī, seem to dominate Buddhist monasticism well into the Christian era when large Buddhist universities began to grow up around large monastic centers. All of this latter growth, of course, goes far beyond the scope of this brief introduction, and in this regard I refer the reader to Sukumar Dutt's *Buddhist Monks and Monasteries of India* for a responsible treatment of the subject.

Description of the Basic Text

What is of critical importance here is the means by which communal life at the monasteries was regulated. Of the three traditional "baskets" of the Buddhist canon, one devotes itself totally to these issues: the Vinaya Piṭaka or "Basket of Discipline." It is only through a careful understanding of the traditional monastic disciplinary literature that we can begin to see how Buddhism was able to prosper and grow throughout its early history, despite many sectarian divisions.

Properly speaking, the Vinaya Piṭaka is composed of three parts: Sūtravibhaṅga, Skandhaka, and Appendices. However, any consideration of Buddhist monastic discipline must be taken in broad spectrum, focusing not just on that portion of the monastic law which was canonized but on Vinaya literature in general, thus affording us an opportunity to view the developmental process going on within the early Buddhist community in the first few centuries following Buddha's death. Consequently, we can include the Prātimokṣa and the Karmavācanās, although not considered to be canonical in the strictest sense, under the heading of paracanonical Vinaya literature,[31] and the commentaries and miscellaneous texts under the heading of noncanonical Vinaya literature. Thus we arrive at the following schema:

- I. Paracanonical Vinaya literature
  - A. Prātimokṣa
  - B. Karmavācanā
- II. Canonical Vinaya literature
  - A. Sūtravibhaṅga
  - B. Skandhaka
  - C. Appendices
- III. Noncanonical Vinaya literature
  - A. Commentaries
  - B. Miscellaneous texts

It is my contention that this schema purports to describe the chronological development of monastic disciplinary texts fully as much as it provides a description of the structure of Vinaya literature. It is the general intention of this study to focus on the earliest strata of Vinaya literature (i.e., the Prātimokṣa), and the specific intention to provide translations of two Prātimokṣa texts (from Sanskrit) hitherto not rendered into English. The first step in such an undertaking, of course, is to provide a capsule view of the structure and contents of the Prātimokṣa.

The Prātimokṣa is an inventory of offenses, being primarily "a collection of liturgical formularies governing the conduct of the Bhikṣus and Bhikṣuṇis."[32] Many scholars have attempted to explicate the etymological meaning of the term Prātimokṣa, but these pursuits remain, for the most part, speculative.[33] The Prātimokṣa was recited by the monks at each Poṣadha day, and regarding its function, I.B. Horner candidly states:

> This recitation served the double purpose of keeping the rules fresh in the minds of the monks and nuns, and of giving each member of the monastic community the opportunity, while the rules were being repeated or recited, to avow an offence that he or she had committed.[34]

For each breach of the rules, appropriate punitive measures are indicated. Since the Prātimokṣa concerns both monks and nuns, it is twofold (Bhikṣu Prātimokṣa and Bhikṣuṇī Prātimokṣa). The monks' Prātimokṣa contains eight categories of offenses, classified "according to the degree of gravity."[35] These eight categories of offenses will now be listed and explained.

1. *Pārājika Dharmas*

These four offenses are the most serious that can be committed by the bhikṣu. They include: (1) sexual intercourse, (2) theft, (3) deprivation of life (of a human), and (4) false proclamation of superhuman faculties.[36] Mention of these four offenses is not distinct to the Prātimokṣa or Sūtravibhaṅga, as we find them, for example, elsewhere in the Pāli Vinaya.[37] Violation of any one of the pārājika dharmas results in permanent expulsion from the saṃgha. It should be noted that the term pārājika remains a puzzle. I.B. Horner renders it "defeat," following Rhys Davids and Oldenberg.[38] E. J. Thomas notes that "Buddhaghosa interprets pārājika as 'suffering defeat,' and the Mūlasarvāstivādins appear to do the same. . . ."[39] Recently, however, Gustav Roth has thrown some new light on the subject by interestingly reexamining Sylvain Lévi's suggestion of an earlier form of the term: pārācika.[40]

2. *Saṃghāvaśeṣa Dharmas*

These thirteen offenses represent, following the pārājika dharmas, the most severe breach of monastic discipline. Five offenses deal with sexual transgressions, two with dwelling places, two with false accusation, two with schisms, one with a monk who is difficult to speak to,[41] and one with monks who corrupt families. The first nine of these become offenses at once, whereas the final four do not become offenses until the third admonition of the monk involved.[42] The section of saṃghāvaśeṣa dharmas is unique in that it represents the only class of Prātimokṣa offenses which contains provisions for disciplinary action (in the text itself). When a monk is culpable of a saṃghāvaśeṣa offense, he is subjected to a probationary period [parivāsa] for as many days as the offense was concealed. If the offense was confessed at once, the parivāsa period is reduced to nil. When the parivāsa is completed, a further period called mānatva[43] must also be spent. It is interesting to note that an entire vastu (i.e., chapter) in the Skandhaka portion of the Vinaya, the Pārivāsika-vastu, is devoted to these issues. The term saṃghāvaśeṣa, like pārājika, is problematic. No etymological rendering of the term seems to make much sense. However, a careful discussion of the term, stressing the plausibility of the variant saṃghātiśeṣa (as in the Māsāṃghika text translated below) is presented by Gustav Roth (in "Terminologisches aus dem Vinaya der Mahāsāṃghika-Lokottaravādin")[44] and also Sylvain Lévi (in "Sur une langue précanonique du Bouddhisme").[45] Regarding this class of offenses, Horner notes:

> It is not impossible that originally the various Saṅghas which were really sub-divisions of the whole Saṅgha, exercised their jurisdiction over each individual member only in the case of the Saṅghādisesa offences, only coming later to exercise such jurisdiction in the case of all classes of offence. If this is so, we do well, I think, to underline the formalities which the Saṅghādisesa offenses entailed, and were very likely alone in so doing at first. For by this means some early feature of the Order's history may be kept in mind.[46]

3. *Aniyata Dharmas*

These two offenses include cases whereby a monk may be accused by a trustworthy female lay follower [upāsikā] and dealt with according to her dictate. If a monk should sit together with a woman in a secret place which is convenient for sexual intercourse, he may be charged with a pārājika, saṃghāvaśeṣa, or pāyantika (discussed below) offense, according to what actually transpired. This is case 1. If a monk should sit together with a woman in a place unfit for indulging in sexual intercourse but suitable for speaking to her in lewd words, he may be charged with a saṃghāvaśeṣa or pāyantika offense, the pārājika rule of unchastity having been ruled out. This is case 2. Due to the variable manner in which the monk may be charged, expressing the variety of monastic offenses open to him, this category of offenses is referred to as "undetermined offenses." The two offenses in this category reflect an outstanding and somewhat surprising degree of trust in the female lay follower.

4. *Niḥsargika-Pāyantika Dharmas*

There are thirty offenses in this class, violation of which requires expiation and forfeiture, as can be seen from the class title. I. B. Horner notes, "From internal evidence, pācittiya [Skt. pāyantika] is a (minor) offence to be confessed, āpatti desetabbā [Skt. āpatti deśayitavyā], a state common to all the Nissaggiyas [Skt. Niḥsargikas]."[47] The niḥsargika-pāyantika dharmas are arranged in three vargas or sections of ten rules each. The following is Thomas' description:[48]

> 1. Ten rules concerning robes.
> These refer to the length of time during which an extra robe might be kept, to repair and exchange of robes, and to receiving them as alms. He might not ask a lay person for a robe unless he had lost his own, nor might he suggest the kind he was to receive.
>
> 2. Ten rules for rugs and the use of money.
> The material of which the rug was made was prescribed, and it had to be used for six years. The monk might accept the material for it under certain conditions. Gold and silver must not be accepted or used in transactions, and buying and selling were forbidden.
>
> 3. Then rules concerning bowl, medicine, and robes.
> A monk might not keep an extra bowl beyond ten days, nor exchange his bowl if it was broken in less than five places. Medicine (ghee, butter, oil, honey, raw sugar) must not be stored more than seven days. There are special rules for robes in the rainy season and for having them woven. Nothing intended to be given to the order was to be applied by the monk to his own use.

If we tabulate the offenses, we discover that sixteen refer to robes, five to rugs, four to money and appropriating saṃgha property, two to sheep's wool, two to bowls, and one to medicines. This is the first class of offenses in the Prātimokṣa in which the numbering system employed by the various schools becomes widely divergent.[49] In commenting on the nature of the forfeiture and confession, and on the general value of this form of punishment, I. B. Horner again provides us with a valuable insight:

> As a general rule, the Padabhājaniya [Old Commentary] states that forfeiture and confession were to be made to an Order, that is to any part of the whole Order, five monks or more, living within a boundary, sīmā, or within one residence, āvāsa; or to a group, gaṇa, of monks, that is to a group of from two to four monks; or to an individual monk. When the article has been forfeited and the offence confessed, the offence was to be acknowledged, in the first two instances, by "an experienced, competent monk"; in the third by the monk to whom the forfeiture and confession had been made. The forfeited article was then given back to the monk who, having acquired it wrongfully, had forfeited it.
>
> The value of the nissaggiya-pācittiya [Skt. niḥsargika-pāyantika] type of penalty was, I think, in the eyes of the framer or framers of the Pātimokkha [Skt. Prātimokṣa] rules, its deterrent effect on the commission of further similar offences, and its redemptive power for each particular offender. It was apparently held that an offence whose penalty was of this nature was annulled by confessing it and having it acknowledged, combined with this hardly more than symbolic act of forfeiting the article wrongfully acquired. This involved some formality, but evidently the offence was not considered bad enough to warrant the offender's permanent loss of the goods he had obtained improperly.[50]

Regarding the terms niḥsargika and pāyantika, several of the alternate readings should be pointed out. For niḥsargika, we find (for the most part): nissarigika, naissargika, naisargika, and naiḥsargika. For pāyantika, we also find: pāyattikāḥ, papattikā, pāpantikā, pācittiyakā, pātayantikā, prāyaścittikā, pācittiya, payti, pāyacchitika, pācchita, and pācattika.[51]

5. *Pāyantika Dharmas*

There are ninety offenses in this category,[52] violation of which require expiation. Although the numbering pattern in this class of rules is extremely divergent in the various schools, an examination of the contents of the rules yields surprising results. The vast majority of rules (seventy-four) may be grouped under five major headings:[53]

1. Moral rules (lying, etc.)—twenty-three rules
2. Conduct with women—fourteen rules
3. Food and drink—sixteen rules

4. Dharma, Vinaya, and their application—eleven rules
5. Use of requisites—ten rules

The remaining rules (sixteen) may be grouped under three further rubrics, each containing a lesser number of items:

1. Behavior in the vihāra—six rules
2. Travel—five rules
3. Various types of destruction—five rules

The placement of the rules into these categories is somewhat arbitrary, and several of the rules are actually coterminous. The various Prātimokṣa texts generally group the rules numerically in divisions of ten rules. Some texts supply uddānas or summaries at the end of each section of ten rules, presumably as a memory aid for the monk, and one text (the Mahāsāṃghika) even provides a summary of the vargas at the end of the entire section. E. J. Thomas, primarily because of the use of the term vihāra and the denotation of furniture common to the saṃgha, is of the following opinion:

> Several rules in this section show a more developed communal life than that implied in the Sanghādisesa rules, and the whole section has probably been collected or put into shape at a later period than the previous rules.[54]

6. *Pratideśanīya Dharmas*

The pratideśanīya section contains four straightforward offenses which are to be confessed: (1) partaking of food obtained through the intervention of a nun, (2) not reproving a nun for giving orders (pertaining to the meal) while a meal is being served, (3) accepting food from a family which is undergoing training, and (4) obtaining food while living in a dangerous setting, without having it announced as such beforehand (unless the monk is ill).

7. *Śaikṣa Dharmas*

This group of rules is the most disparate in the entire Prātimokṣa. The number of śaikṣa dharmas varies in the various texts from 66 in the Chinese Mahāsāṃghika version to 113 in the Chinese Sarvāstivādin version.[55] Dr. Pachow describes the śaikṣa dharmas in the following manner:

> The nature of these rules is essentially concerned with the daily conduct

and decorum of the Bhikṣus such as: walking, moving to and fro, looking, dressing, contracting, and stretching and so forth. They do not come under any penal section inasmuch as there will not be any sanction or punishment for their breaches or violations. The violation of any of them by a Bhikṣu is not considered to be a criminal act but simply bad manners.[56]

8. *Adhikaraṇa-Śamatha Dharmas*

These seven rules represent a system by which offenses may be resolved. The first, saṃmukhavinaya, literally means "in the presence of." The Samathakkhandhaka of the Pāli Vinaya explains this by the presence of the individual, the Saṃgha, the Dharma, and the Vinaya.[57] The second, smṛtivinaya, literally means "verdict based on recollection." However, the Samathakkhandhaka makes it clear that it is a verdict of innocence and outlines five requirements for such a decision: (1) that the monk is pure and faultless, (2) that he is accused, (3) that he asks for dismissal of the charge, (4) that the saṃgha gives the smṛtivinaya decision, and (5) that the saṃgha is complete.[58] The third, amūḍhavinaya, literally means "verdict of past insanity." The Samathakkhandhaka notes three criteria for granting such a verdict: (1) the offense was not remembered, (2) the offense was remembered and confessed, and (3) the monk remains insane.[59] The fourth, yadbhūyaṣikīya, literally means "decision of the majority." The Samathakkhandhaka, however, states that when a decision of the majority is not reached, monks at another āvāsa may be consulted.[60] I. B. Horner suspects that this method was not contemplated, referring to a passage in which voting by tickets was used to resolve the legal question.[61] The fifth, tatsvabhāvaiṣīya, literally means "special nature" (of the accused monk). The Samathakkhandhaka notes three occasions for carrying out this against the monk: if he is (1) a maker of fights, (2) a maker of quarrels, or (3) a maker of disputes.[62] The sixth, tṛṇaprastāraka, literally means "cover (as) with grass." The Samathakkhandhaka explains that when monks are engaged in dispute, many unbecoming things may be said. Monks should gather together under the direction of an experienced monk, confess their collective fault, and unless it is a grave sin [sthūlavadya] or connected with the laity [gṛhapatisaṃyukta], enact this procedure.[63] The seventh, pratijñākāraka, literally means "verdict which effects confession." The Samathakkhandhaka advises that acts must not be carried out against a monk without his acknowledgment.[64] The adhikaraṇa-śamatha dharmas are discussed at length in Sukumar Dutt's

Early Buddhist Monachism [Chapter VI: The Internal Polity of a Buddhist Sangha, pp. 113–145 (revised edition)]. Strangely enough, we also find an explanation of this class of rules in the Sāmagāma Sutta of the Majjhima Nikāya (Sutta No. 104).

These eight classes of rules comprise the monks' Prātimokṣa Sūtra. The nuns' Prātimokṣa consists of the same classes of rules as the monks' Prātimokṣa, but the aniyata dharmas are omitted. We also find that the number of rules in the nuns' Prātimokṣa is considerably larger than in the monks' version, many rules having been inserted specifically for females.[65] In any case, the texts are preceded by a series of verses praising the disciplined life, and also by a ritual formulary. A series of verses, often concurring with several verses in the Dhammapada or Udānavarga, also follow the text proper, uniformly mentioning the six Buddhas immediately antecedent to Śākyamuni Gautama and Gautama himself.[66] Since the texts translated in this study reveal themselves to be ritual liturgies in the fullest sense of the word, we must now investigate the process by which the ritualization of this basic disciplinary code took place.

Ritualization of the Prātimokṣa

Although etymological explanations of the term Prātimokṣa were earlier noted to be speculative, and for the most part beside the point, some of the leading notions should be reviewed, for reasons that will soon become apparent. Rhys Davids and Oldenberg derive Prātimokṣa from prati √muc, taken in the sense of disburdening or getting free.[67] E. J. Thomas also favors derivation from √muc, but he renders it "that which binds, obligatory."[68] Winternitz associated the word with redemption, based primarily on his reading of the Jātakas.[69] Dr. Pachow notes:

> In the Chinese and Tibetan translations, this is interpreted as: Deliverance, liberation, or emancipation for each and every one and at all occasions, that is "prati" stands for "each, every" and "mokṣa" for "Deliverance."[70]

And the derivations from √muc go on and on. Against this we find the evidence of the Pāli Mahāvagga, declaring Pātimokkha (the Pāli equivalent of Prātimokṣa) to be the face, the head of all good dharmas [mukhaṃ etaṃ, pamukhaṃ etaṃ kusalānaṃ dhammānaṃ].[71] With the exception of the Mahāvagga passage, each of our Western interpreters seems to commit one huge error in his interpretation of the term: etymological judgment was colored by the preconceived notion that Prātimokṣa, since it was a monastic code, had to be rendered accordingly. What if Prātimokṣa, at the inception of the word into Buddhist vocabulary, had nothing to do with the outline and confession of offenses? Sukumar Dutt throws considerable light on this suggestion by interpreting Prātimokṣa in quite a different sense:

> Pātimokkha, however, can be equated to Skt. Prātimokṣa, which from its etymological parts lends itself to interpretation as something serving for a bond, the prefix Prati meaning "against" and the root Mokṣa meaning "scattering" (kṣepaṇe iti kavikalpadrumaḥ), though I have not been able to discover any instance of the use of the word precisely in this sense in Sanskrit. I should prefer to take the etymological interpretation of the word as bond. . . .[72]

To determine what led Dr. Dutt to such a bold statement, so obviously abandoning the orthodoxy of the time, we are necessarily led to an examination of the Prātimokṣa's original nature, content, and function, since the two problems are thoroughly intertwined. Dr. Dutt assesses the state of the early Buddhist saṃgha:

> The Buddhist Sangha existed originally as a sect of the Parivrājaka community of the sixth century B.C., and it rested on the basis of a common Dhamma and had at first no special Vinaya of its own. It is impossible to say at what point of time, but certainly very early in its history, the sect of the Buddha, the Cātuddisa Bhikkhu-sangha [Skt. Cāturdiśa Bhikṣu-saṃgha], devised an external bond of union: it was called Pātimokkha.[73]

What was the nature and content of this earliest Prātimokṣa? The Mahāpadāna Sutta of the Dīgha Nikāya provides a brief glimpse. We may recall that this sutta mentions the six Buddhas immediately preceding Śākyamuni Gautama, expounding at length a story concerning Vipaśyin, the first of these previous Buddhas. Of utmost importance are three verses in the third chapter of the text (Nos. 26, 27, and 28). The first two verses relate that at the end of each six-year period the monks are enjoined to journey to the town of Bandumatī to recite the Prātimokṣa. The text of this Prātimokṣa is as follows:

> Khantī paramaṃ tapo titikkhā
> Nibbānaṃ paramaṃ vadanti Buddhā.

Na hi pabbajito parūpaghāti,
Samaṇo hoti paraṃ viheṭhayanto.

Sabbapāpassa akaraṇaṃ, kusalassa upasampadā,
Sacittapariyodapanaṃ, etaṃ Buddhāna sāsanaṃ.

Anupavādo anupaghāto pātimokkhe ca saṃvaro,
Mattaññutā ca bhattasmiṃ pantañ ca sayanāsanaṃ,
Adhicitte ca āyogo, etaṃ Buddhāna sāsanan ti.[74]

Its translation:

Enduring patience is the highest austerity,
nirvāṇa is the highest say the Buddhas;
for he who injures others is not a monk,
he who violates others is not a śramaṇa.

Not to do any evil, to attain good,
to purify one's own mind; this is the Teaching
of the Buddhas.

Not speaking against others, not harming others,
and restraint according to the Prātimokṣa,
moderation in eating, secluded dwelling,
and the practice of adhicitta; this is the
Teaching of the Buddhas.[75]

These verses are not distinct to the Dīgha Nikāya. They also appear as verses 183–185 of the Dhammapada, but even more significantly they are among the verses appended to the Prātimokṣa Sūtras of the various schools (although attributed to others of the six Buddhas).[76] It is not unreasonable to suppose that each verse (of those appended to the Prātimokṣa Sūtras) represented the original Prātimokṣa of a particular Buddha, the favorability of this hypothesis being heightened by the fact that at least one version of a Prātimokṣa Sūtra (the Sanskrit Mahāsāṃghika text) refers to each verse as a Prātimokṣa.[77] I conjecture that the inclusion of these verses in the fully developed Prātimokṣa Sūtras of the various schools represents an admission of the earlier form of Prātimokṣa, designed to provide the mature texts with added religious and historical authority. Regarding the function of the earliest Prātimokṣa, Dutt remarks:

> The Buddhist Sangha had rested originally on a community of faith and belief, on a Dhamma, but an external bond of union, a Pātimokkha, was afterwards devised serving to convert the Sect into a re-

> ligious Order, and this Pātimokkha originally consisted in periodical meeting for the purpose of confirming the unity of the Buddha's monk-followers by holding a communal confession of faith in a set form of hymn singing. This custom seems to me to be indicated by the story of Vipassī [Skt. Vipaśyin].[78]

Recently Dutt's theses have been accepted by at least two modern scholars: Bhikshu Sangharakshita in *The Three Jewels. An Introduction to Modern Buddhism* and Peter A. Pardue in *Buddhism*, although neither indicates Dutt as the source of his inspiration.[79]

It is beyond doubt that relatively early in the history of the Buddhist saṃgha the Prātimokṣa evolved into a monastic code, eventually developing into the formalized ritual mentioned above. Sukumar Dutt seems to think that the Prātimokṣa as bond or union being transformed into a monastic code took place shortly after Buddha's death, his reasoning being founded on his reading of the account of the council of Rājagṛha, in the Pāli Vinaya, about which he says:

> The canonical account of this "council," as I have already suggested, cannot be relied upon. It is based on a vague tradition of what happened in the long, long past. But we may read it between the lines. In the reported proceedings, the term, Pātimokkha, is nowhere mentioned, but all the heads of misdemeanour on the part of a Bhikkhu are listed except the Sekhiyas [Skt. Śaikṣas] and the procedural rules of Adhikaraṇa-samatha [Skt. Adhikaraṇa-śamatha]. The reason for the studied omission of the word, Pātimokkha, is not far to seek if we assume that at the time when the proceedings were put into shape, the Bhikkhus understood by Pātimokkha something quite different from a code of Vinaya rules. . . . The code, whatever its original contents, became after the First Council the bond of association of the Buddhist Bhikkhus, and was called Pātimokkha (Bond). Thus the old name for a confession of faith came to be foisted on something new, a code of Prohibitions for a Bhikkhu.[80]

One might object that although Prātimokṣa is not mentioned in the council account, it is mentioned in other parts of the Skandhaka text. However, these references to Prātimokṣa occur almost exclusively in the Poṣadhavastu and Poṣadhasthāpanavastu, sections which have been shown by Frauwallner to be both intimately related and late, indicating their formal, ritualistic nature.[81] Unfortunately Dr. Dutt does not state his case strongly enough or make full use of the sources available to him. At the end of the eleventh chapter of the Cullavagga (in the Pāli Vinaya), the proceedings of the council are described as a vinayasaṃgīti, rendered by I.B. Horner as "chanting of discipline."[82] Is it not possible that this chanting of Vinaya was of the same nature and function of the earliest Prātimokṣa, outlined above? In addition, when Upāli is questioned in the chapter, the text does not say that this interrogation concerned Prātimokṣa, but rather Vinaya.[83] Upāli's answers, replete with names of categories of offenses, pose no problem. Obviously rules for conduct existed, many probably even propounded by the Buddha, but these had not been as yet codified into a rigid structure. On this point, Dr. Pachow notes:

> Gautama Buddha, of course, was a reformer in some respects but as the conception of morality had been so well established before his time, that he had simply to accept their fundamental principles, and cast new rules in order to suit the requirements of his disciples, under unusual circumstances.[84]

After the Buddha's death, and most probably after the alleged first council, the monks set out to gather together those precepts, outlined by Upāli as Vinaya, into a code. We have already seen that Prātimokṣa was to be the title of the code. There is no mistaking the existence of this bare code. Examples of it being so regarded are numerous in the Nikāyas. We repeatedly find terms such as pātimokkha-saṃvara-saṃvuto, "constrained by the restraints of the Pātimokkha," and the like.[85] In addition, the ritual formulary preceding the Prātimokṣa as we have it today is found not in the Sūtravibhaṅga, as we should expect, but in the Poṣadhavastu (a section where it is out of place).[86] Sukumar Dutt goes as far as to say, "The Sutta-Vibhaṅga, in fact, regards the Pātimokkha as a mere code, while the Mahāvagga [in the Khandhaka] regards it as a liturgy,"[87] raising another vital question: What is the relationship between the Prātimokṣa and the Sūtravibhaṅga? To be more specific, Oldenberg succinctly outlines the problem:

> The question is, therefore, whether the ordinances originally appeared with the explanatory notes as in the Vibhaṅga, the Pātimokkha being subsequently extracted from it; or whether the Pātimokkha alone was the older portion, the additional matter of the Vibhaṅga being the work of a subsequent revision.[88]

I do not wish to dwell on this point, since Oldenberg himself conclusively verifies the antiquity of the Prātimokṣa:

> In dealing with this question, it should, in the first place, be observed,

> that if we read the ordinances of the Pātimokkha without the commentary of the Vibhaṅga, we find that they constitute one uninterrupted whole; and, moreover, it frequently happens that one rule refers to the one immediately preceding it, in a manner that would be altogether unintelligible if the two had been originally separated by the intervening explanations of the Vibhaṅga.
>
> So, too, both the nature and effect of the explanations themselves seem conclusively to point to their later origin. Sometimes they extend the application of the rule, at others limit their operation, while occasionally they give directions for preventing their evasion. In some cases also the explanations substitute an entirely new rule, based upon a development of the law which took place since the framing of the rules.[89]

In addition to the introductory formulary being out of place in the bare Prātimokṣa code, the interrogatory formula, concluding each category of rules, also does not fit. An example of this last point might be taken with regard to the adhikaraṇa-śamatha dharmas. No offenses are actually stated, hence the declaration of purity following these rules is indeed superfluous.[90]

Before we examine the actual process by which the Prātimokṣa developed into a formalized ritual, two further points need emphasis: (1) the flexibility of the Prātimokṣa during its formative period, and (2) the relative date of its finalized root form. That the Prātimokṣa text was flexible during its growth period is unquestionably attested to by the inclusion of a substantial amount of late material in its final form. For example, in the Theravādin, Mahāsāṃghika, and Mūlasarvāstivādin pāyantika dharma section, we find the term akṛtānudharmeṇa [not performed according to Dharma]. We cannot find an explanation of this technical term anywhere in the Prātimokṣa. In fact, it is only in the Pāṇḍulohitakavastu that the term is explained.[91] The Sūtravibhaṅga does, however, note that the utkṣepaṇīyakarma is anticipated as penalty for such an offense, but again, this second new term (as well as other, similar, punitive terms) is unknown to the Prātimokṣa. Sukumar Dutt notes:

> Then, again, the classification of offences does not appear to have been made on any initially recognized principle, but is more or less haphazard and promiscuous suggesting, if not actually later additions and alterations, at least the elasticity of the original code which offered opportunities for them.[92]

Also regarding the flexibility of the emerging Prātimokṣa code, we have some evidence that the earliest form of the code contained a considerably smaller number of rules than the final form. Although Pachow cites the Sammatīya Prātimokṣa to contain only about 200 rules,[93] our most reliable source in the numbers game seems to be the Pāli. In its final form this Pātimokkha contains 227 rules. However, several sources indicate a figure of something more than 150 śiksāpadas [sādhikaṃ diyaḍḍhasikkhāpada-sataṃ].[94] Several scholars have entertained a series of arithmetic gymnastics in explaining the disparity of 77 rules (plus or minus). B. C. Law, for example, suspects that because the adhikaraṇa-śamatha dharmas, as well as the śaikṣa dharmas, were unnamed at the first council, they may have been later additions. To arrive at the proper number, he disposes of the former group somehow and declares the correct figure to be 152 (i.e., 227 total rules minus 75 śaikṣa dharmas; if he also subtracted the adhikaraṇa-śamatha dharmas, he would end up with the untenable result of having *less than* 150 rules).[95] Sukumar Dutt comes very close to making the same assertion, but he adds that these two sections of rules "were considered to be of a somewhat different character from the rest."[96] Although Dutt is correct to a degree, Pachow points out the futility of such approaches, noting that some of the śaikṣa material is extremely old.[97] Other ploys to account for the roughly 150 rules, perhaps just as untenable, might have been set forth. For example, if one charts the place at which each rule is said to have been promulgated, we discover that an overwhelming majority (roughly 170 rules) was set forth at Śrāvastī. This figure is no more unreasonable than the others suggested (especially in view of the Pāli qualifier sādhikaṃ, "something more than"), and probably could be further supported by emphasizing the many rainy seasons spent there by the Buddha. This hypothesis was most likely not employed (and I assume that I am not the first to consider it, although I have not seen it in print) because scholars generally ascribe very little reliability to place names mentioned in the Pāli Canon.

In view of the materials presented above, we can tentatively propose several conclusions concerning the date of the earliest root Prātimokṣa text. First, the oldest portions of this text, indeed very ancient, may date from 500–450 BC. Due to the flexibility of the early text, its period of growth to completion must have taken a considerable period of time, perhaps 50 to 100 years. Thus it was probably in its final root form by about 400 BC. Accepting Oldenberg's thesis concerning the relationship between the Prātimokṣa and the Sūtravibhaṅga, we can assume that the latter text was composed soon after the completion of the Prātimokṣa. However short this period may have been, it was certainly significant, for by the time of the composition of the Sūtravibhaṅga, no new additions to the Prātimokṣa were admitted, thus accounting for the new terms for offenses mentioned in the Sūtravibhaṅga: sthūlātyaya [grave offense], duṣkṛta [light offense], and durbhāṣita [offense of improper speech]. We might say that the development of the Karmavācanās and the Skandhaka, taken together, parallels that of the Prātimokṣa and the Sūtravibhaṅga, although not being quite so ancient. Clearly, by the time of completion of the Skandhaka, the root Prātimokṣa text had already developed into a ritual text, regarded as such by the former.

The ritual form of the Prātimokṣa is intimately bound up with the Buddhists' acceptance and observance of the Poṣadha ceremony; thus Poṣadha, or the Buddhist Sanskrit form of upavasatha [fast day], must be examined first. The story is a familiar one, related in the Poṣadhavastus of the various Vinayas. King Śreṇīya Bimbisāra, the well-known patron of Buddhism, observed that various groups within the parivrājaka community came together on the eighth, fourteenth, and fifteenth of each fortnight to speak their respective Dharmas. In so doing, they gained adherents and prospered, arousing in Bimbisāra the question as to why Buddha's followers did not observe this practice. Being possessed of the necessary amount of audacity, the king approached Gautama and questioned him on this point, suggesting that the bhikṣu-saṃgha also hold these fortnightly meetings. Recognizing the wisdom of Bimbisāra's recommendation, the Buddha decided to adopt it, altering it to suit his followers' needs. As Gokuldas De points out:

> But, the Buddha's injunction to his disciples regarding the observance of this ceremony of Uposatha [the Pāli form for Poṣadha] was that, instead of discussing the Dharma which was also conceded later on among themselves only, they should recite on this particular day the "Sikkhāpadas" embodying the code of rules for their own guidance, to be henceforward known as the Pātimokkha.[98]

Dr. Dutt comments on the change in function of this ceremony:

> But though Uposatha observance was a widespread popular custom, the Buddhist Bhikkhus adapted it to their own uses and purposes; they made it fit in with their congregational life. Its form was changed: it became a confessional service, an instrument of monastic discipline.[99]

Before coming to the Prātimokṣa itself, it should be noted that two further points regarding the Poṣadha ceremony were changed. First, the observance days were reduced to two with the eighth day of the fortnight being excluded.

Precautions were taken to avoid excessive observance. Second, extreme care was taken to establish a meeting hall for the Poṣadha ceremony and delineate proper boundaries [sīmā] for each āvāsa, already verifying the fact that various saṃghas existed in several places.

At first, the only business of the Poṣadha ceremony was the Prātimokṣa recital.[100] Accordingly, the bare Prātimokṣa text had to be transmuted into liturgical form. The first thing necessary was to add an introduction [nidāna] to the text. This nidāna is spoken by an elder, competent monk who first calls the saṃgha to order, announces the recitation of the Prātimokṣa to be at hand, calls for the careful attention of the saṃgha, extols the confession of faults, denotes silence as an affirmation of innocence, and emphasizes conscious lying to be a serious impediment to a monk's progress.[101] However, it is essential to note that in addition to the above, the elder monk, before calling for the careful attention of the monks, remarks that the first duty of the saṃgha is to declare complete purity.[102] That declaration of complete purity, pariśuddhi, is a prerequisite to the Prātimokṣa Sūtra recitation is attested to elsewhere. In the Poṣadhasthāpanavastu, the Buddha refuses to recite the Prātimokṣa because one of the monks present in the assembly is not completely pure.[103] If the Prātimokṣa Sūtra recitation, in fact, served anything more than a purely ritual function, why must complete purity be declared *before* the ceremony? With preannounced complete purity, the only offenses subject to confession during the actual recitation would be those that were remembered while the recitation was in progress or those concealed previously but now confessed. Both of these cases were likely to be the exception rather than the rule. At the conclusion of the nidāna we find a statement indicating that there is comfort [phāsu], i.e., absolution, for one confessing a previously unconfessed fault, thus adding to our premise of the artificiality and purely ritual function of the ceremony, for the possiblity of an offense for which confession would not suffice (such as a pārājika dharma) is not entertained at all. After adding the nidāna to the bare text, the next requisite was to add interrogatory portions at the end of each class of rules. These statements consisted of a threefold repetition of the question: Are you completely pure in this matter? Immediately following the interrogation was the declaration of the elder monk: Since there is silence, the Venerable Ones are completely pure in this matter. Thus do I understand. Apparently the confession of even one fault was not anticipated by the Prātimokṣa leader, again illustrating the solely ritualistic function of the formulary. I pointed out earlier that the interrogatory text is utterly misplaced after the adhikaraṇa-śamatha portion of the Prātimokṣa, but I mention it here only to conjecture that it was incorporated to maintain the symmetry of the ritual. In addition to the nidāna and the interrogatory sections added to the root text, verses before and after the text were included, many of these corresponding to the speculated Prātimokṣas of the previous six Buddhas (as well as that of Śākyamuni Gautama). Unfortunately, not all of these verses have been traced in the various recensions of the canon, and it might prove enlightening to do so. Nevertheless, Schayer's comment on the inclusion of unusual passages in formalized texts is particularly pertinent here:

> There arises a further question: why have those texts not been suppressed in spite of their contradictory non-canonical character? There is only one answer: evidently they have been transmitted by a tradition old enough and considered to be authoritative by the compilers of the canon.[104]

Later, when other functions were added to the Poṣadha ceremony (such as monastic decisions carried out according to the Karmavācanā method), Prātimokṣa recital began to occupy a lesser position. De remarks:

> Naturally when other items of business were introduced into its [the Poṣadha's] observance, the main one, i.e., the recital of Pātimokkha, failed to attract much attention of the members which it originally did being the only item. Good care therefore must be taken to ensure its recital and uphold the purity of the saṃgha according to its several provisions.[105]

However:

> As to the effect of this Uposatha on the members of the Order we may observe that the different Saṃghas which quickly grew up in large numbers all over India, especially in the North, freely transacting their respective business in very different manners had now to mind a particular work which concerned every individual of every Saṃgha in a way common to all.[106]

What does the ritualization of the Prātimokṣa, with its artificiality and lesser role in the Poṣadha ceremony, mean in terms of the ethical dimension of Buddhist life? Most assuredly it does not mean that the ethical ideal had been abandoned by the Buddhists in the course of time. Rather, it seems to indicate a shift in the thrust of Buddhist ethics. With the rise of individual saṃghas, it was more apparent than ever that each saṃgha needed an ethical guideline or foundation to preserve its collective life and maintain its individual integrity. With the maturation of the monastic order in Buddhism it also became critically apparent that pragmatic considerations indeed had to be reckoned with. By having all offenses (except those cited above) confessed and dealt with *before* the actual Poṣadha ceremony, more time was freed for other monastic concerns. Thus the ritualized recitation of the Prātimokṣa becomes intensely meaningful. It seems to become the *formal embodiment* of a tradition, by this time long in practice, of expecting and demanding the highest cultivation of an ethical life by practitioners of Buddhism. In so doing, the ritualization of the Prātimokṣa reveals not that ethics and morality were overlooked, but rather that they continued as strongly as ever, simply recast into the formalistic mold that Buddhist monastic life had adopted. Considered in this perspective, Prātimokṣa is not just monastic "glue" holding the saṃgha together but the common ground on which the internally enforced ethical life is manifested externally in the community.

Conclusions

It is clear that in the second century following Buddha's parinirvāṇa, Buddhism was beset by an extensive sectarian movement. Since André Bareau has already presented a definitive and discerning study of the so-called Hīnayāna sects,[107] I shall not review this topic here but simply note that it is quite difficult to read Bareau without concluding that doctrinal matters solely were responsible for the sectarian movement. Other scholars have taken the opposite approach. Dr. Ankul Chandra Banerjee, for example, notes:

> We are told that there was little matter of dispute on Dharma between the different sects but it was Vinaya on which they differed and this ultimately led to the origin of so many schools of Buddhism. Thus we find that the texts of the Āgamas or the Piṭakas were accepted more or less by all the schools, while those of Vinaya varied in the different schools. Even in Buddha's life-time Vinaya, i.e., rules of discipline, sometimes formed the subject-matter of dispute but it subsided at the instance [sic] of the Great Teacher. It, however, produced a result of far-reaching importance. The difference in the interpretation of the Vinaya rules became very serious to the masters of Vinaya (Vinaya-dharas) and was the occasion for their separation. Thus arose the different schools with different rules of Vinaya.[108]

Banerjee overstates his case as severely as Bareau. More likely, the sectarian movement was a product of *both* doctrinal and disciplinary issues. Nevertheless, it is not unreasonable to suppose that one should expect to find Vinayas for all (or at least the majority) of the Hīnayāna sects. However, this is clearly not the case, for many of these sects were indeed short-lived, disappearing before they could leave anything more than scanty evidence of their existence. We find fully developed Vinayas of only six schools: Mahāsāṃghikas, Theravādins, Mahīśāsakas, Dharmaguptakas, Sarvāstivādins, and Mūlasarvāstivādins. Even a casual perusal of the records of the travels of the Chinese pilgrims Fa-hien, Hsüan-tsang, and I-tsing reveals these six schools to be the most forceful and persistent of the Hīnayāna sects. It cannot be mere coincidence that the schools with the most developed Vinayas prospered while the others dissipated, and with this in mind, we can proceed to an examination of the texts at hand.

Notes

1 Hermann Oldenberg, ed., *The Vinaya Piṭakaṃ*, 5 vols.; reprint (London: Luzac & Company, for P.T.S., 1964), Vol. I, pp. 21–22 (Mahāvagga I.12.1–4). The translation is mine. Later the ordination formula shifts again to be included as a specific Karmavācanā.

2 Bhikshu Sangharakshita, *The Three Jewels. An Introduction to Modern Buddhism* (Garden City, N.Y.: Anchor Books, 1970), p. 142.

3 H. Saddhatissa, *Buddhist Ethics* (New York: George Braziller, 1970), p. 55, n. 2. I have paraphrased, replacing the Pāli terms with their more familiar Sanskrit equivalents.

4 Nalinaksha Dutt, *Early Monastic Buddhism* (Calcutta: Calcutta Oriental Book Agency, 1960), pp. 252–261. Dr. Dutt reviews here not only the Pāli sources but also the Abhidharmakośa.

5 Saddhatissa, *Buddhist Ethics*, p. 81.

6 Oldenberg, *The Vinaya Piṭakaṃ*, Vol. I, p. 21, and also I. B. Horner, trans., *The Book of the Discipline*, 6 vols. (London: Luzac & Company, for P.T.S., 1938–1966), Vol. IV, p. 28, n. 4.

7 Nārada Thera, ed. and trans., *Dhammapada* (Colombo: Vajirārāma, 1963), p. 304.

8 Oldenberg, *The Vinaya Piṭakaṃ*, Vol. I, p. 58 (Mahāvagga I.30.4).

9 Sukumar Dutt, *Early Buddhist Monachism*, revised ed. (Bombay: Asia Publishing House, 1960), p. 102. I am quoting Dutt's translations, which he mislabels Mahāparinibbāna ii, 27, rather than the correct verse, ii, 22.

10 Horner, *The Book of the Discipline*, Vol. IV, p. 51 (Mahāvagga I.22.16).

11 Sukumar Dutt, *Buddhist Monks and Monasteries of India* (London: George Allen & Unwin, 1962), pp. 58–59.

12 Oldenberg, *The Vinaya Piṭakaṃ*, Vol. I, p. 106 (Mahāvagga II.6.1).
13 *Ibid.* (Mahāvagga II.7.1–2). The other side of a body of water could only be chosen when there was a reliable bridge or boat.
14 *Ibid.*, p. 111 (Mahāvagga II.13.1–2).
15 *Ibid.*, p. 216 (Mahāvagga II.23.1).
16 S. Dutt, *Early Buddhist Monachism*, p. 150.
17 S. Dutt, *Buddhist Monks and Monasteries of India*, p. 59.
18 Oldenberg, *The Vinaya Piṭakaṃ*, Vol. I, p. 39 (Mahāvagga I.22.17–18).
19 James Legge, trans., *A Record of Buddhistic Kingdoms*, reprint (New York: Dover Publications, 1965), pp. 55–63.
20 S. Dutt, *Buddhist Monks and Monasteries of India*, p. 59. The brackets are mine.
21 Oldenberg, *The Vinaya Piṭakaṃ*, Vol. II, p. 153 (Cullavagga VI.3.6).
22 See the Ghoṭamukha Sutta, No. 94 in the Majjhima Nikāya.
23 S. Dutt, *Buddhist Monks and Monasteries of India*, p. 60.
24 See Oldenberg, *The Vinaya Piṭakaṃ*, Vol. I, pp. 139–140 (Mahāvagga III.5.6) and Vol. II, p. 159 (Cullavagga VI.4.10); see also S. Dutt, *Early Buddhist Monachism*, pp. 150–151.
25 S. Dutt, *Early Buddhist Monachism*, pp. 154–156. I have tried to correct some of Dutt's mistakes here. Also see Oldenberg, *The Vinaya Piṭakaṃ*, Vol. II, pp. 175–177 (Cullavagga VI.21.1–3) and 160 (Cullavagga VI.5.2), and H. Kern, *Manual of Indian Buddhism*, reprint (Delhi: Indological Book House, 1968), p. 83.
26 These are mentioned outside the Vinaya. See Kern, *Manual of Indian Buddhism*, p. 83.
27 Oldenberg, *The Vinaya Piṭakaṃ*, Vol. I, p. 137 (Mahāvagga III.2.1–2), and Vol. II, p. 167 (Cullavagga VI.11.3–4).
28 *Ibid.*, Vol. II, p. 146 (Cullavagga VI.1.2).
29 S. Dutt, *Buddhist Monks and Monasteries of India*, p. 93.
30 *Ibid.*, p. 97.
31 On this point, see, for example, Sukumar Dutt, *The Buddha and Five After Centuries* (London: Luzac & Company, 1957), p. 76. Dr. Dutt notes, "The Pātimokkha forms no part of the Pāli canon, even though the bulk of the Vinaya-piṭaka is based upon it; it is embedded, however, in the ancient commentary called Sutta-vibhaṅga on the canon." In using the term paracanonical, I have followed Louis Renou and Jean Filliozat, *L'Inde Classique*, Tome II (Paris: Imprimerie Nationale, 1953), p. 351 (par. 1980).
32 W. Pachow, *A Comparative Study of the Prātimokṣa*, in *Sino-Indian Studies* [Volumes IV, 1–4 and V, 1 (1951–1955)], IV, 1, p. 19.
33 For a review of these attempts, see Horner, *The Book of the Discipline*, Vol. I, pp. xii–xiv. Also see Pachow, *A Comparative Study of the Prātimokṣa*, Vol. IV, 1, pp. 19–23.
34 Horner, *The Book of the Discipline*, Vol. I, p. xii.
35 E. J. Thomas, *The History of Buddhist Thought*, reprint of 2nd ed. (London: Routledge & Kegan Paul, 1963), p. 16.

36 On these offenses Horner, *The Book of the Discipline*, Vol. I, pp. xx–xxiv, remarks:

> Evidently the aim of the strictures on unchastity, with which Pārājika I. is concerned, was partly to bring the monks into line with members of other preceding and contemporary sects whose members, having renounced the household state, had to be celibate. This notion already had history behind it by the time the Sakyan Order of monks came into being. It was a notion based as much on common sense, as on the conviction that restraint and self-taming were indespensible factors in the winning of the fruit of a monk's life. (pp. xx–xxi)
>
> Stealing is ranked as a Pārājika (Pār. II.), or the gravest kind of offence, not merely because civilisation agrees that, for various reasons, it is wrong to take something not given. It was particularly reprehensible for a Sakyan monk to steal, since at the time of his entry into the Order he morally renounced his claim to all personal and private possessions, and should henceforth have regarded anything he used as communal property, lent to him for his needs. (p. xxi)
>
> No doubt the depriving of life ranked as a Pārājika offence (Pār. III.) partly because it is the very opposite of ahiṃsā, non-violence, non-injury, which was an idea prevalent in India before the advent of Sakya. Again, the teaching on rebirth and the allied teaching on karma, both pre-Sakyan notions, would hold that the murderer, in consequence of his deed, obstructs his progress through the worlds, until he has worked off the fruit of his action. (pp. xxii–xxiii)
>
> At present I can only suggest that the fourth Pārājika, of which I have shortly spoken elsewhere, is concerned more with a monk's spiritual state than with his behaviour. In this it differs from the sīlas [Skt. śīlas], and more interesting still, from the other Pātimokkha rules. (p. xxiv)

The brackets in this quotation are mine.

37 Oldenberg, *The Vinaya Piṭakaṃ*, Vol. I, pp. 96–97 (Mahāvagga I.78.1–5).

38 Horner, *The Book of the Discipline*, Vol. I, p. xxvi.

39 Thomas, *The History of Buddhist Thought*, p. 16, n. 2.

40 See Gustav Roth, "Terminologisches aus dem Vinaya der Mahāsāṃghika-Lokottaravādin," *Zeitschrift der deutschen morgenländischen Gesellschaft*, 118 (1968), 341–343; see also Sylvain Lévi, "Sur une langue précanonique du Bouddhisme," *Journal Asiatique*, *Série X*, XX (Novembre-Décembre, 1912), 505–506.

41 Horner, *The Book of the Discipline*, Vol. I, pp. xxviii–xxix, notes that "difficult to speak to" (dubbacajātika in Pāli) is rendered in the Old Commentary (Oldenberg, *The Vinaya Piṭakaṃ*, Vol. III, p. 178) in precisely the same way as Anumāna's description, in the 15th Sutta of the Majjhima Nikāya, of a monk who is unfit to be taught or instructed. She then cites Buddhaghosa's commentary (Papañcasūdanī, II, p. 67) which declares that the Ancients referred to this Sutta as the Bhikkhu-pātimokkha, and she ponders whether this rule represents an especially old portion of the Pātimokkha.

42 The final four saṃghāvaśeṣa dharmas contain, in their text, a threefold admonition for the monk to abandon his evil course. For an example of this admonition, refer to these rules in the translation below.

43 This term is also found as mānāpya in various sources. To cite a few: Thomas, *The History of Buddhist Thought*, p. 18, n. 2; Etienne Lamotte, *Histoire du Bouddhisme Indien des origines à l'ère Śaka* (Louvain: Publications Universitaires, 1958), p. 183; and Ankul Chandra Banerjee, *Sarvāstivāda Literature* [Calcutta: D. Banerjee (Calcutta Oriental Press Private Limited), 1954], p. 228.

44 In *Zeitschrift der deutschen morgenländischen Gesellschaft*, 118 (1968), 343–345.

45 In *Journal Asiatique, Série X*, XX (Novembre-Décembre, 1912), 503–504.

46 Horner, *The Book of the Discipline*, Vol. I, p. xxxii.

47 *Ibid.*, Vol. II, p. vii. I have added Sanskrit equivalents in brackets for the Pāli words employed by Horner and shall continue to do so wherever pertinent throughout.

48 Thomas, *The History of Buddhist Thought*, p. 19.

49 Refer to the Appendix below, and see also Valentina Rosen, ed. and trans., *Der Vinayavibhaṅga Zum Bhikṣu Prātimokṣa Der Sarvāstivādins* (Berlin: Deutsche Akademie der Wissenschaften zu Berlin. Institut für Orientforschung, 1959), pp. 43–45.

50 Horner, *The Book of the Discipline*, Vol. II, p. xii. The brackets are mine.

51 See Roth, "Terminologisches aus dem Vinaya der Mahāsāṃghika-Lokottaravādin," pp. 345–347, Lévi, "Sur une langue précanonique du Bouddhisme," pp. 506–507, and Ryōzaburō Sakaki, ed., *Mahāvyutpatti*, 2 vols. (Kyōto: Shingonshū Kyōto Daigaku, 1925), Vol. I, pp. 530–531 (No. 8360).

52 Pachow, *A Comparative Study of the Prātimokṣa*, Vol. IV, 1, p. 27, illustrates this point, noting that the Pāli text and the Chinese Mahāsāṃghika text have 92 rules, while the Chinese Mahīśāsaka version has 91 rules. The Sanskrit texts of the Mahāsāṃghika and Mūlasarvāstivādin schools have 92 and 90 rules, respectively (see the translations below).

53 These headings have been outlined by Thomas, *The History of Buddhist Thought*, p. 20. However, I deviate considerably from his placement of the rules into the various categories.

54 Thomas, *The History of Buddhist Thought*, p. 20.

55 Pachow, *A Comparative Study of the Prātimokṣa*, Vol. IV, 1, p. 27.

56 *Ibid.*, Vol. IV, 2, p. 69.

57 Oldenberg, *The Vinaya Piṭakaṃ*, Vol. II, p. 93 (Cullavagga IV.14.16).

58 *Ibid.*, Vol. II, p. 80 (Cullavagga IV.4.11).

59 *Ibid.*, Vol. II, pp. 82–83 (Cullavagga IV.6.2).

60 *Ibid.*, Vol. II, p. 94 (Cullavagga IV.14.17).

61 Horner, *The Book of the Discipline*, Vol. III, pp. 153–154, n. 6. See also Oldenberg, *The Vinaya Piṭakaṃ*, Vol. II, pp. 84–85 (Cullavagga IV.9.1–IV.10.2).

62 Oldenberg, *The Vinaya Piṭakaṃ*, Vol. II, p. 4 (Cullavagga I.4.1) and p. 86 (Cullavagga IV.12.3).

63 *Ibid.*, Vol. II, pp. 86–88 (Cullavagga IV.13.1–4).

64 *Ibid.*, Vol. II, p. 83 (Cullavagga IV.7).
65 See Gustav Roth, "Bhikṣuṇīvinaya and the Bhikṣu-Prakīrṇaka and Notes on the Language," *Journal of the Bihar Research Society*, LII, 1–4 (January-December, 1966), 32, and Ernst Waldschmidt, ed. and trans., *Bruchstücke des Bhikṣuṇī-Prātimokṣa der Sarvāstivādin* (Leipzig: Deutsche morgenländischen Gesellschaft in Kommission bei F.A. Brockhaus, 1926), pp. 2–3.
66 The verses preceding and following the Prātimokṣa Sūtra are absent in the Theravāda version, and the ritual formulary is found not only before the text but also in the Mahāvagga. See Oldenberg, *The Vinaya Piṭakaṃ*, Vol. I, pp. 102–104 (Mahāvagga II.3.1–8).
67 Thomas W. Rhys Davids and Hermann Oldenberg, trans., *Vinaya Texts*, 3 vols., reprint (Delhi: Motilal Banarsidass, 1965), Vol. I, pp. xxvii-xxviii.
68 Thomas, *The History of Buddhist Thought*, p. 15, n. 1.
69 Moriz Winternitz, *A History of Indian Literature*, 2 vols. (Calcutta: University of Calcutta, 1927, 1933), Vol. II, p. 22, n. 2.
70 Pachow, *A Comparative Study of the Prātimokṣa*, Vol. IV, 1, p. 20.
71 Oldenberg, *The Vinaya Piṭakaṃ*, Vol. I, p. 103 (Mahāvagga II.3.4).
72 S. Dutt, *Early Buddhist Monachism*, pp. 72–73.
73 *Ibid.*, p. 70. The brackets are mine.
74 Thomas W. Rhys Davids and J. Estlin Carpenter, eds., *The Dīgha Nikāya*, 3 vols., reprint (London: Luzac & Company, for P.T.S.,1966), Vol. II, pp. 49–50.
75 The translation is mine, as are all others in the body of this paper.
76 Pachow, *A Comparative Study of the Prātimokṣa*, Vol. IV, 1, pp. 40–45.
77 Refer to W. Pachow and Ramakanta Mishra, eds., "The Prātimokṣa Sūtra of the Mahāsāṃghikas," *Journal of the Gaṅgānāth Jhā Research Institute*, X, 1–4 (November-February-May-August, 1952–1953), Appendix, pp. 42–45.
78 S. Dutt, *Early Buddhist Monachism*, p. 73. The brackets are mine.
79 Refer to Sangharakshita, *The Three Jewels*, pp. 198–200, and also see Peter A. Pardue, *Buddhism* (New York: The Macmillan Company, 1968), pp. 24–25.
80 S. Dutt, *Early Buddhist Monachism*, pp. 73–74. For a complete discussion of materials related to Buddhist councils, see my article "A Review of Scholarship on the Buddhist Councils," *The Journal of Asian Studies*, 33, 2 (February 1974), 239–254.
81 Erich Frauwallner, *The Earliest Vinaya and the Beginnings of Buddhist Literature*, *Serie Orientale Roma*, Vol. VIII (Rome: Instituto per il Medio ed Estremo Oriente, 1956), p. 112 (and 113), n. 1. For an appraisal of Frauwallner's Vinaya theories, refer to my review article in *The Journal of Asian Studies*, 32, 4 (August 1973), 669–678.
82 Oldenberg, *The Vinaya Piṭakaṃ*, Vol. II, p. 292; also see Horner, *The Book of the Discipline*, Vol. V, pp. xv and 405 (Cullavagga XI.1.16).
83 See Oldenberg, *The Vinaya Piṭakaṃ*, Vol. II, pp. 286–287; also see Horner, *The Book of the Discipline*, Vol. V, pp. 396–397 (Cullavagga XI.1.7).
84 Pachow, *A Comparative Study of the Prātimokṣa*, Vol. IV, 2, p. 81.

85 V. Trenckner, ed., *The Majjhima Nikāya*, Vol. I, reprint (London: Luzac & Company, for P.T.S., 1964), p. 33.

86 See Frauwallner, *The Earliest Vinaya*, p. 79. Rhys Davids and Oldenberg in *Vinaya Texts*, Vol. I, pp. xv–xvi, regard the formulary as part of the Old Commentary [Padabhājaniya], but there is little basis for this. Also see Oldenberg, *The Vinaya Piṭakaṃ*, Vol. I, p. xix, which states, "The Mahāvagga gives precepts concerning the recital of the Pātimokkha, which puts it beyond a doubt that the name Pātimokkha refers here to that text which we also possess under the same name."

87 S. Dutt, *Early Buddhist Monachism*, p. 75. The brackets are mine.

88 Oldenberg, *The Vinaya Piṭakaṃ*, Vol. I, pp. xvi–xvii.

89 *Ibid.*, p. xvii.

90 S. Dutt, *Early Buddhist Monachism*, p. 77.

91 Frauwallner, *The Earliest Vinaya*, pp. 107–109.

92 S. Dutt, *Early Buddhist Monachism*, pp. 78–79. For a discussion of the substantive differences in the Prātimokṣa texts of the various Hinayana schools, see my article "The Prātimokṣa Puzzle: Fact Versus Fantasy," *Journal of the American Oriental Society*, 94, 2 (April-June, 1974), 168–176.

93 Pachow, *A Comparative Study of the Prātimokṣa*, Vol. IV, 1, p. 23.

94 See, for example, V. Trenckner, ed., *The Milindapañho*, reprint (London: Luzac & Company, for P.T.S., 1962), pp. 143, 243, and 272; also see Richard Morris, ed., *The Aṅguttara Nikāya*, Vol. I, 2nd ed., revised (London: Luzac & Company, for P.T.S., 1961), pp. 230 (III.83.1), 231 (III.85.1), 232 (III.86.1), and 234 (III.87.1).

95 B. C. Law, *A History of Pāli Literature*, 2 vols. (London: Kegan Paul, Trench, Trübner & Co., 1933), Vol. I, p. 21.

96 S. Dutt, *Early Buddhist Monachism*, p. 76.

97 Pachow, *A Comparative Study of the Prātimokṣa*, Vol. IV, 1, pp. 25–26.

98 Gokuldas De, *Democracy in Early Buddhist Saṃgha* (Calcutta: Calcutta University Press, 1955), p. 61. The brackets are mine.

99 S. Dutt, *Early Buddhist Monachism*, p. 84.

100 This is pointed out by several scholars. For example, see De, *Democracy in Early Buddhist Saṃgha*, p. 63.

101 For an example of this nidāna, refer to pp. 3–5 of the Sanskrit Mahāsāṃghika text, cited in note 77 above.

102 For a discussion of pariśuddhi, see Horner, *The Book of the Discipline*, Vol. IV, pp. vi and xv.

103 Frauwallner, *The Earliest Vinaya*, pp. 111–112.

104 Stanislaw Schayer, "Precanonical Buddhism," *Archiv Orientalni*, VII (1935), 124.

105 De, *Democracy in Early Buddhist Saṃgha*, p. 72. The brackets are mine.

106 *Ibid.*

107 A. Bareau, *Les Sectes Bouddhiques du Petit Véhicule* (Saigon: École Francaise D'Extreme Orient, 1955).

108 Banerjee, *Sarvāstivāda Literature*, p. 30.

II

The Sanskrit Prātimokṣa Sūtras of the Mahāsāṃghikas and Mūlasarvāstivādins: A Preview

Description of the Texts

In discussing the two texts translated in this study a description of the two manuscripts consulted is a good starting point.

Mahāsāṃghika

The Sanskrit Bhikṣu Prātimokṣa Sūtra owes its discovery to Rāhula Sāṅkṛtyāyana, who, in 1934, traveled from Patna to Tibet in search of manuscripts. "Braving all danger and hardships,"[1] he found a series of Mahāsāṃghika Vinaya texts (the text under discussion being one of these) preserved on palm leaves in the Sa-lu monastery near Śi-ga-rtse, which he photographed. The photographic prints were then entrusted to the Bihar Research Society in Patna for editing. The text which I have translated was edited by W. Pachow and Ramakanta Mishra as "The Prātimokṣa Sūtra of the Mahāsāṃghikas" and published in the *Journal of the Gaṅgānāth Jhā Research Institute*. They describe the text to consist of forty-four folios, the script of which "is similar to that of the Pala Dynasty of Bengal in the 11th century AD."[2] The script is further referred to as Proto-Maithili by Gustav Roth.[3] Concerning the scribe, the editors note:

> On folio 44B there is a description:—
>
> "Śākyabhikṣu śrīvijayabhadra likhitamidam" claiming that the Ms. was copied by Bhikṣu Vijaya Bhadra. This may be a partial truth, because on a careful scrutiny we found that up to folio 23B the bold handwriting is definitely different from the remaining folios. And from

time to time there were corrections or additions on the margin of the folios attempted by different hands. It seems quite certain that the text was copied by more than one Indian Bhikṣu in the 11th century AD when it was brought to Tibet (the actual date we are unable to decide) and kept in the safe custody in a monastery, a few Tibetans tried to scribble a few remarks on folio 44B—the last page of the Ms. Possibly it had been undisturbed until Mahāpandit Rahula Sāṅkṛtyāyana arranged to have it photographed some ten years ago.[4]

Mūlasarvāstivādin

The Sanskrit Bhikṣu Prātimokṣa Sūtra was among the sixty-two items unearthed at Gilgit in Kaśmīr. The text translated in Chapter V below is that edited by Ankul Chandra Banerjee as *Prātimokṣa-Sūtram* [*Mūlasarvāstivāda*]. The text is described by the editor to have been "written on birchbark in Gupta characters of the 5th or 6th century AD."[5] Dr. Banerjee's manuscript was somewhat fragmentary, the gaps having been filled by Sanskrit reconstructions from the Tibetan, referred to as an "infallible guide," and from Finot's Sarvāstivādin Prātimokṣa edition, as well as the *Mahāvyutpatti.*[6] In 1960 Lokesh Chandra noted that Professor Banerjee had utilized only one of the two Mūlasarvāstivādin Bhikṣu Prātimokṣa Fragments in the Gilgit collection, identifying Banerjee's manuscript as No. 3.[7] Chandra therefore edited the remaining fragment (No. 2) as "Unpublished Gilgit Fragment of the Prātimokṣa-Sūtra" and published it in *Wiener Zeitschrift für die Kunde Süd- und Ostasiens.* Unquestionably, the new manuscript filled many of the lacunae in Banerjee's text.

Critique

Corollary to a description of the two texts translated is an appraisal of the editing on the part of Pachow and Mishra on the one hand and Banerjee on the other. Since the original texts were inaccessible to me, the task, of course, is inordinately more difficult. Nevertheless, several statements can be made in this regard.

Mahāsāṃghika

At the outset, Pachow and Mishra note that there is little distinction between various pairs of syllables, examples being pa-ya and sa-ma.[8] Being well versed in the Chinese materials on Vinaya, Pachow, when in doubt, relied on these.[9] Gustav Roth has pointed out several editorial errors made by Pachow and Mishra, and for illustrative purposes, I shall cite three examples:

1. Incorrect and repeated reading of bhikṣū for bhikṣu, a masculine nominative singular form.[10]
2. Incorrect reading of śikṣā for śaikṣā in the introduction to this section of rules.[11]
3. Incorrect reading of ovadikā trayājñapteḥ for ovayikā eṣā jñaptiḥ in the introductory formulary preceding the recitation of the rules.[12]

There are other deficiencies in the manuscript, many of which I am now inclined to assign to the editors rather than the scribe, as the result of a study of Gustav Roth's work on the subject, to which, until recently, I had no access. This is no case of arbitrarily picking and choosing sources of reliance. Roth's work is carefully documented, much more so than Pachow and Mishra's, and it represents a thoroughly sound grammatical approach, enhanced by the earlier research carried out by several German scholars. Regardless of where the blame lies for the poor quality of the editing of the manuscript, I have sought to remedy this insufficiency in my translation and footnotes. Lest I appear too harsh on the editors, it should be noted that the Mahāsāṃghika text is indeed a difficult one grammatically, and its editing is an extremely arduous task for anyone not thoroughly schooled in the numerous Buddhist Hybrid Sanskrit variants.

At first glance it seems almost impossible to make any generalizations concerning the grammar of this text. However, if we take into account the work of others with regard to Mahāsāṃghika-Lokottaravādin texts, a glimmer of light begins to show through. Edgerton has said this of the Mahāvastu:

> Perhaps the most difficult and corrupt, as also probably the oldest and most important, of all BHS [Buddhist Hybrid Sanskrit] works is the Mahāvastu. . . . It was edited by Émile Senart in three stout volumes, 1882–1897. Senart's extensive notes often let the reader perceive the despair which constantly threatened to overwhelm him.[13]

Against this we have the testimony of Gustav Roth:

> A disciple of the great Pāṇini, of course, will not see correct Sanskrit in the language of the Bhikṣuṇī-Vinaya. And it cannot be so, because it is a language of its own which is virtually different from what is understood as correct Sanskrit. I would call this language the Prakrit-cum-

quasi-Sanskrit of the Ārya Mahāsāṃghika-Lokottaravādins.[14]

Roth appears to offer a thoroughly reasonable explanation for both the aberrant grammar and striking affinities found in all the Mahāsāṃghika-Lokottaravādin texts. In this regard he writes:

> The regular recurrence of Prakritic forms shows that they cannot be taken for grammatical mistakes. They belong to the stock of the language. A later attempt to render the text in Sanskrit brought Sanskritic case and verb-endings into the text which stand side by side of Prakritic forms. This led to the composite character of the language with which we have to deal. Yet we can observe regular return of certain forms in stereotype phrases to some extent which determine distinct features of its own.[15]

Roth goes on:

> Exactly the same state of affairs can be observed in texts like Bhi-Vi [Bhikṣuṇī-Vinaya] and Mv [Mahāvastu]. This inscription [i.e., one from Mathurā, cited by Roth] illustrates how Sanskrit endings slowly creep in, which cannot displace the Prakritic endings wholly, they just take their place by the side of them. . . . This coexistence of Prakrit and Sanskrit forms side by side has to be acknowledged as the new type of a language through and through composite in its nature.[16]

To Roth's citation of the Bhikṣuṇī-Vinaya and the Mahāvastu, we can now add the Bhikṣu Prātimokṣa Sūtra, lending further credence to his argument, one with which I concur completely. In fact, due to the striking similarities between the language of the Mahāsāṃghika-Lokottaravādin texts and the Mathurā inscriptions edited by Heinrich Lueders and Klaus Janert and dated from the first century BC to the end of the first century AD, it is possible to ascribe the date of final compilation of these texts to this period (which Roth does).[17]

Mūlasarvāstivādin

The editing of the Mūlasarvāstivādin text is less difficult to assess than the preceding, thanks to Lokesh Chandra's publication of the missing portions of Banerjee's manuscript. First, Banerjee's training and experience attest to his proficiency in working with Sanskrit materials. At the time of the publication of his manuscript, he was Lecturer in Pāli and Sanskrit at Calcutta University (as stated on the title page of the publication). In 1949 he edited

"Bhikṣukarmavākya," a manuscript also included in the Gilgit collection, affording him an opportunity to examine both the general character of the Gilgit Sanskrit manuscripts and the style of the Mūlasarvāstivādin Vinaya texts. If we compare the reconstructed portions of Banerjee's manuscript to those of Chandra's, we find a most striking similarity. In the majority of cases the two versions are, in fact, identical. In the cases where there is disparity we find that these fall into the following categories:

1. Banerjee does not separate the compounds as often as Chandra.
2. The Tibetan vocabulary often employs synonyms for words in Chandra's Sanskrit text.
3. The case endings infrequently differ in the two texts, but they always carry the same intention.
4. The syntax is sometimes at divergence.
5. Banerjee (and this is rare) has made an incorrect reconstruction.

Now it is obvious that of these categories, none but point 5 alters the meaning of Banerjee's text in any way. We should note, however, that the Mūlasarvāstivādin text did not pose nearly as much of a grammatical obstacle as the Mahāsāṃghika, thus providing perhaps less challenge to the editor.

There seems no question that the text, grammatically, is considerably removed from strong Prakritic influences. Gustav Roth notes that with the second century AD, the Sanskrit renaissance began to touch the Middle Indic regions,[18] and it is not unreasonable to date this text somewhat after this time. Since the text was composed in Gupta characters of the fifth or sixth century AD (as noted above), we seem fairly certain in dating the text's finalization between AD 100 and 600. Since the sect name Mūlasarvāstivādin does not appear in any records until the seventh century AD, the latter date appears more satisfactory.

Before concluding this chapter, I would be remiss if I did not offer a brief note concerning the translations and their annotation. Structurally, I have tried to adhere as closely as possible to that set forth in the texts. The language of the texts, as well as my punctuation, is sometimes cumbersome. Nevertheless, I have felt justified in doing so, primarily because we must remember that, as presented in the manuscripts, we are dealing with texts that are both solemnly ritualistic and formal. To attempt to render these sūtras in a literal and flowing style would most certainly do considerable injustice to the solemnity and formality of the ritual. In this I follow the pattern set by my predecessors. I have patently avoided making any omissions of repetitive passages, based on my firm belief that such omissions, usually represented by dots, dashes, and the like, are untrue to the primary language. The translations are arranged with corresponding passages in each version facing each other for easy comparison. This technique has worked especially well in, for example, Hofinger's *Étude sur la concile de Vaiśālī.* I have done my best in the notes to provide a helpful guide to reading and understanding the two texts, explaining problematic Vinayic points wherever expedient. Unusual vocabulary renderings and commentary passages are cited when indicated. Grammatical and phonological peculiarities have been omitted here but can be obtained by those interested in the extremely interesting variants present in Buddhist Hybrid Sanskrit texts.[19]

Notes

1 W. Pachow and Ramakanta Mishra, "The Prātimokṣa Sūtra of the Mahāsāṃghikas," *Journal of the Gaṅgānāth Jhā Research Institute*, IX, 2–4 (February-May-August, 1952), 245. Hereafter, this article shall be referred to as "Prātimokṣa Article," so as not to be confused with the actual text, published by the same two scholars and having the same title as this explanatory article.

2 *Ibid.*, pp. 247–248.

3 Gustav Roth, "Bhikṣuṇīvinaya and Bhikṣu-Prakīrṇaka and Notes on the Language," *Journal of the Bihar Research Society*, LII, 1–4 (January-December, 1966), 30.

4 Pachow and Mishra, "Prātimokṣa Article," pp. 248–249.

5 Ankul Chandra Banerjee, ed., *Prātimokṣa-Sūtram* [*Mūlasarvāstivāda*] (Calcutta: Calcutta Oriental Press Ltd., 1954), p. 2.

6 *Ibid.*, p. 3.

7 Lokesh Chandra, ed., "Unpublished Gilgit Fragment of the Prātimokṣa-Sūtra," *Wiener Zeitschrift für die Kunde Südund Ostasiens*, IV (1960), 1.

8 Pachow and Mishra, "Prātimokṣa Article," p. 248.

9 *Ibid.*

10 Roth, "Bhikṣuṇīvinaya and Bhikṣu-Prakīrṇaka and Notes on the Language," p. 47.

11 Gustav Roth, "Terminologisches aus dem Vinaya der Mahāsāṃghika-Lokottaravādin," *Zeitschrift der deutschen morgenländischen Gesellschaft*, 118 (1968), 340 (and n. 16).

12 *Ibid.*, p. 348.

13 Franklin Edgerton, *Buddhist Hybrid Sanskrit Grammar and Dictionary*, 2 vols. (New Haven: Yale University Press, 1953), Vol. I, p. 10 [par. 1.73]. The brackets are mine.

14 Roth, "Bhikṣuṇīvinaya and Bhikṣu-Prakīrṇaka and Notes on the Language," p. 38.

15 *Ibid.*

16 *Ibid.*, p. 39. The brackets are mine.

17 *Ibid.*, pp. 39 and 51.

18 *Ibid.*, p. 51.

19 Refer to my Ph.D. thesis (The University of Wisconsin, 1971), which provides copious grammatical notes and queries.

III

The Sanskrit Prātimokṣa Sūtras of the Mahāsāṃghikas and Mūlasarvāstivādins: Translations

The Prātimokṣa Sūtra of the Mahāsāṃghikas

Prefatory Verses

Homage to the Blessed One, free from passion

1. This Prātimokṣa was set forth by the Buddha, whose fame is widespread among the knowers of the three worlds, who is well celebrated by the lord of gods and lords of men, who is the servant of the world, and who is the Wise One among the protectors.[1]
2. Having heard that Prātimokṣa spoken by the Sugata, [which provides] release from the pains of becoming, the self-possessed, filled with restraint regarding the six sense organs, put an end to birth and death.
3. Be diligent and of pure śīla, having removed that which the Buddha [has declared to be] the fault of bad śīla, the impure, and the illusory, and after a long time, you will obtain the three jewels.[2]
4. The Śramaṇa who is intent upon śīla crosses over; the Brāhmaṇa who is intent upon śīla crosses over. One who is intent upon śīla is worthy of worship by men and gods; accordingly, there is Prātimokṣa for one intent upon śīla.
5. I will deliver that pure śīla, approved by many Buddhas, which will exist as long as the earth-foundation remains, in the middle of the saṃgha for the welfare of the world and its gods.[3]

Introductory Verses

1. What is the good of life for those who cover their hearts here with the nets of akuśalamūla, like high clouds cover the sky?
   And life is very good for those who quickly drive the nets of akuśalamūla to destruction here, like darkness struck by the sun.
2. What is the use of Poṣadha to those acting with inferior śīla? Those who have fallen into the net of old age and death are devoured by conjectures about immortality.
   And Poṣadha has purpose for those acting with faultless śīla; those who put an end to old age and death, as the self-possessed crush Māra into dissolution.
3. What is the use of Poṣadha to those who are shameless, who have transgressed the śīla of good conduct, who are disposed to improper liveli-

The Prātimokṣa Sūtra of the Mūlasarvāstivādins

[Prefatory and Introductory Verses]

Homage to the Omniscient One

1–2. Having bowed down before the Chief One in the world, who crossed over the boundless attachment to suffering, who was a flag of glory celebrated in the three worlds, whose lion's roar made apparent the roar of the True Dharma, who reached the jeweled treasure of omniscience,[1]* whose feet were rubbed by the crest-jewels of Brahmā's egg, I will explain the treasury of jewels, which is the moral precepts relating to omniscience, in the middle of the community of monks.[2]*

3. This Prātimokṣa is called the essence, the heart and foundation of the limitless and unfathomable water of the ocean of Vinaya of the Buddha.

4. This is the compendium of the True Dharma written by the King of the True Dharma.
This great treaty consists of articles of precepts for the monks who are like a guild of merchants.

5. This is the medicine for impeding the venom of those corrupted by bad śīla.
This is the goad stick for youths bewildered by their youthfulness.

6. This is the raft for crossing over the deep ocean of saṃsāra.
[This is] the foremost guide for a king.

7. This stands like a ladder for ascending the city of release.
It has been proclaimed, "When I enter Nirvāṇa, this [Prātimokṣa] will be your Teacher."[3]*

8. The hearing of the Prātimokṣa is hard to obtain in ten millions of ages; even going beyond, to grasp and to bear [it] is much more difficult to obtain.

9. Happy is the birth of Buddhas, happy is the knowledge of the Dharma;
Happy is the concord in the saṃgha, happy is the tapas of the Śramaṇas.[4]*

10. Happy is the sight of the noble ones, happy also is association with the truth;
Absence of the sight of the ignorant should be a constant happiness.[5]*

11. Happy is seeing the disciplined ones, happy is seeing the learned ones;
And seeing the arhants is happy (i.e., good) for the removal of rebirths.

12. Happy is the river, happy is the bank of the river, happy is the person who has acquired Dharma;

hood, and who speak as if immortal?
And Poṣadha has purpose for those who are modest, who follow the śīla of good conduct, who are disposed to proper livelihood, and who are resolved toward pure śīla.

4. What is the use of Poṣadha to those whose actions are of wicked śīla; those who are thrown aside from the Teaching of the Teacher like a corpse from the ocean?
And Poṣadha has purpose for those who have been instructed here in the three dhātus,[4] who are of pure hands and liberated minds, like the sky.
5. What is the use of Poṣadha to those by whom the six sense organs are not constantly guarded, who have fallen into the realms of Māra, and who are deprived of right conduct?
And Poṣadha has purpose for those by whom the six sense organs are constantly well guarded, those emancipated by the Instruction of the Teacher, and those disposed to the Teaching in the instruction of the Conqueror.
6. What is the use of Poṣadha to those who cite their own [good] śīla, but who cite the bad śīla of their fellow Brahmacārins, men, gods, and the Teacher?
And Poṣadha has purpose for those whose śīla is not to be considered blameworthy, who always speak conscientiously of the yoga[5] of the world with its gods.
7. What is the use of Poṣadha to those who have turned away from the Teaching of the Teacher; to those by whom the misfortunes and five sins are practiced?
And Poṣadha has purpose for those established in the Teaching of the Ten-Powered One, the Fully Enlightened One, the All-Seeing One, and who walk [on] the paths of love.
8. There is now Poṣadha for those in whose hearts the Teacher, Dharma, and Saṃgha[6] dwell, and who have not abandoned the discipline, exposition, dwelling together, satisfaction, and instruction of the Teacher. There is unconditioned knowledge for those having attended to the King of Dharma.
9. Those who are continually pure [receive the helping] hand and Poṣadha. Those of continual purity and undefiled actions [belong to] the saṃgha.
10. As long as the core of the saṃgha shall not be endangered with regard to the Prātimokṣa Sūtra, so long will the True Dharma and unity in the saṃgha stand.

Happy is the attainment of prajñā, happy indeed is the destruction of egotism.

13. Happy is the condition of those learned ones who have made fixed intentions and subdued their senses;
[Happy is the condition] of those gone to old age in peaceful forests, of those having spent their youthfulness in forests.

11. As long as there are explainers and comprehenders of the Jewel of Dharma, so long will the True Dharma stand, for the welfare of the whole world.
12. Therefore, you should be united together harmoniously, be dignified, serve one another, and understand the King of Dharma.
    Grief is permanently subdued in the state of Nirvāṇa.

Introduction

Leader: So many people who have passed beyond, who are well disposed, skilled in purity, who have attained the final end, and who are of [good] conduct have been counted by counting sticks and are seated [here]. No nuns are here. Let the Venerable Ones announce the complete purity and consent of the monks who have not arrived, and having announced it, make it known which monk is the conveyer of consent of the nuns.[7] And here no one is unordained, disposed to passion, a matricide, a patricide, the murderer of an arhant, a schism-maker in the saṃgha, an evil-minded devourer of the blood of the Tathāgata, an offender of the nuns, a dweller among thieves, a dweller with all kinds [of people], expelled, an attacker of the body,[8] or delighted with oneself.[9] Therefore, pay respect to the Śrāvakas of the Blessed One, who are always pure and of completely pure śīla. O Venerable Sirs, let the saṃgha hear me. Today is the fourteenth day in the bright half of the lunar month, Poṣadha day for the saṃgha. So many nights have passed, so many remain. What preliminaries of the saṃgha should be done?
Response: The Śrāvaka-saṃgha of the Blessed One has little that should be done.
Leader: O Venerable Sirs, let the saṃgha hear me. Today is the fifteenth day in the bright half of the lunar month, Poṣadha day for the saṃgha. If it is the right time for the saṃgha, in this place, in as much [area] as[10] has been accepted by the Bhikṣu-saṃgha, measuring a fathom in all directions, the saṃgha, on this occasion, should perform Poṣadha on the fifteenth day and recite the Prātimokṣa Sūtra.[11] You should follow what has been instructed here.
O Venerable Sirs, in this place, in as much [area] as has been accepted by the Bhikṣu-saṃgha, measuring a fathom in all directions, the saṃgha, on this occasion, shall perform Poṣadha on the fifteenth day and recite the Prātimokṣa Sūtra. Since there is silence, that seems good to the saṃgha. Thus do I understand.

[Introduction]

Leader: O Venerable Ones, so many hot seasons have passed, so many remain. Life passes, old age and death approach. The Teaching of the Teacher is diminishing. Yoga should be practiced by the Venerable Ones with diligence. The Tathāgatas, Arhants, Fully Enlightened Ones obtained the wholesome bodhipakṣya dharmas, indeed conducive to bodhi, by diligence. What preliminaries of the Śrāvaka-saṃgha of the Blessed One should be done?
Response: Little, there is little to be done.
Leader: Let the Venerable Ones announce the complete purity[6]* and consent of those who have not arrived, and having announced it, make it known.

14. Bowing down to the Lion of the Sākyas, and a reverential salute having been made, I will proclaim the Prātimokṣa, and let one hear that Vinaya from me.
15. And having heard that, let one act here as proclaimed by the great sage; by making an effort [and] by being without [even] minute sins.
16. For one who constantly, quickly, and with effort pursues his horse-like mind with statements from the mouth [of the Buddha], Prātimokṣa is like the bit of a bridle from which one hundred sharp thorns are shot.
17. The great-minded ones who do not turn away from the proper station [even] by mere words, are indeed horse-like men who will be victorious in the battle of the kleśas.
18. But for the unrestrained ones to whom this is not known to be a bridle, and is not even desired in their hearts, in the battle of the kleśas, they will be bewildered by confusion.

Old age and death come near, life is corrupted, pleasure declines, the True Dharma ceases, the explainers blow out the torch of Dharma, and the comprehenders become limited. The moments, half-seconds, instants, nights, days, half-months, months, seasons, and years pass by. Lives are like the flowing of the swift water of a mountain stream, not even abiding having been removed from the saṃskāras. It should be accomplished by the Venerable Ones with diligence. Why? Because it is the law of the Tathāgatas, Arhants, Fully Enlightened Ones who accomplished it with diligence. Thus do we say: one who has accomplished it with diligence destroys the greatest substratum of existence.[12] It is accomplished by the Venerable Ones through that diligence. Seeing the ten conditions, the Tathāgatas, Arhants, Fully Enlightened Ones pointed out the moral discipline and the higher śīla to the Śrāvakas, and preached the Prātimokṣa Sūtra. What are the ten? They are as follows:[13]

1. For the unity of the saṃgha
2. For the prosperity of the saṃgha
3. For the suppression of small-statured men
4. For the enjoyment and comfort of the skillful monks
5. For the carelessness of the unfavorable ones
6. For the threefold becoming of the pure ones
7. For the removal of the āsravas[14] relating to this life
8. For the state of nonproclamation of sins of the āsravas relating to life after death

So that this teaching may be well guarded, freely[15] exposed, clearly delineated, even among men and gods, the Tathāgatas, Arhants, Fully Enlightened Ones, seeing the ten conditions, pointed out the moral discipline and higher śīla to the Śrāvakas, and preached the Prātimokṣa Sūtra.

O Venerable Ones, I will recite the Prātimokṣa Sūtra. I will speak, and you should listen to it obediently and aptly, and reflect on it. For whom there may be a fault,[16] let him confess it. If there is no fault, [one] should be silent. By being silent, I will know the Venerable Ones are completely pure. Just as, O Venerable Ones, there is an explanation for a monk questioned individually, so it will be proclaimed in this or that form in the assembly of monks up to the third time. For whatever monk, being questioned in this way up to the third time in the assembly of monks, who does not reveal an existing fault which is remembered, there is the speaking of a deliberate lie. The speaking of a deliberate lie has been declared by the Blessed One to be an obstructive condition.[17] Therefore, an existing fault should be revealed

Leader: O Venerable Sirs, let the saṃgha listen. Today is the fourteenth or fifteenth day [of the lunar month], Poṣadha day for the saṃgha. If it seems good [and the saṃgha] should agree that it is the right time for the saṃgha, the saṃgha should perform Poṣadha and recite the Prātimokṣa Sūtra recitation. This is the motion.
Response: O Venerable One, we will make Poṣadha and recite the Prātimokṣa Sūtra recitation.

Leader: For whom there may be a fault, it should be confessed by that one. If there is no fault, [one] should be silent. By being silent, we will understand the Venerable Ones to be completely pure. Just as there is an explanation for a monk questioned individually in this or that form, so also there is the threefold public proclamation in the assembly of monks. For whatever monk, being questioned in this way three times in the assembly of monks, who does not reveal an existing fault which is remembered, there is the speaking of a deliberate lie. Speaking a deliberate lie, O Venerable Ones, has assuredly been declared by the Blessed One to be an obstructive condition. Therefore, an existing fault should be revealed by a fallen monk, remembering [the offense and] hoping for purity. By revealing it, there is comfort for him, but by not revealing it, there is none. O Venerable Ones, the introduction of the Prātimokṣa Sūtra recitation has been recited by me. Therefore, I ask the Venerable Ones—Are you completely pure in this matter? A second and also a third time I ask—Are you completely pure in this matter? Since there is silence, the Venerable Ones are [completely pure] in this matter. Thus do I understand.

by a fallen monk, remembering [the offense and] hoping for purity. Having revealed it, there will be comfort for him, but by not revealing it, there is none.[18]

The Four Pārājika Dharmas

Now, O Venerable Ones, the four pārājika dharmas come up in the half-monthly Prātimokṣa Sūtra recitation.

1. Whatever monk, having undertaken the proper course and training of the monks, should, not having rejected the training and revealed his weakness, engage in sexual intercourse,[19] even so much as with an animal, this monk is pārājika, expelled [from the monastic community]; he is not to obtain dwelling together with the monks.

This moral precept was prescribed by the Blessed One, with regard to the Venerable Yaśikakalandakaputra, in Vaiśālī, in the afternoon[20] of the twelfth day of the fifth half-month in the winter, in the fifth year after perfect enlightenment. [At that time] the shadow cast by one sitting with his face toward the north was equal to one and one half man. When this moral precept has been laid down, that which has been declared [therein] is to be conformed to. This is called Dharma and Anudharma.[21]

2. Whatever monk should, by means of theft, take from a village or forest that which, belonging to others, has not been given, in such a form of theft that kings, having seized [him], would slay, restrain, or banish [him], saying, "O man, you are a thief, you are a fool, you are a robber"; this monk, taking in such manner that which has not been given, is pārājika, expelled; he is not to obtain dwelling with the monks.[22]

This moral precept was prescribed by the Blessed One, with regard to the Venerable Dhanika, King Śreṇīya Bimbisāra, and the monk Pāṃsukulika, in Rājagṛha, in the afternoon of the ninth day of the second half-month in the winter, in the sixth year after perfect enlightenment. [At that time] the shadow cast by one sitting with his face toward the north was equal to two and one half men. When this moral precept has been laid down, that which has been declared [therein] is to be conformed to. This is called Dharma and Anudharma.

3. Whatever monk should, with his own hand, deprive one that has human form[23] of life, obtain an assassin for him, instigate him to death, or praise the nature of death to him, saying, "O man, what use is this dreadful, sinful life which is a poison to you? Death is better for you than life"; should [the

The Four Pārājika Dharmas

Now, O Venerable Ones, the four pārājika dharmas come up in the half-monthly Prātimokṣa Sūtra recitation.

1. Whatever monk, having undertaken the proper course and training of the monks, should, not having rejected the training and not having revealed his weakness in the training, indulge in sexual intercourse, an unchaste thing, even so much as with an animal, this monk is pārājika, expelled.

2. Whatever monk, having gone to a village or forest, should take from others what is not given, in a manner considered to be theft, and by such form of theft, a king or king's minister, having seized him, would slay, bind, or banish him, saying, "O man, you are a thief, you are a fool, you are a robber"; should the monk take in this way what is not given, this monk is pārājika, expelled.

3. Whatever monk should intentionally, with his own hand, deprive a human or one that has human form[7]* of life, supply him with a knife, search for an assassin for him, instigate him to death, or praise the nature of death, saying, "O man, what use is this dreadful, impure, sinful life to you? O man,

monk] purposefully, with an impure mind, instigate him in many ways to death, or praise the nature of death to him, and that man should die[24] by that means and no other, this monk is pārājika, expelled; he is not to obtain dwelling together with the monks.

This moral precept was prescribed by the Blessed One, with regard to the wanderer Mṛgadaṇḍika and the attendants of many ill monks, in Vaiśālī, in the afternoon of the tenth day of the third half-month in the winter, in the sixth year after perfect enlightenment. [At that time] the shadow cast by one sitting with his face toward the east was equal to two and one half men. When this moral precept has been laid down, that which has been declared [therein] is to be conformed to. This is called Dharma and Anudharma.

4. Whatever monk, unknowing and not understanding, should boast with regard to himself of having superhuman faculties, sufficient insight and knowledge into Dharma, like the nobles, and a specific and particular spiritual realization,[25] saying, "Thus do I know, thus do I see"; and then, at a later time, being questioned or not being questioned, this fallen monk desiring purity [should say]: "Not knowing, I spoke in this way, and O Venerable Ones, I said that I know and also that I see; I spoke vainly, falsely, idly"; unless this was spoken because of pride, this monk is pārājika, expelled; he is not to obtain dwelling together with the monks.[26]

This moral precept was prescribed by the Blessed One, with regard to the monk Ābhimānika[27] and the many village dwelling monks, in Śrāvastī, in the afternoon of the thirteenth day of the fourth half-month in the winter, in the sixth year after perfect enlightenment. [At that time] the shadow cast by one sitting with his face toward the north was equal to one and one half man. When this moral precept has been laid down, that which has been declared [therein] is to be conformed to. This is called Dharma and Anudharma.

Summary:[28] (1) sexual intercourse, (2) taking what is not given, (3) slayer of one having human form, and (4) asserting that one may have superhuman faculties.

O Venerable Ones, the four pārājika dharmas have been recited. Whatever monk, having fallen here, into one or another fault, is pārājika, expelled; he is not to obtain dwelling together with the monks. As before, so after; as after, so before; he is pārājika, expelled; he is not to obtain dwelling together with the monks. Therefore, I ask the Venerable Ones—Are you completely pure in this matter? A second time I ask the Venerable Ones—Are you completely pure in this matter? Also a third time I ask the Venerable Ones—Are you completely pure in this matter? Since there is silence, the Venerable Ones are completely pure in this matter. Thus do I understand.

death is better than life for you"; should [the monk] purposefully, being of one opinion, instigate him in many ways to death, or recommend the nature of death to him, and he (i.e., that man) should die by that [means], this monk is pārājika, expelled.

4. Whatever monk, unknowing and not understanding, should boast of having superhuman faculties, sufficient knowledge and the specific spiritual realization of the nobles, and insight and a state of comfort[8]* which are inexistent and unobtained [by him], saying, "I know this, I see this"; and at a later time, the fallen [monk], desiring purity, being questioned or not being questioned, should say, "O Venerable Ones, I said I know, I see, [but it was] worthless, vain, false speaking"; unless [spoken] because of pride, this monk is pārājika, expelled.

O Venerable Ones, the four pārājika dharmas have been recited by me. Whatever monk, having committed one or another fault, is not to obtain dwelling or eating together with the monks. As before, so after; he is pārājika, expelled. Therefore, I ask the Venerable Ones—Are you completely pure in this matter? A second and also a third time I ask the Venerable Ones—Are you completely pure in this matter? Since there is silence, the Venerable Ones are completely pure in this matter. Thus do I understand.

The Thirteen Saṃghātiśeṣa Dharmas

Now, O Venerable Ones, the thirteen saṃghātiśeṣa dharmas come up in the half-monthly Prātimokṣa Sūtra recitation.

1. Intentional emissions[29] of semen, except in a dream, [constitute] a saṃghātiśeṣa.

2. Whatever monk, excited by passion, with perverted mind, should come into bodily contact with a woman, namely, taking her hand, taking her hair, delighting in one or another of her limbs, or should take pleasure in touching and caressing her body,[30] that is a saṃghātiśeṣa.

3. Whatever monk, excited by passion, with perverted mind, should speak to a woman with wicked words concerned with unlawful sexual intercourse, as a young man [would speak] to a young woman, that is a saṃghātiśeṣa.

4. Whatever monk, excited by passion, with perverted mind, should speak, in the presence of a woman, in praise of [sexual] service [with the body] to himself, saying, "Sister, this is the highest of services; that a woman, with this act connected with sexual intercourse, should serve [or] attend to a śramaṇa like me who is well disciplined, virtuous, and chaste"; that is a saṃghātiśeṣa.

5. Whatever monk should undertake to act as a go-between, or should personally bring a man to a woman or a woman to a man, as a wife, or a lover, or even if it is [the body of] a nun,[31] that is a saṃghātiśeṣa.

6. When a monk himself is begging to have a hut built which has no donor, being intended for himself, it should be made [according to measure]. This is the measure: in length, twelve spans of the Sugata-span; in width, seven spans inside. Various monks should be brought to mark out the site. A site not involving slaughter and good for roaming about should be marked out by these monks. If the monk, by begging himself, should cause a hut to be built which has no donor, being intended for himself, on a site which involves destruction or is not good for roaming about, should not bring the monks to mark out the site, or should exceed the measure on an unmarked site which is not good for roaming about, that is a saṃghātiśeṣa.

7. When a monk is having a large vihāra built, with a donor and intended for himself, monks should be brought to the woods to mark out the site. A site not involving slaughter and good for roaming about should be marked out by these monks. If the monk should have a large vihāra built, with a donor and intended for himself, on a site not good for roaming about, or should he not bring the monks to mark out the site, in this unmarked site, not good for roaming about, there is a saṃghātiśeṣa.

The Thirteen Saṃghāvaśeṣa Dharmas

Now, O Venerable Ones, the thirteen saṃghāvaśeṣa dharmas come up in the half-monthly Prātimokṣa Sūtra recitation.

1. Intentional emission of semen, except during a dream, is a saṃghāvaśeṣa.

2. Whatever monk, with perverted mind, should come into bodily contact with a woman, taking her hand, taking her arm, taking her hair, touching one or another of her limbs, or should indulge in stroking her limbs, that is a saṃghāvaśeṣa.

3. Whatever monk, with perverted mind, should speak to a woman with wicked, evil, or vulgar words connected with sexual intercourse, just as a young man [speaks] to a young woman, that is a saṃghāvaśeṣa.

4. Whatever monk, with perverted mind, should recommend, in front of a woman, [sexual] service with the body to himself, saying, "Sister, this is the highest of services; namely, that one should serve with this act connected with sexual intercourse, a monk like me who is well disciplined, virtuous, and chaste"; that is a saṃghāvaśeṣa.

5. Whatever monk should undertake to act as a go-between, [bringing] a man to a woman or a woman to a man, so much as for a wife, a lover, or even for a moment, that is a saṃghāvaśeṣa.

6. When a monk, by begging himself, is having a hut built, having no donor and intended for himself, the hut should be built according to measure. This is the measure for the hut: in length, twelve spans of the Sugata-span; in width, seven spans inside. Monks should be brought by that monk for viewing the site. The site should be viewed by those monks who are brought to not involve slaughter and be good for roaming about. If the monk should have a hut built, for which he begged himself, having no donor and intended for himself, on a site which involves destruction and is not good for roaming about, or should he not bring monks to view the site, or should he exceed the measure on a site which has not been viewed by the monks who were not brought, that is a saṃghāvaśeṣa.

7. When a monk is having a large vihāra built, with a donor and intended for the saṃgha, monks should be brought by that monk for viewing of the site. Hence, the site should be viewed by those monks who are brought to not involve slaughter and be good for roaming about. If the monk is having a large vihāra built, which has a donor and is intended for the saṃgha, on a site which is not good for roaming about, or should he not bring the monks for viewing of the site, that is a saṃghāvaśeṣa.[9]*

8. Whatever monk, ill-tempered, corrupt, and angry because of malice toward a monk, should accuse a pure, faultless monk of a groundless pārājika dharma, thinking, "Thus indeed,[32] I will cause this monk to fall from the pure life"; and at a later time, when he (i.e., the corrupt monk) is being questioned or not being questioned, that legal question is [determined to be] groundless, that thing is the grasping of a groundless legal question; and [if] that monk stands fast in his malice,[33] saying, "I spoke because of malice"; that is a saṃghātiśeṣa.
9. Whatever monk, ill-tempered, corrupt, and angry because of malice toward a monk, taking up something merely as a pretext for a legal question connected with something else, should accuse a non-pārājika monk of a pārājika offense, thinking, "I will cause this monk to fall from the pure life"; and at a later time, when he (i.e., the corrupt monk) is being questioned or not being questioned, that legal question is [determined to be] connected with something else, that thing is the grasping of a legal question connected with something else, merely as a pretext; and [if] that monk stands fast in his malice, saying, "I spoke because of malice"; that is a saṃghātiśeṣa.
10. Whatever monk should proceed toward a division of a saṃgha which is harmonious,[34] or having taken up a legal question conducive to a schism, and should persist in taking it up, that monk should be spoken to thus[35] by the monks: "Do not, O Venerable One, proceed toward a division of a saṃgha which is harmonious, or taking up a legal question conducive to a schism, persist in taking it up. Let the Venerable One come together with the saṃgha, for the saṃgha is harmonious, united, on friendly terms, without dispute, and dwells comfortably under one rule,[36] like milk and water, illuminating the Teaching of the Teacher." And should that monk, being spoken to thus by the monks, abandon that course, this is good. If he should not abandon it, that monk should be questioned and admonished by the monks up to three times for the abandonment of that course. Should he, being questioned and admonished up to three times, abandon that course, this is good. Should he not abandon it, having taken up that course, and persist in taking it up, that is a saṃghātiśeṣa.
11. If there are one, two, three, or many monk-comrades of a schism-minded monk, who take his side and follow him, and these monks together with men should say to those [other] monks, "Do not, O Venerable Ones, say anything, good or bad, about this monk. This monk speaks according to the Dharma and this monk speaks according to the Vinaya; and this monk takes up our wish and objective, and having taken [them up], obtains [them]. That which seems good and pleases this monk also seems good and

8. Whatever monk, angry because of hostility, should accuse a pure monk of a groundless pārājika dharma, thinking, "Just so, I will cause him to fall from the pure life"; and at a later time, when he is being examined or not being examined, that legal question of his [is determined to be] groundless, and the monk should stand fast because of hostility, saying, "I spoke in hostility"; that is a saṃghāvaśeṣa.
9. Whatever monk, angry because of hostility, taking up something merely as a pretext for a legal question connected with something contrary or other, should accuse a pure monk of a pārājika dharma, thinking, "Just so, I will cause him to fall from the pure life"; and at a later time, when he is being examined or not being examined, that legal question [is determined to be] connected with something else, that thing is used merely as a pretext pointing to something [else], and the monk should stand fast in his hostility, saying, "I spoke because of hostility"; that is a saṃghāvaśeṣa.
10. Whatever monk should proceed toward a division of a saṃgha which is harmonious, or having taken up a legal question conducive to causing a schism, should persist in taking it up, that monk should be spoken to thus by the monks: "The Venerable One should not proceed toward a division of the saṃgha which is harmonious, or having taken up a legal question conducive to causing a schism, persist in taking it up. Let the Venerable One come together with the saṃgha, for the saṃgha is harmonious, united, on friendly terms, without dispute, and dwells in a happy condition under a one-pointed Dharma exposition, being like milk and water, demonstrating the Teaching[10]* of the Teacher. Abandon, O Venerable One, such a course which causes a schism in the saṃgha." If that monk, being spoken to by the monks, should abandon that course,[11]* this is good. If he should not abandon it, he should be examined and instructed a second and a third time for the abandonment of that course. Should he, being examined and instructed a second and a third time, abandon that course, this is good. If he should not abandon it, that is a saṃghāvaśeṣa.
11. If there are one, two, three, or many monk-comrades of a monk who is a speaker of disunion, and should these monks say to those [other] monks, "Do not, O Venerable Ones, say anything good or bad about this monk. Why? This monk, O Venerable Ones, speaks according to the Dharma and according to the Vinaya, and taking up our wish and objective, obtains [them]. This monk speaks knowingly and not unknowingly, and that which pleases this monk also pleases and seems good to us." These monks [siding with the schism-maker] should be spoken to thus by the monks: "Do not let the Venerable Ones speak this way. That monk does not speak according

pleases us. This monk speaks knowingly and not unknowingly." These monks [siding with the schism-maker] should be spoken to thus by the [other] monks: "Do not, O Venerable Ones, speak thus. This monk does not speak according to the Dharma and this monk does not speak according to the Vinaya. This monk speaks against the Dharma and this monk speaks against the Vinaya. Not knowing, this monk speaks unknowingly. Do not, O Venerable Ones, take delight in a schism in the saṃgha. Just, O Venerable Ones, delight in the totality of the saṃgha. Let the Venerable Ones come together with the saṃgha, for the saṃgha is harmonious, united, on friendly terms, without dispute, and dwells comfortably and happily under one rule, like milk and water, illuminating the Teaching of the Teacher." Should those [schismatic] monks, having been spoken to thus by the [other] monks, abandon that course, this is good. If they should not abandon it, those monks should be questioned and admonished by the monks up to three times for the abandonment of that course. Should they, being questioned and admonished up to three times, abandon that course, this is good. Should they not abandon it, having taken up that course, and persist in taking it up, that is a saṃghātiśeṣa.

12. If a monk who is difficult to speak to,[37] being spoken to by the monks in accordance with the Dharma and in accordance with the Vinaya, concerning the moral precepts in the training included in the exposition, makes himself one who is not to be spoken to, saying, "Do not, O Venerable Ones, say anything to me, either good or bad, and also I will not ask anything, good or bad, of the Venerable Ones. Let the Venerable Ones abstain from speaking to me"; that monk should be spoken to thus by the monks: "Do not, O Venerable One, being spoken to by the monks in accordance with the Dharma and in accordance with the Vinaya, concerning the moral precepts in the training included in the exposition, make yourself one who is not to be spoken to; let the Venerable One make himself one who is to be spoken to, and then the monks will speak to the Venerable One in accordance with the Dharma and in accordance with the Vinaya, concerning the training. Also let the Venerable One speak to the monks in accordance with the Dharma and in accordance with the Vinaya, concerning the training. Thus, by mutual speech and by mutual helping to eliminate faults, shall the community[38] of the Blessed One, the Tathāgata, the Arhant, the Fully Enlightened One increase." Should that monk, being spoken to thus by the monks, abandon that course, this is good. Should he not abandon it, that monk should be questioned and admonished by the monks up to three times for the abandonment of that course. Should he, being questioned and ad-

to the Dharma and according to the Vinaya.[12]* [Do not say that that monk], taking up our wish and objective, obtains [them]. [Do not say] that monk speaks knowingly and not unknowingly, and that which pleases and seems good to that monk also seems good to you. Also, O Venerable Ones, do not take delight in a schism in the saṃgha. Again, do not [allow] a schism in the saṃgha to [provide] delight for the Venerable Ones. Let the Venerable Ones come together with the saṃgha, for the saṃgha is harmonious, on friendly terms, without dispute, and dwells in a happy condition under a one-pointed Dharma exposition, being one like milk and water, demonstrating the Teaching of the Teacher. Do not, O Venerable One,[13]* persist toward a division of the saṃgha. Abandon this form of speech which causes a division in the saṃgha." These [schismatic] monks should be examined and instructed a second and a third time by the [other] monks for the abandonment of that course, and should they, being examined and instructed a second and a third time, abandon that course, this is good. If they should not abandon it, that is a saṃghāvaśeṣa.

12. If many monks who are corrupters of families and practitioners of evil should dwell near a certain village or town and the families corrupted by these [monks] should be seen, heard, or known of, these monks should be spoken to thus by the monks: "The Venerable Ones are corrupters of families and practitioners of evil, and the families corrupted by you are seen, heard, and known of. Depart, O Venerable Ones, from this āvāsa. You have lived here long enough!" If these [evil] monks should say to those [other] monks: "The monks, O Venerable Ones, are followers of desire, followers of malice, followers of delusion, and followers of fear. They banish some monks because of faults such as these, but do not banish some [other] monks"; the monks should be spoken to thus: "Do not, O Venerable Ones, speak in this way; that some monks are followers of desire, followers of malice, followers of delusion, and followers of fear; that they banish some monks because of faults such as these, but do not banish some [other] monks. Why? These monks are not followers of desire, followers of malice, followers of delusion, and followers of fear, but you Venerable Ones are indeed corrupters of families and practitioners of evil. The families corrupted by you are seen and heard, and your evil practices are seen, heard, and known of. [You] monks, O Venerable Ones, are followers of desire, followers of malice, followers of delusion, and followers of fear. Abandon this form of speech." These [evil] monks should be spoken to thus by the monks. If they should abandon it, this is good. If they should not abandon it, they should be examined and instructed a second and a third time for the abandon-

monished up to three times, abandon that course,[39] this is good. Should he not abandon it, having taken up that course, and persist in taking it up. that is a saṃghātiśeṣa.

13. If monks who are corrupters of families and practitioners of evil dwell near a certain village or city or town, and their evil practices are seen and heard, and the corrupted families are seen and heard, these monks who are corrupters of families and practitioners of evil should be spoken to thus by the monks: "The evil practices of the Venerable Ones are seen and heard, and the corrupted families are seen and heard. Let the Venerable Ones who are practitioners of evil and corrupters of families depart from this āvāsa. You have lived here long enough!" If the [evil] monks, being spoken to thus by the [other] monks, should say to those [other] monks: "The saṃgha, O Venerable Ones, is a follower of desire; the saṃgha, O Venerable Ones, is a follower of malice; the saṃgha, O Venerable Ones, is a follower of delusion; the saṃgha, O Venerable Ones, is a follower of fear; and the saṃgha banishes some monks because of faults such as these, but does not banish some [other] monks"; these [evil] monks should be spoken to thus by the [other] monks: "Do not, O Venerable Ones, speak thus. The saṃgha of monks is not a follower of desire; the saṃgha is not a follower of malice; the saṃgha is not a follower of delusion; the saṃgha is not a follower of fear; and the saṃgha does not banish some monks because of faults such as these while not banishing some [other] monks. The evil practices of the Venerable Ones are seen and heard, and the corrupted families are seen and heard. Let the Venerable Ones who are practitioners of evil and corrupters of families depart from this āvāsa. You have lived here long enough!" Should those monks, being spoken to thus by the monks, abandon that course, this is good. Should they not abandon it, these [evil] monks should be questioned and admonished by the monks up to three times for the abandonment of that course. Should they, being questioned and admonished up to three times, abandon that course, this is good. Should they not abandon it, having taken up that course, and persist in taking it up, that is a saṃghātiśeṣa.

Summary: (1) intentional [emissions of semen], (2) taking the hand, (3) [wicked] speech, (4) praise of [sexual] service, (5) acting as a go-between, (6–7) two [forms of dwelling]: hut and vihāra, (8–9)[40] by a messenger to the saṃgha, (10) proceeding to a schism, (11) following [a schismatic] monk, (12) one who is difficult to speak to, and (13) corrupters of families.

O Venerable Ones, the thirteen saṃghātiśeṣa dharmas have been recited: nine which become faults at once[41] and four which do not become faults up to the third admonition. If a monk falls into one or another of these faults, ment [of that course]. Should they, being examined and instructed a second and a third time, abandon [that course], this is good. If they should not abandon it, that is a saṃghāvaśeṣa.

13. If some monk here who is difficult to speak to, being spoken to by the monks in accordance with the Dharma and in accordance with the Vinaya, concerning the moral precepts included in the exposition and included in the Sūtras of the Sugata, makes himself one who is not to be spoken to, saying, "Do not, O Venerable Ones, say anything to me, either good or bad, and also I will not say anything good or bad to the Venerable Ones. Let the Venerable Ones abstain from speaking to me, and also I will abstain from speaking to you"; that monk should be spoken to thus by the monks: "You, O Venerable One, being spoken to by the monks in accordance with the Dharma and in accordance with the Vinaya, concerning the moral precepts included in the exposition and included in the Sūtras of the Sugata, make yourself one who is not to be spoken to. Let the Venerable One make himself one who is to be spoken to. Let the monks speak to the Venerable One in accordance with the Dharma and in accordance with the Vinaya, and also let the Venerable One speak to the monks in accordance with the Dharma and in accordance with the Vinaya, for thus, through mutual speech and through mutual helping to eliminate faults, will the community of the Blessed One, the Tathāgata, the Arhant, the Fully Enlightened One, be bound together. Do not let the Venerable One make himself one who is not to be spoken to." That monk should be spoken to thus by the monks. If he should abandon that course, this is good. If he should not abandon it, he should be examined and instructed a second and a third time for the abandonment of that [course]. Should he, being examined and instructed a second and a third time, abandon that course, this is good. If he should not abandon it, that is a saṃghāvaśeṣa.

O Venerable Ones, the thirteen saṃghāvaśeṣa dharmas have been recited by me: nine which become faults at once and four which do not become faults up to the third admonition. If a monk has fallen into one or another of these [faults], so much time [parivāsa] should be spent by that [monk], even unwillingly, as he knowingly conceals it. When that monk, even unwillingly, has completed the parivāsa, six more nights should be spent [undergoing] mānatva in the saṃgha. When the mānatva has been completed, the monk, with satisfied mind, should be pardoned by the āvarhaṇa ceremony[14*] by the Bhikṣu-saṃgha, done according to Dharma. If the Bhikṣu-saṃgha is a group of twenty, that monk should be reinstated. If a Bhikṣu-saṃgha should reinstate that monk while being a group of twenty

so many days parivāsa should be spent by that monk, even unwillingly, as he knowingly conceals it. When the monk has completed[42] the parivāsa, six more days should be spent [undergoing] mānatva in the Bhikṣu-saṃgha. When the mānatva has been observed, the monk should answer the summons made according to Dharma. If the Bhikṣu-saṃgha is a group of twenty, that monk should be reinstated. If, having reinstated that monk, that Bhikṣu-saṃgha is lacking by even one monk from being a group of twenty, that monk is not reinstated and the monks are blameworthy. This is the proper conduct here.[43]

Therefore, I ask the Venerable Ones—Are you completely pure in this matter? A second time I ask the Venerable Ones—Are you completely pure in this matter? Also a third time I ask the Venerable Ones—Are you completely pure in this matter? Since there is silence, the Venerable Ones are completely pure in this matter. Thus do I understand.

The Two Aniyata Dharmas

Now, O Venerable Ones, the two aniyata dharmas come up in the half-monthly Prātimokṣa Sūtra recitation.

1. Whatever monk should sit down[44] with a woman, one with the other,[45] in secret, on a concealed, convenient seat,[46] and a trustworthy upāsikā,[47] having seen that one, should accuse him according to one or another of three dharmas: [either] with a pārājika, saṃghātiśeṣa, or pācattika dharma, that monk, admitting that he was so seated, should be dealt with according to one or another of three dharmas: [either] a pārājika, saṃghātiśeṣa, or pācattika dharma; or by whichever dharma that trustworthy upāsikā, having seen him, should say. So that monk should be dealt with according to that dharma. This is an aniyata.

2. If there is not a seat which is concealed and convenient, but sufficient to speak to a woman with wicked words connected with unlawful sexual intercourse, whatever monk should sit down with a woman, one with the other, on such a seat, and a trustworthy upāsikā, having seen that one, should accuse him according to one or another of two dharmas: [either] with a saṃghātiśeṣa or pācattika dharma, that monk, admitting that he was so seated, should be dealt with according to one or another of two dharmas: [either] a saṃghātiśeṣa or pācattika dharma; or by whichever dharma that trustworthy upāsikā, having seen him, should say. So that monk should be dealt with according to this or that dharma. This is an aniyata.

lacking by even one [monk], that monk is not reinstated and the monks are blameworthy. This is the proper conduct. Therefore, I ask the Venerable Ones—Are you completely pure in this matter? A second and also a third time I ask the Venerable Ones—Are you completely pure in this matter? Since there is silence, the Venerable Ones are completely pure in this matter. Thus do I understand.

The Two Aniyata Dharmas[15*]

Now, O Venerable Ones, the two aniyata dharmas come up in the half-monthly Prātimokṣa Sūtra recitation.

1. Whatever monk should sit down with a woman, one with the other, in secret, on a concealed seat suitable to have sexual intercourse, and if a trustworthy upāsikā should accuse [him] of one or another of three dharmas: [either] with a pārājika, saṃghāvaśeṣa, or pāyantika dharma, that monk, admitting that he was so seated, should be dealt with according to one or another of three dharmas: [either] a pārājika, saṃghāvaśeṣa, or pāyantika dharma; or by whichever dharma that trustworthy upāsikā should accuse that monk. So should that monk be dealt with by this or that dharma. This is an aniyata.

2. Whatever monk should sit down with a woman, one with the other, in secret, on a concealed seat not suitable to have sexual intercourse,[16*] and if a trustworthy upāsikā should accuse [him] of one or another of two dharmas: [either] with a saṃghāvaśeṣa or pāyantika dharma, that monk, because of admitting that he was so seated, [should be dealt with] according to one or another of two dharmas: [either] a saṃghāvaśeṣa or pāyantika dharma; or by whichever dharma that trustworthy upāsikā should accuse that monk. So should that monk be dealt with by this or that dharma. This is an aniyata.

O Venerable Ones, the two aniyata dharmas have been recited by me.

Summary: (1) a concealed seat, and (2) a secret seat.

O Venerable Ones, the two aniyata dharmas have been recited. Therefore, I ask the Venerable Ones—Are you completely pure in this matter? A second time I ask the Venerable Ones—Are you completely pure in this matter? Also a third time I ask the Venerable Ones—Are you completely pure in this matter? Since there is silence, the Venerable Ones are completely pure in this matter. Thus do I understand.

The Thirty Niḥsargika-Pācattika Dharmas

Now, O Venerable Ones, the thirty niḥsargika-pācattika dharmas come up in the half-monthly Prātimokṣa Sūtra recitation.

1. When the robes have been made up by the monks, and the kaṭhina ceremony has been suspended,[48] an extra robe may be worn by a monk up to ten days. Should he wear it beyond that, that is a niḥsargika-pācattika.

2. When the robes have been made up by the monks, and the kaṭhina ceremony has been suspended, if a monk should be separated from one or another of the three robes, even for one night, except with the permission of the saṃgha,[49] that is a niḥsargika-pācattika.

3. When the robes have been made up by the monks, and the kaṭhina ceremony has been suspended, should a robe be produced for a monk at the wrong time, it may be accepted by the monk if he wishes. Having accepted that robe, it should be made up quickly, and should that robe, because of the preparation [involved], not be completed for that monk, that robe should be laid aside by the monk for a month at the most when hope exists for the completion of the deficiency. Should he lay it aside in excess of that, whether hope exists or not [for the completion of the deficiency], that is a niḥsargika-pācattika.

4. Whatever monk should accept a robe from an unrelated[50] nun, except in exchange, that is a niḥsargika-pācattika.

5. Whatever monk should have an old robe washed, dyed, or beaten by an unrelated nun, that is a niḥsargika-pācattika.

6. Whatever monk should ask an unrelated householder or householder's son for a robe, except at the right time, that is a niḥsargika-pācattika. Under those circumstances, this is the right time: if the monk is one whose robe has been stolen. This is the right time in this matter.

7. If it seems good to a monk whose robe has been stolen to ask an unrelated householder or householder's son for a robe, and that one (i.e., the house-

Therefore, I ask the Venerable Ones—Are you completely pure in this matter? A second and also a third time I ask the Venerable Ones—Are you completely pure in this matter? Since there is silence, the Venerable Ones are completely pure in this matter. Thus do I understand.

The Thirty Niḥsargika-Pāyantika Dharmas

Now, O Venerable Ones, the thirty niḥsargika-pāyantika dharmas come up in the half-monthly Prātimokṣa Sūtra recitation.

1. When a monk has been provided with a [set of] robes,[17*] and the kaṭhina ceremony has been suspended, an extra, optional robe may be worn up to ten days. Should he wear it beyond that, that is a niḥsargika-pāyantika.

2. If a monk who has been provided with a [set of] robes, when the kaṭhina ceremony has been suspended, should be separated, outside the sīmā,[18*] from one or another of the three robes, even for one night, except with the permission of the saṃgha, that is a niḥsargika-pāyantika.

3. A robe accruing to a monk at the wrong time: when he has been provided with a [set of] robes, and the kaṭhina ceremony has been suspended, may be accepted by that monk if he wishes. Having accepted that robe, and making it up quickly, it should be worn if it is completed. If it is not completed, that robe should be laid aside by that monk for a month at the most when hope exists that he may complete the deficiency of the robe. Should he lay it aside in excess of that, that is a niḥsargika-pāyantika.

4. Whatever monk should have an old robe washed, dyed, or beaten by an unrelated nun, that is a niḥsargika-pāyantika.

5. Whatever monk should accept a robe from a nearby,[19*] unrelated nun, except in exchange, that is a niḥsargika-pāyantika.

6. Whatever monk, having approached an unrelated householder or householder's wife, should ask for a robe, except at the right time, that is a niḥsargika-pāyantika. Under those circumstances, this is the right time: when a monk is one whose robe has been stolen, whose robe has been destroyed, whose robe has been burned, whose robe has been washed away, whose robe has been carried off [by wind]. This is the right time in this matter.

7. When a monk whose robe has been stolen, whose robe has been destroyed, whose robe has been burned, whose robe has been washed away, or whose

holder or householder's son), in consenting, should offer[51] him [material for] many robes, then [material for] an inner and upper robe at the most should be accepted by that invited monk. Should he accept in excess of that, that is a niḥsargika-pācattika.

8. When different robe prices, having been intended for a monk, have been prepared by two householders who are not related[52] [to the monk], thinking, "Having purchased a robe with these robe prices, we will present such and such named monk with a robe"; then if that monk, approaching, but not having been previously invited, should [seek to] procure a gift,[53] saying, "It would be good if you Venerable Ones, having purchased a robe with these robe prices, present such and such named monk with a robe, both [prices] for one."[54] In obtaining the robe, having taken up the desire for something excellent, there is a niḥsargika-pācattika.

9. When various robe prices, having been intended for a monk, have been prepared by two [people] who are not related [to the monk]: a householder and a householder's wife, thinking, "Having each purchased a robe with these various robe prices, we will each present such and such named monk with a robe"; then if that monk, approaching, but not having been previously invited, should [seek to] procure a gift, saying, "It would be good if you, the Venerable One and the lady, having purchased a single robe with these various robe prices, present such and such named monk with such and such a single robe, both [prices] for one." In obtaining the robe, having taken up the desire for something excellent, there is a niḥsargika-pācattika.

10. In case a certain king or king's minister should send forth robe prices by a messenger, having been intended for a monk, and [that messenger], having approached the monk, should say to that monk: "These robe prices, having been intended for the Noble One, have been sent via messenger by such and such named king or king's minister. Let the Noble One accept these"; that messenger should be spoken to thus by the monk: "It is not good, O Venerable One, for a monk to accept the robe prices, but we do accept a robe which is given properly at the right time."[55] Thus addressed, the messenger should say to the monk: "Is there, O Noble One, someone who does the work of the monks." The vaiyyāvṛtyakaras[56] should be pointed out by the monk desiring [a robe]—either ārāmikas[57] or vaiyyāvṛtyakaras of the monks, saying, "O Venerable One, these do the work of the monk." Thus addressed and having approached the vaiyyāvṛtyakaras, that messenger should say to those

robe has been carried off [by wind], having approached an unrelated householder or householder's wife, should ask for a robe, if that faithful [wife] or Brāhmaṇa householder should offer that one excessively, regarding [material for] many robes, [material for] an inner and upper robe at the most should be accepted from that one by the monk, if he wishes. Should he accept in excess of that, that is a niḥsargika-pāyantika.

8. If robe prices are assembled, having been intended for a monk, by an unrelated householder or householder's wife, thinking, "Such named monk will approach, and I, having purchased such and such a robe with these robe prices, will present him with a robe, properly, at the right time"; and if one monk, approaching, but not having been previously invited, [seeking to] obtain a gift, should say to that unrelated householder or householder's wife: "These are robe prices which, having been assembled by the Venerable One, are intended for me. Indeed it is good for you, O Venerable One, that you should, having purchased such and such a robe with the robe prices, present [me] with a robe, properly, at the right time"; in the obtaining of the robe, there is a niḥsargika-pāyantika.

9. If various robe prices are assembled, having been intended for a monk, by an unrelated householder and a householder's wife, thinking, "The monk will approach, and we, [having each purchased a robe] with these various [robe prices], will present that one with the two robes, one by one, properly, at the right time"; and if that monk, approaching, but not having been previously invited, [seeking to] procure a gift, should say to that unrelated householder or householder's wife: "These are various robe prices which, having been assembled by the Venerable One, are intended for me. Indeed it is good. Let the Venerable Ones, having purchased such and such a robe with the various robe prices, present [me] with a robe, properly, at the right time, both [prices] for one [robe]"; in the obtaining of the robe, having taken up the desire for something excellent, there is a niḥsargika-pāyantika.

10. If robe prices have been sent forth in the hand of a messenger, having been intended for a monk, by a king, or king's minister, or Brāhmaṇa, or householder, or townsman, or country dweller, or wealthy man, or wealthy merchant, or caravan leader, then that messenger, taking up those prices, should go up to where the monk is, and having approached, should say to that monk: "The Noble One should know that robe prices have been sent forth, having been intended for you, by a king, or king's minister, or Brāhmaṇa, or householder, or townsman, or country dweller, or wealthy man, or wealthy merchant, or caravan leader. Let the Noble One, having taken up compassion, accept [the robe prices]." That messenger should be spoken

vaiyyāvṛtyakaras: "It would be good if you venerable vaiyyāvṛtyakaras, having purchased a robe with these robe prices, present such named monk with a robe, properly and not improperly, at the right time." That messenger, having instructed those vaiyyāvṛtyakaras and approaching (i.e., returning to) the monk, should say to that monk: "Those vaiyyāvṛtyakaras, having been pointed out by the Noble One, have been instructed by me. Approach them and they will present you with a robe, properly and not improperly, at the right time." When the sought after robe is desired by the monk, having approached the vaiyyāvṛtyakaras, the vaiyyāvṛtyakaras should be asked and apprised once, twice, or three times [for the robe]. When the Venerable Ones are being requested and apprised once, twice, or three times concerning the robe for the monk, should he (i.e., the monk) obtain that robe, this is good. If he should not obtain [the robe], the monk should stand silently on this spot[58] four, five, or six times at most. Should the monk obtain that robe, standing silently in this spot four, five, or six times at most, this is good. If he should not obtain [the robe], and asks in excess of that [in order to] obtain that robe, in the obtaining of the robe, there is a niḥsargika-pācattika. If he should not obtain [the robe], he should go himself [to the place] from which these robe prices were sent by the king or king's minister, or a messenger[59] should be sent by the monk, saying, "These robe prices which were sent by the Venerable Ones, having been intended for such named monk, are not of any use for that monk. Let the Venerable Ones make use of their own things so that [your wealth] will not be lost."[60] This is the proper course [in this matter].

Summary: (1) ten days, (2) separation, (3) improper time, (4) acceptance, (5) washing, (6) asking, (7–8) two: inner and outer robe, (9) regarding a gift, and (10) king. First section.

11. Whatever monk should have a new rug[61] made of pure black sheep's wool,[62] that is a niḥsargika-pācattika.

12. When a monk is having a new rug made, two portions of pure black sheep's wool should be taken, the third of white, and the fourth of tawny.[63] Should he take in excess of that, that is a niḥsargika-pācattika.

13. Whatever monk should have a new rug made of sheep's wool mixed with silk, that is a niḥsargika-pācattika.

14. When a monk has a new rug made, it should be used, willingly, for six years. If that monk, after that,[64] either casting aside or not casting aside the old rug, should have another new rug made, having taken up the desire for something excellent, except with permission, that is a niḥsargika-pācattika.

to thus by that monk: "Go, venerable messenger. It is ruin for monks to accept robe prices, but we do accept a robe, having obtained it[20]* properly, at the right time." That messenger should say to that monk: "Is there some vaiyyāvṛtyakara of the Noble Ones who undertakes the work of the Noble Ones?" The vaiyyāvṛtyakara should be pointed out by the monk desiring a robe—either an ārāmika or an upāsaka, saying, "These vaiyyāvṛtyakaras, O messenger, undertake the work of the monks." Then that messenger, taking up the robe prices, should go up to where the vaiyyāvṛtyakara is, and having approached, should say to that vaiyyāvṛtyakara: "You should know, O venerable vaiyyāvṛtyakara, that such named monk will approach, and you, having purchased such and such a robe with these robe prices, should present him with a robe, properly, at the right time." Then that messenger, having admonished and instructed that vaiyyāvṛtyakara properly and thoroughly, should go up to where that monk is, and having approached, should say to that monk: "That vaiyyāvṛtyakara who was pointed out by the Noble One has been instructed. You should approach him at the right time, and he will present you with a robe, properly, at the right time." The vaiyyāvṛtyakara, having been approached by the monk desiring a robe, should be requested and reminded two or three times: "I am, O venerable vaiyyāvṛtyakara, in need of a robe; I am, O venerable vaiyyāvṛtyakara, in need of a robe." If, having been requested and reminded two or three times, that robe is obtained, this is good. If he should not obtain it, he should stand silently in this spot up to four, five, or six times. If, standing silently in this spot up to four, five, or six times, he should obtain the robe, this is good. If he should not obtain it, he should not pursue it[21]* beyond that. If [he should further exert himself] for the obtainment of the robe, in obtaining the robe, there is a niḥsargika-pāyantika. If he should not obtain [the robe], he should go himself to the place from which these robe prices were brought, or a trusted messenger should be sent, saying, "These robe prices which were sent by the Venerable Ones, having been intended for such named monk, do not serve any use for that monk. Let the Venerable Ones know your own wealth. Do not let your wealth go to ruin."

11. Whatever monk should have a new rug made of silk, that is a niḥsargika-pāyantika.

12. Whatever monk should have a new rug made of pure black sheep's wool, that is a niḥsargika-pāyantika.

13. When a monk is having a new rug made, two portions of pure black sheep's wool should be taken, the third of white, and the fourth of tawny. If a monk should have a new rug made, not taking up two portions of pure

15. When a monk is having a rug for sitting on[65] made, then a portion equal to a Sugata-span should be taken from the old rug, on all sides, to disfigure the new [rug]. If a monk should have a new rug for sitting on made without taking up [the required portion of the old rug], that is a niḥsargika-pācattika.
16. Sheep's wool may accrue to a monk when he is traveling on a road.[66] It may be accepted by the monk if he wishes, and having accepted it, it may be carried by him[67] up to three yojanas when there is no other carrier. Should he carry it in excess of that, whether there is another carrier or not, that is a niḥsargika-pācattika.
17. Whatever monk should have sheep's wool washed, dyed, or combed out by an unrelated nun, that is a niḥsargika-pācattika.
18. Whatever monk should, with his own hand, acquire gold or silver, or should have [another] acquire it [for him], even so much as to say: "Deposit it here," or should consent to its having been deposited, that is a niḥsargika-pācattika.
19. Whatever monk should undertake activity in various sorts of buying and selling, namely, that he should buy this, or buy from there, or say: "Buy so much," that is a niḥsargika-pācattika.
20. Whatever monk should undertake activity in various sorts of sales in gold or silver, that is a niḥsargika-pācattika.

Summary: (11–12) two portions of pure black [sheep's wool], (13) mixed with silk, (14) six years, (15) [rug for] sitting, (16) road, (17) should comb out, (18) with his own hand, (19) buying and selling, and (20) activity in sales. Second section.

21. An extra bowl may be kept by a monk for ten days at the most. Should he keep it in excess of that, that is a niḥsargika-pācattika.
22. Whatever monk, having taken up the desire for something excellent,[68] should get another new bowl when his [old] bowl has been repaired in less than five places, that is a niḥsargika-pācattika, and that bowl should be forfeited to the assembly of monks by that monk. That which is the last bowl in that assembly of monks should be given to that monk, [saying:] "This bowl, O Venerable One, should be kept by you until it breaks."
23. These are the medicines which should be partaken of [69] by the sick, namely: clarified butter, oil, honey, and molasses. It is allowed that such unprepared [medicines], having been accepted, may be laid aside for seven days, to be eaten by a sick monk, and the remainder should be thrown out. Should he chew or consume in excess of that, or not throw out the remainder, that is a niḥsargika-pācattika.
24. Whatever monk, having given a robe to [another] monk, and later, being

black sheep's wool, the third of white, and the fourth of tawny, that is a niḥsargika-pāyantika.

14. When a monk is having a new rug made, having been made, it should be used, even unwillingly, for six years. If the monk, before the six years are up, either casting aside or not casting aside that old rug, should have another new rug made, except with the permission of the saṃgha, that is a niḥsargika-pāyantika.

15. When a monk is having a rug for sitting on[22*] made, a Sugata-span should be taken from the old rug for sitting on, on all sides, to disfigure the new [rug]. If a monk should use a new rug for sitting on, not taking up a Sugata-span from the old rug for sitting on, on all sides, to disfigure the new [rug], that is a niḥsargika-pāyantika.

16. Should sheep's wool accrue to a monk when on a journey, it may be accepted by that monk if he wishes, and having accepted it, it may be carried by him up to three yojanas when there is no carrier. Should he carry it in excess of that, that is a niḥsargika-pāyantika.

17. Whatever monk should have sheep's wool washed, dyed, or combed out by an unrelated nun, that is a niḥsargika-pāyantika.

18. Whatever monk should, with his own hand, acquire gold or silver, or cause it to be acquired,[23*] that is a niḥsargika-pāyantika.

19. Whatever monk should undertake various activities in money, that is a niḥsargika-pāyantika.

20. Whatever monk should undertake various [kinds of] buying and selling, that is a niḥsargika-pāyantika.

21. An extra bowl may be kept by a monk for ten days at the most. Should he maintain it in excess of that, that is a niḥsargika-pāyantika.

22. Whatever monk, having taken up the desire for something excellent, should seek another new bowl when his [old] bowl, which is fit for use, has been repaired in less than five places, [is guilty], in the obtaining of the bowl, [of] a niḥsargika-pāyantika. That bowl should be forfeited to the assembly of monks by that monk. That which is the last bowl in that assembly of monks should be given to that monk, saying: "This [bowl] is for you, O monk. It should be depended on, and should not be changed. Having taken it up, it should be used gradually until it is entirely broken." This is the proper course in this matter.

23. Whatever monk, by begging yarn himself, should have a robe woven by an unrelated weaver, in the obtaining of that robe, there is a niḥsargika-pāyantika.

24. If an unrelated householder or householder's wife should have a robe

malicious, angry because of malice, and ill-tempered, should snatch away, should cause to be snatched away,[70] or take away that monk's robe, or should say: "I did not give [the robe] to you," that is a niḥsargika-pācattika.

25. Thinking, "A month of the hot season remains," a varṣāśāṭikā[71] robe may be searched about for by a monk. Thinking, "half-month remains," having made it up, it should be put on.[72] If a monk should search about for a varṣāśāṭikā robe with more than [a month remaining], and having made it up, should put it on, that is a niḥsargika-pācattika.

26. Whatever monk, himself having asked for yarn, should have a robe woven[73] by a weaver, that is a niḥsargika-pācattika.

27. If an unrelated householder or householder's son should have a robe woven by a weaver, having been intended for a monk, and if the monk, approaching, but not having been previously invited, should [seek to] procure a gift, saying: "That is good, O Venerable One; make this robe long, make it wide, make it well-woven,[74] make it well-formed,[75] and make it well-scraped. If you do so, we will collect some money for you: a measure of gold, or a half-measure of gold, or alms food, or a sum necessary for alms food";[76] and if that monk, speaking thus, should not collect some money: a measure of gold, or a half-measure of gold, or alms food, or a sum necessary for alms food, in obtaining the robe, there is a niḥsargika-pācattika.

28. Should a special robe accrue to a monk ten days before the full moon of Kārtika, three months [of the rains having passed], it may be accepted by a monk, thinking it is special. Having accepted it, it should be laid aside until the time of the giving of robes. Should he lay it aside in excess of that, that is a niḥsargika-pācattika.

29. If a monk, having spent the three months of the rainy season up to the full moon or Kārtika, dwells on a bed and seat in a forest which is held to be fearful, dangerous, and doubtful, one or another robe of the three robes may be laid aside, inside a house, by the monk if he wishes. Should there be any reason for that monk to stay away from that robe, that monk may stay away from that robe for six days at the most. Should he stay away in excess of that, except with permission regarding the length,[77] that is a niḥsargika-pācattika.

30. Whatever monk should knowingly confiscate for himself wealth belonging to the saṃgha, accumulated in the saṃgha, that is a niḥsargika-pācattika.

Summary: (21) bowl, (22) repair, (23) medicine, (24) not snatching, (25) varṣāśāṭikā, (26–27) two [rules regarding] a weaver, (28) ten days before, (29) rains, and (30) confiscation. Third section.

woven by an unrelated weaver, having been intended for a monk, and if that monk, approaching, but not having been previously invited, in [seeking to] procure a gift, should say to that weaver: "Know, O venerable weaver, that this robe which is being woven has been intended for me. That is good, O venerable weaver. Make the robe wide, well-scraped, well-formed, and well-beaten. If you do so, we, in order to obtain the robe, will collect some money for the venerable weaver, namely: alms food, the substance in a begging bowl, or the provisions in a begging bowl"; in the obtaining of the robe, there is a niḥsargika-pāyantika.

25. Whatever monk, having given a robe to a monk, and afterwards, being angry, mad, wrathful,[24]* and ill-tempered, should snatch away or cause [the robe] to be snatched away, and should say to him, in taking it back: "Moreover, O monk, I did not give the robe to you"; that robe and that remainder[25]* should be forfeited by that [angry] monk to the one who made use of it, and that is a niḥsargika-pāyantika.

26. Should a special robe accrue to a monk ten days before the full moon of Kārtika, it may be accepted by that monk if he wishes. Having accepted it, it should be held until the time of the giving of robes. Should he hold it in excess of that, that is a niḥsargika-pāyantika.

27. When many monks are [spending] the rains on beds and seats in forests which are held to be doubtful, [full of] various fears, and abundantly dangerous, one or another robe of the three robes may be laid aside, inside a house, by the forest [dwelling] monk if he wishes. Should there be any reason such as that for a forest [dwelling] monk to go outside the sīmā, that forest [dwelling] monk may stay away, outside the sīmā, from that robe for six nights at the most. Should he stay away in excess of that, that is a niḥsargika-pāyantika.

28. When a month of the hot season remains, a varṣāśāṭikā robe may be searched about for by a monk. When a half-month remains, having made it up, it should be put on. If a monk should search about for a varṣāśāṭikā robe with less than a month of the hot season remaining, or should put it on, having made it after a half-month of the hot season remains, that is a niḥsargika-pāyantika.

29. Whatever monk should knowingly confiscate for himself, individually, wealth belonging to and accumulated in the saṃgha, that is a niḥsargika-pāyantika.

30. These are the proper medicines which have been declared by the Blessed One to be partaken of by sick monks: clarified butter, oil, honey, and molasses. These, having been held by him for seven days at the most, to be

O Venerable Ones, the thirty niḥsargika-pācattika dharmas have been recited. Therefore, I ask the Venerable Ones—Are you completely pure in this matter? A second time I ask the Venerable Ones—Are you completely pure in this matter? Also a third time I ask the Venerable Ones—Are you completely pure in this matter? Since there is silence, the Venerable Ones are completely pure in this matter. Thus do I understand.

The Ninety-Two Pācattika Dharmas

Now, O Venerable Ones, the ninety-two pācattika dharmas come up in the half-monthly Prātimokṣa Sūtra recitation.

1. In speaking a conscious lie, there is a pācattika.
2. In insulting speech,[78] there is a pācattika.
3. In slander of monks, there is a pācattika.
4. Whatever monk should knowingly open up[79] to further actions, legal questions which have been appeased and determined by the saṃgha according to Dharma and according to Vinaya, saying: "This act which should be done again, will be [done]"; having done it for just this reason and not another, the opening up is a pācattika for that monk.
5. Whatever monk, being a doer of the improper, should teach Dharma to a woman in excess of five or six words,[80] except with a wise man [present], that is a pācattika.
6. Whatever monk should speak Dharma, step by step, to an unordained man, that is a pācattika.
7. Whatever monk should, in the presence of an unordained person, boast with regard to himself, of having superhuman faculties, sufficient noble insight and knowledge, and a specific spiritual realization,[81] saying: "Thus do I know, thus do I see"; if it is a fact,[82] that is a pācattika.
8. Whatever monk should knowingly speak of the grave offense of a monk to an unordained person, except when permission for the explanation has been made,[83] that is a pācattika.
9. Whatever monk, when the wealth belonging to the saṃgha is being distributed, should knowingly, having first given his consent,[84] afterwards raise objections as: "The Venerable Ones, as a vehicle of friendship, confiscate for some person or other, wealth belonging to the saṃgha, accumulated in the saṃgha"; that is a pācattika.
10. Whatever monk, when the half-monthly Prātimokṣa Sūtra is being recited, should say: "What is the use, O Venerable Ones, of reciting these

used as a stored supply, should be consumed by the sick monk if he wishes. Should he eat in excess of that, that is a niḥsargika-pāyantika.[26]*.

O Venerable Ones, the thirty niḥsargika-pāyantika dharmas have been recited by me. Therefore, I ask the Venerable Ones—Are you completely pure in this matter? A second and also a third time I ask—Are you completely pure in this matter? Since there is silence, the Venerable Ones are completely pure in this matter. Thus do I understand.

The Ninety Pāyantika Dharmas

Now, O Venerable Ones, the ninety pāyantika dharmas come up in the half-monthly Prātimokṣa Sūtra recitation.

1. In speaking a conscious lie, there is a pāyantika.
2. In speaking of the defects of men, there is a pāyantika.
3. In slander of monks, there is a pāyantika.
4. Whatever monk should knowingly open up to further actions, a legal question established by the entire saṃgha according to Dharma, that is a pāyantika.

5. Whatever monk should teach Dharma to a woman in excess of five or six words, except in the presence of a wise man, that is a pāyantika.
6. Whatever monk should speak Dharma, step by step, to an unordained man, that is a pāyantika.
7. Whatever monk should speak of the grave offense [of a monk] to an unordained person, except with consent of the saṃgha, that is a pāyantika.

8. Whatever monk should speak of the superhuman faculties [of himself] to an unordained person, if it is a fact, that is a pāyantika.
9. Whatever monk, having first given his consent, should afterwards say: "The Venerable Ones, for the sake of friendship, seek to confiscate for their personal use, accumulated wealth belonging to the saṃgha"; that is a pāyantika.

10. Whatever monk, when the half-monthly Prātimokṣa Sūtra recitation is being recited, should say: "What is the use, O Venerable Ones, of reciting these lesser and minor precepts in the half-monthly Prātimokṣa Sūtra rec-

lesser and minor moral precepts, since they are conducive to remorse, distress, and perplexity for the monks"; in reviling the precepts, there is a pācattika.

Summary: (1) lie, (2) insult, (3) slander, (4) open up [a legal question], (5) Dharma instruction, (6) step by step, (7) specific [spiritual realization], (8) speaking, (9) regarding friendship, and (10) reviling [precepts]. First section.

11. In destruction of all sorts of seeds and vegetables, there is a pācattika.

12. In causing annoyance by doing this,[85] there is a pācattika.

13. In vexing or abusiveness,[86] there is a pācattika.

14. Whatever monk, arranging or having a couch, chair, cushion,[87] square blanket,[88] rug with long hair,[89] or pillow[90] arranged[91] in an open space in a bhikṣu-vihāra belonging to the saṃgha, and setting it out, should neither remove it nor have it removed, or should go away without asking [permission], that is a pācattika.

15. Whatever monk, arranging or having a bed on the ground arranged in a bhikṣu-vihāra belonging to the saṃgha, and setting it out, should neither remove it nor have it removed, or should go away without asking [permission], that is a pācattika.

16. Whatever monk, ill-tempered, corrupt, and angry because of malice, should throw out or cause a monk to be thrown out of a bhikṣu-vihāra belonging to the saṃgha, even going so far that he should say: "Go away, O monk"; that is a pācattika.

17. Whatever monk, although not arriving until the beds for the monks had been previously arranged, should knowingly arrange a bed in the middle of a bhikṣu-vihāra belonging to the saṃgha, saying: "For whom this will bear [a burden], he should go away"; having done it for just this reason and not another, the removal [of a monk] is a pācattika for that monk.

18. Whatever monk should sit down or lie down[92] on a chair or couch having removable legs,[93] in an elevated hut in a bhikṣu-vihāra belonging to the saṃgha, that is a pācattika.

19. Whatever monk, knowingly, should sprinkle or have grass or clay[94] sprinkled with water containing living creatures, that is a pācattika.

20. When a monk is having a large vihāra built, situated where there is little grass,[95] having taken up preparation for the window holes[96] and the bolt with regard to the door frame,[97] means[98] for covering it two or three times should be determined. Should he determine in excess of that, situated where there is little grass, that is a pācattika.[99]

itation, as they are conducive to remorse, sorrow, perplexity, regret, and contrition for the monks"; in the transgression of the moral precepts, there is a pāyantika.

11. In the destruction of all sorts of seeds and vegetables, there is a pāyantika.
12. In vexing or abusiveness,[27*] there is a pāyantika.
13. In violating orders,[28*] there is a pāyantika.
14. Whatever monk, placing down or throwing down a cushion, couch, chair, or four-cornered pillow in an open space belonging to the saṃgha, should then, neither removing nor having it removed, go away without asking[29*] a competent monk [for permission], except when there is a reason, that is a pāyantika.
15. Whatever monk, spreading out or causing a bed of grass or a bed of leaves to be spread out in a vihāra belonging to the saṃgha, should then, neither removing nor having it removed, go away without asking a competent monk [for permission], except when there is a reason, that is a pāyantika.
16. Whatever monk, being angry, mad, wrathful, and ill-tempered, should throw out or cause a monk to be thrown out of a vihāra belonging to the saṃgha, except when there is a reason, that is a pāyantika.
17. Whatever monk, although not arriving until [the beds] for the monks had been previously obtained, and having intruded, should knowingly sit down or lie down on a seat in a vihāra belonging to the saṃgha, saying: "For whom this will be a burden, he should go away"; having done it for just this reason,[30*] that is a pāyantika.
18. Whatever monk should knowingly sit down or lie down, by force, on a chair or couch having removable legs, in an elevated hut[31*] in a vihāra belonging to the saṃgha, that is a pāyantika.
19. Whatever monk should knowingly sprinkle or have grass, refuse, or clay sprinkled with water containing living creatures, that is a pāyantika.
20. When a monk is having a large vihāra built, having taken up preparations, consisting of earth, for the window holes and for the placing of the bolt with regard to the door frame, means for covering it two or three times with grass should be determined. Should he determine in excess of that, that is a pāyantika.[32*]

Summary: (11) seed, (12) causing annoyance, (13) abusiveness, (14) couch, (15) bed, (16) throwing out, (17) previously arrived, (18) elevated [hut], (19) water, and (20) covering. Second section.

21. Whatever monk, being unauthorized, should admonish a nun, that is a pācattika.
22. Whatever monk, even if authorized, should admonish a nun at the wrong time: when the sun has gone down [or] when dawn has not yet arisen,[100] that is a pācattika.
23. Whatever monk, intending to admonish, should, having not invited a qualified monk, approach the nuns' quarters,[101] except at the right time, that is a pācattika. Under those circumstances, this is the right time: when a nun who should be admonished and instructed becomes ill. This is the right time in this matter.
24. Whatever monk should speak thus to a monk: "For the sake of material good, O Venerable One, the monk admonishes a nun"; that is a pācattika.
25. Whatever monk should sit down with a nun, one with the other, in secret, that is a pācattika.
26. Whatever monk, proceeding with a nun, should go on a journey, even to another village, except at the right time, that is a pācattika. Under those circumstances, this is the right time: when the road is considered to be doubtful, dangerous, and fearful. This is the right time in this matter.
27. Whatever monk, proceeding with a nun, should board one boat [together], going upstream or downstream, except for crossing to the opposite shore, that is a pācattika.
28. Whatever monk should give a robe to an unrelated nun, except in exchange, that is a pācattika.
29. Whatever monk should sew or have a robe sewn for an unrelated nun, that is a pācattika.
30. Whatever monk should knowingly eat alms food which a nun caused to be cooked, except if it was previously undertaken by the householder,[102] that is a pācattika.

Summary: (21) unauthorized, (22) even if authorized, (23) admonishment, (24) material good, (25) sitting, (26) going on a journey, (27) boat, (28) give [a robe], (29) sew, and (30) cause [food] to be cooked. Third section.

31. Alms food in a village may be eaten by a monk who is not ill for up to one day. In eating in excess of that, there is a pācattika.
32. In eating out of turn,[103] except at the right time, that is a pācattika. Under those circumstances, this is the right time: the time of illness or the

21. Whatever monk, not having been authorized by the saṃgha, should admonish nuns, by possession of such a dharma, that is a pāyantika.
22. Whatever monk, even if authorized by the saṃgha, [should admonish nuns] at a time when the sun has gone [down], that is a pāyantika.
23. Whatever monk should say to a monk: "The monks admonish the nuns for the sake of some material goods"; that is a pāyantika.
24. Whatever monk should give a robe to an unrelated nun, except in exchange, that is a pāyantika.
25. Whatever monk should make a robe for an unrelated nun, that is a pāyantika.

26. Whatever monk should go on a journey with a company of nuns, even to another village, except at the right time, that is a pāyantika. Under those circumstances, this is the right time: when the road the company is traveling on is considered to be doubtful, dangerous, and fearful. This is the right time in this matter.
27. Whatever monk, proceeding with a company of nuns, should board one boat, going upstream or downstream, except for crossing to the opposite shore, that is a pāyantika.
28. Whatever monk should sit down with a woman, one with the other, on a secret, concealed seat, that is a pāyantika.
29. Whatever monk should stand with a nun, one with the other, in a secret, concealed [place], that is a pāyantika.
30. Whatever monk should knowingly eat alms food which a nun caused to be cooked, except if it was previously undertaken by the householder, that is a pāyantika.
31. In eating out of turn, except at the right time, there is a pāyantika. Under those circumstances, this is the right time: a time of illness, a time of work, a time of going on a journey, or a time of the giving of robes. [This is the right time in this matter.]
32. One [meal of] alms food may be eaten by a monk who is not ill, dwelling in a village. Should he eat in excess of that, that is a pāyantika.
33. Should many monks approach families, if faithful Brāhmana householders should invite them for food[33]* such as barley-gruel and meal, two or three bowls full may be accepted by those monks if they wish. Should

time of the giving of robes. This is the right time in this matter.
33. Whatever monk who has eaten what is offered and risen from his seat, should chew or consume hard food or soft food that has not been left over, that is a pācattika.
34. Whatever monk, in seeking to annoy,[104] should knowingly invite a monk who has eaten what is offered and risen from his seat, [to eat] hard food or soft food that has not been left over, or should say: "Come, O monk, chew and consume"; that is a pācattika.
35. Whatever monk should put food which was not given, or is unacceptable, in his mouth, except water for rinsing the teeth,[105] that is a pācattika.
36. In eating at the wrong time, there is a pācattika.
37. In eating [food] that has been laid aside [as a store], there is a pācattika.
38. If a family should invite a monk who has approached for barley-gruel[106] early in the morning, up to three bowls full may be accepted by the invited monk. Having accepted it, the two [bowls full] should be carried outside,[107] and having carried the two [bowls full] outside, sharing it with monks who are not ill, it should be chewed and consumed. Having accepted in excess of that, and having carried the two [bowls full] outside, should he chew or consume it, sharing or not sharing it with monks who are not ill, that is a pācattika.
39. These are foods which are regarded as excellent,[108] namely: clarified butter, oil, honey, molasses, milk, curds, fish, and meat. Whatever monk who is not ill, asking or having families asked for such foods which are regarded as excellent, for himself, should chew or consume them, that is a pācattika.
40. In a group meal, except at the right time, there is a pācattika. Under those circumstances, this is the right time: a time of illness, time of the giving of robes, time of going on a journey, time of being boarded on a boat, the great time,[109] and the meal time of the śramaṇas. This is the right time in this matter.

Summary: (31) [alms food] in a village, (32) [eating] out of turn, (33) [food] offered, (34) [seeking] to annoy, (35) [food] that is not given, (36) [eating] at the wrong time, (37) [food] laid aside, (38) barley-gruel, (39) asking [for excellent food], and (40) group meal. Fourth section.
41. Whatever monk who is not ill, desiring to warm himself because of his shivering, should kindle or cause a fire to be kindled of grass, wood, cow dung, sweepings,[110] or rubbish, except at the right time, that is a pācattika.
42. Whatever monk should lie down in the same house with an unordained person for more than two or three nights, that is a pācattika.

they accept in excess of that, that is a pāyantika. Having accepted two or three bowls full, and going outside the ārāma, [the bowls full] should be shared by those monks with [other] monks, and it (i.e., the food) should be eaten by each. This is the proper course in this matter.

34. Whatever monk who has eaten what is offered, should chew or consume hard food or soft food that has not been left over, that is a pāyantika.

35. Whatever monk, in seeking to annoy,[34]* should knowingly invite a monk who has eaten what is offered, for hard food or soft food that has not been left over, saying: "Chew this, O Venerable One, consume this"; having done it for just this reason, that is a pāyantika.

36. In a group meal, except at the right time, there is a pāyantika. Under those circumstances, this is the right time: a time of illness, a time of work, a time of going on a journey, a time of being boarded on a boat, the time of a great meeting, and the meal time of the śramaṇas. This is the right time in this matter.

37. Whatever monk should chew or consume hard food or soft food at the wrong time, that is a pāyantika.

38. Whatever monk should chew or consume hard food or soft food which has been stored up, that is a pāyantika.

39. Whatever monk should put food in his mouth which was not given, except for water or a tooth-pick, that is a pāyantika.

40. These are foods for the monks declared by the Blessed One to be excellent, namely: milk, curds, fresh butter, fish, meat, and dried flesh. Whatever monk who is not ill, asking for such excellent foods from different families, for himself, should chew or consume them, that is a pāyantika.

41. Whatever monk should knowingly consume water containing living creatures, that is a pāyantika.

42. Whatever monk, knowingly intruding on a family with food, should sit down on a seat, that is a pāyantika.

43. Whatever monk should knowingly stand concealed amidst a family with food, that is a pāyantika.

44. Whatever monk should give, with his own hand, hard food or soft food to a male ascetic, female ascetic, or male wanderer, that is a pāyantika.

45. Whatever monk should go to see an army fighting, that is a pāyantika.

46. If there is some reason for a monk to go to see an army fighting, that monk may stay amongst that army for two or three nights at most. Should he stay in excess of that, that is a pāyantika.

47. If a monk, dwelling amongst an army for two nights, should go to maneuvers,[35]* or should enjoy[36]* the [battle] banner,[37]* the head of the

43. Whatever monk, having given his consent for formal acts of the monks, and afterwards being ill-tempered, corrupt, and angry because of malice, should say: "My consent was not given, my consent was improperly given; these formal acts are incomplete, these formal acts are improperly done, for I do not give my consent to the formal acts of those [monks]"; that is a pācattika.

44. Whatever monk should say to a monk: "Come, O Venerable One, we will enter a village for alms food, and I will have some [alms food] given to you"; if he, either causing some [alms food] to be given to him or not, should afterwards, seeking to dismiss him, say: "Go, O Venerable One. Neither talking nor sitting with you is pleasant for me"; having done it for just this reason and not another, the dismissal is a pācattika for that monk.

45. Whatever monk should say to the monks: "O Venerable Ones, as I understand the Dharma taught by the Blessed One, indulgence in these which have been declared by the Blessed One to be obstructive conditions is not sufficient for a hindrance"; that monk should be spoken to thus by the monks: "Do not, O Venerable One, speak thus. Do not, O Venerable One, by understanding the obstructive conditions as inexistent,[111] declare this about the Blessed One, for indulgence in these, the same obstructive conditions which have been declared by the Blessed One, is sufficient for a hindrance." And should that monk, being spoken to thus by the monks, abandon that course, this is good. Should he not abandon it, that monk should be questioned and admonished by the monks up to three times for the abandonment of that course. Being questioned or admonished up to the third time, should he abandon that course, this is good. If he should not abandon it, that monk should be sent away by the harmonious saṃgha. This sending away is a pācattika for that monk.

46. Whatever monk should knowingly eat, dwell, or lie down in the same house with a monk who has been sent away by the harmonious saṃgha in accordance with Dharma and in accordance with Vinaya, and who, acting as he speaks,[112] has not abandoned that evil view and has not made Anudharma, that is a pācattika.

47. If a male novice[113] should say: "O Venerable Ones, as I understand the Dharma taught by the Blessed One, indulgence in these which have been declared by the Blessed One to be obstructive desires is not sufficient for a hindrance"; that male novice should be spoken to thus by the monks: "Do not, O venerable male novice, speak thus. Do not, O venerable male novice, by understanding the obstructive desires as inexistent, declare this about the Blessed One, for indulgence in these, the same obstructive desires which

army, the battle array, or inspection of the army, that is a pāyantika.
48. Whatever monk, being angry, mad, and ill-tempered, should strike a blow to a monk, that is a pāyantika.
49. Whatever monk, being angry, mad, wrathful, and ill-tempered, should threaten a blow [with a weapon] to a monk, even so much as to make a threatening gesture with the hand,[38]* that is a pāyantika.
50. Whatever monk should knowingly conceal the grave offense of a monk, that is a pāyantika.
51. Whatever monk should say to a monk: "Come, O Venerable One, we will approach families, and I will have them give you hard food and soft food, as much as is apt"; if he, having caused excellent hard food and soft food to be given to that one, as much as is apt, should afterwards, seeking to dismiss him, say: "Go, O Venerable One. There is no pleasure for me with you, but talking and sitting alone is pleasant for me,"[39]* thinking, "This monk will be dismissed"; having done it for just this reason and not another, that is a pāyantika.
52. Whatever monk who is not ill, desiring to warm himself, should put together or have a fire put together, that is a pāyantika.
53. Whatever monk, having given his consent to a monk for formal acts of the saṃgha [done] according to Dharma, and afterwards, being angry, mad, wrathful, and ill-tempered, should raise objections,[40]* saying: "Take away [my consent]. I did not give consent to the monk for those [acts]"; that is a pāyantika.
54. Whatever monk should lie down in the same house with an unordained person for more than two nights, that is a pāyantika.
55. Whatever monk should say: "As I understand the Dharma taught by the Blessed One, indulgences in these which have been declared by the Blessed One to be obstructive conditions are not sufficient for a hindrance"; that monk should be spoken to thus by the monks: "Do not, O Venerable One, speak thus: 'As I understand the Dharma taught by the Blessed One, indulgences in these which have been declared by the Blessed One to be obstructive conditions are not sufficient for a hindrance.' Do not speak [this] about the Blessed One. False accusation against the Blessed One is not good, and also the Blessed One has not said that. The obstructive conditions, O Venerable One, have been declared by the Blessed One in many ways to really be obstructive, and indulgences [in them] are sufficient for a hindrance. Abandon such an evil view, O Venerable One." If that monk, being spoken to by the monks, should abandon that course, this is good. If he should not abandon it, he should be examined and instructed two or

have been declared by the Blessed One, is sufficient for a hindrance." And should that male novice, being spoken to thus by the monks, abandon that course, this is good. Should he not abandon it, that male novice should be questioned and admonished by the monks up to three times for the abandonment of that course. Being questioned or admonished up to the third time, should he abandon that course, this is good. Should he not abandon it, that male novice should be driven away by the monks, saying: "From this day on, O venerable male novice, the Blessed One, the Tathāgata, the Arhant, the Fully Englightened One should not be mentioned as your teacher, and also you cannot obtain gifts. Also, from this day on, for you there is no sleeping in the same house with the monks for two or three nights. Go, move on, flee!" Whatever monk should knowingly meet with, treat affectionately,[114] eat with, dwell with, or lie down in the same house with an expelled male novice who, acting as he speaks, has not abandoned that evil view and has not made Anudharma, that is a pācattika.

48. When a new robe is obtained by a monk, one or another method of disfigurement of three methods for disfigurement should be taken: dark blue, mud, or black colored. If a monk should use a new robe, not taking up [one of the three methods for disfigurement], that is a pācattika.

49. Whatever monk should pick up or cause a jewel or what is considered a jewel to be picked up, except in the ārāma or in the dwelling, that is a pācattika. A jewel or what is considered a jewel should be picked up in the ārāma or in the dwelling by a monk if he wishes, thinking, "This will be for he who will take it." Having done it for just this reason and not another, this is the proper course in this matter.

50. Half-monthly bathing was declared by the Blessed One. Except at the right time, that (i.e., bathing more frequently than half-monthly) is a pācattika. Under those circumstances, this is the right time: thinking, "One and one half months of the hot season remains," and "the first month of the rains"; these two and one half months are the time of heat; [also at] a time of going on a journey, a time of illness, a time of work, a time of wind, and a time of rain. This is the right time in this matter.

Summary: (41) shivering, (42) [sleeping] in the same house, (43) consent, (44) dismissal, (45–47) three obstructions, (48) not made properly, (49) jewel, and (50) bathing. Fifth section.

51. Whatever monk should knowingly consume water containing living creatures, that is a pācattika.

52. Whatever monk should give, with his own hand, hard food or soft food to a male ascetic, female ascetic, male wanderer, or female wanderer, that is a pācattika.

three times for the abandonment of that course. Being examined and instructed two or three times, should he abandon that course, this is good. If he should not abandon it, that is a pāyantika.
56. Whatever monk should knowingly speak to or converse with a person who has not abandoned that evil view, and according to his word,[41]* has not made Anudharma, or should eat, dwell, or lie down in the same house with that one, that is a pāyantika.
57. Should a male novice say: "As I understand the Dharma taught by the Blessed One, indulgences in these which have been declared by the Blessed One to be obstructive conditions are not sufficient for a hindrance"; that male novice should be spoken to thus by the monks: "Do not, O venerable male novice, speak thus: 'As I understand the Dharma taught by the Blessed One, indulgences in these which have been declared by the Blessed One to be obstructive conditions are not sufficient for a hindrance.' Do not speak [this] about the Blessed One. False accusation against the Blessed One is not good, and also the Blessed One has not said that. The obstructive conditions, O male novice, have been declared by the Blessed One in many ways to really be obstructive, and indulgences [in them] are sufficient for a hindrance. Abandon such an evil view, O male novice." If that monk, being spoken to by the monks, should abandon that course, this is good. If he should not abandon it, he should be examined and instructed two or three times for the abandonment of that course. Being examined and instructed two or three times, should he abandon that course, this is good. If he should not abandon it, that male novice should be spoken to thus by the monks: "From this day on, O venerable male novice, the Blessed One, the Tathāgata, the Arhant, the Fully Enlightened One should not be mentioned as your teacher. You should not follow behind one or another Brahmacārin, and as the other male novices obtain [the privilege of] sleeping in the same house with the monks for up to two nights, from this day on, for you this is not allowed. Go away, foolish man, you are expelled." Whatever monk should knowingly treat kindly or meet with a male novice who has been expelled, or should lie down in the same house with that one, that is a pāyantika.
58. When a monk obtains a new robe, one or another of three methods of disfigurement should be taken for disfigurement [of the robe]: dark blue, red, or yellow. If a monk should use a new robe, not taking up one or another of three methods for disfigurement [of the robe]: the dark blue, red, or yellow method of disfigurement, that is a pāyantika.
59. Whatever monk should pick up with his own hand or cause a jewel or what is considered to be a jewel to be picked up, except in the ārāma or in the

53. Whatever monk, knowingly intruding[115] on a family with food, should sit down on a seat, that is a pācattika.
54. Whatever monk should knowingly sit down on a concealed seat amongst a family with food, that is a pācattika.
55. Whatever monk should go to see an army fighting, that is a pācattika.
56. If there is some reason for a monk to go amongst an army, that monk may stay amongst the army for two or three nights. Should he stay in excess of that, that is a pācattika.
57. If a monk, dwelling amongst an army for two or three nights, should go to see an attack,[116] fighting,[117] many military arrays, a banner, or the [battle] front, that is a pācattika.
58. Whatever monk should strike a monk, that is a pācattika.
59. Whatever monk should raise his hand[118] to a monk, that is a pācattika.
60. Whatever monk should knowingly conceal the grave offense, habitually done, of a monk, he should not declare to others: "Why do you act this way?" In knowingly concealing the sin of another, that is a pācattika.

Summary: (51) [water] containing living creatures, (52) male ascetic, (53) intrusion, (54) concealed seat, (55–57) amongst an army, (58) striking, (59) raised hand, and (60) concealing. Sixth section.

61. Whatever monk should intentionally deprive an animal of life, that is a pācattika.
62. Whatever monk should intentionally cause remorse for a monk, thinking, "There will be no comfort for him, even for a moment"; that is a pācattika.
63. Whatever monk, having given a robe to a monk, nun, male novice, female novice, or female probationer, and not having taken it back, should make use of the article which was not taken back, that is a pācattika.
64. Whatever monk should hide or cause the bowl, robe, sitting rug, or needle case of a monk to be hidden, even in jest, that is a pācattika.
65. Whatever monk should frighten a monk, that is a pācattika.
66. In splashing the hands in the water, there is a pācattika.
67. In tickling with the fingers, there is a pācattika.
68. Whatever monk, proceeding with a woman, should go on a journey, even to another village, that is a pācattika.
69. Whatever monk should lie down in the same house with a woman, that is a pācattika.
70. Whatever monk should sit down with a woman, one with the other, in secret, that is a pācattika.

āvāsa, that is a pāyantika. A jewel or what is considered to be a jewel should be picked up by a monk in the ārāma or in the āvāsa, thinking, "This will be for he who will take it." This is the proper course in this matter.
60. Half-monthly [bathing] was declared by the Blessed One. In bathing in excess of that, except at the right time, there is a pāyantika. Under those circumstances, this is the right time: thinking, "One and one half months of the hot season remain," and "the first month of the rains"; these two and one half months, the time of heat remains; [also] at a time of illness, a time of work, a time of rain, and a time of wind and rain. This is the right time in this matter.

61. Whatever monk should intentionally deprive an animal of life, that is a pāyantika.
62. Whatever monk should intentionally cause remorse for a monk, thinking, "There will be no comfort or pleasure for that monk, even for a moment"; that is a pāyantika.
63. In tickling with the fingers,[42]* there is a pāyantika.
64. In playing in the water, there is a pāyantika.
65. Whatever monk should lie down in the same house with a woman, that is a pāyantika.
66. Whatever monk should frighten or cause a monk to be frightened, even in jest,[43]* that is a pāyantika.
67. Whatever monk should hide or cause one or another of the personal belongings[44]* of a monk, nun, male novice, female novice, or female probationer to be hidden: [either a] bowl, robe, sandals, needle case, or girdle, unless there is a reason, that is a pāyantika.
68. Whatever monk, having given[45]* a robe to a monk, and afterwards, not having taken it back, should use it, that is a pāyantika.
69. Whatever monk who is ill-tempered and mad should accuse a pure, faultless monk with a groundless saṃghāvaśeṣa dharma that is a pāyantika.
70. Whatever monk, proceeding with a woman [without a man], should go on a journey, even to another village, that is a pāyantika.

Summary: (61) intentionally [killing], (62) remorse, (63) [a robe] not taken back, (64) should hide, (65) should frighten, (66) [splashing] in the water, (67) [tickling with] fingers, (68) proceeding [with a woman], (69) in the same house [with a woman], and (70) sitting [with a woman]. Seventh section.

71. Whatever monk should knowingly ordain to full monkhood a person less than twenty years old, that person is not ordained and those monks are blameworthy. So this blameworthiness is a pācattika for the monk.[119]

72. Whatever monk, proceeding with a caravan intent on theft, should knowingly go on a journey, even to another village, that is a pācattika.

73. Whatever monk should dig the soil with his own hand or have it dug, even so far as to say: "Dig here"; that is a pācattika.

74. Each invitation may be accepted by a monk for four months. Should he accept in excess of that, unless it is a new invitation or an [invitation] for life, that is a pācattika.

75. Whatever monk, being spoken to thus by the monks: "By not covering yourself, O Venerable One, with these five groups of sins, this precept should be observed"; should that monk say to those monks: "I will not practice according to the speech of the Venerable Ones; not until I see elder monks who are masters of the Sūtras, masters of the Vinaya, and masters of the Mātṛkās; junior monks who are masters of the Sūtras, masters of the Vinaya, and masters of the Mātṛkās; not until I, having approached them, shall ask and they shall make a reply"; that is a pācattika. It should be understood, perceived, and comprehended by a monk desiring instruction.[120]

76. In drinking intoxicating beverages, spirits, and liquors, there is a pācattika.

77. In disrespect to monks, there is a pācattika.

78. Whatever monk, when monks are passing time quarreling, bickering, engaged in dispute and strife, should stand in a place [suitable for] eavesdropping, thinking, "Having heard that which they say, I will absorb it"; having done it for just that reason and not another, in that standing [involving] eavesdropping, there is a pācattika for that monk.

79. Whatever monk, when the saṃgha is engaged in philosophical discussion,[121] rising from his seat, should go away without bidding farewell to a qualified monk, except when there is a cause for the irregular behavior,[122] that is a pācattika.

80. Whatever monk, dwelling on a bed and seat in the forest, should enter a village at the wrong time, not bidding farewell to a qualified monk, except when there is a cause for such irregular behavior, that is a pācattika.

71. Whatever monk, proceeding with a caravan intending theft, should go on a journey, even to another village, that is a pāyantika.
72. Whatever monk should ordain a person less than twenty years old to the state of monkhood, that is a pāyantika. That person is not ordained and those monks are blameworthy. This is the proper course in this matter.
73. Whatever monk should dig the soil with his own hand or have it dug, that is a pāyantika.
74. A four month invitation may be accepted by a monk; in excess of that is a pāyantika, except with regard to a single invitation, a new invitation, an invitation relating to a [special] time, or a permanent invitation. This is the proper course in this matter.
75. Whatever monk, being spoken to [thus] by the monks: "This precept should be practiced by the Venerable One"; should say: "I will not practice according to the words of you who are foolish, stupid, and weak-minded; not until I shall ask monks who are masters of the Sūtras, masters of the Vinaya, and masters of the Mātṛkās"; that is a pāyantika. This precept should be practiced by a monk desiring omniscience, [and also] monks who are masters of the Sūtras, masters of the Vinaya, and masters of the Mātṛkās should be questioned. This is the proper course in this matter.
76. Whatever monk, when the monks are quarreling, bickering, fighting, engaged in dispute, should stand silently as an eavesdropper, thinking, "I will preserve (i.e., remember) that which the monks shall say"; having done it for just this reason, that is a pāyantika.
77. Whatever monk, when the saṃgha is engaged in pious philosophical discussion, rising from his seat, should go away without asking a competent monk for permission, except when there is a reason, that is a pāyantika.
78. In conduct which is disrespectful, there is a pāyantika.
79. In drinking intoxicating beverages, spirits, and liquors, there is a pāyantika.
80. Whatever monk should enter a village at the wrong time without asking a competent monk for permission, except when there is a reason, that is a pāyantika.

Summary: (71) [ordaining one] less than twenty, (72) caravan intent on theft, (73) [digging] the soil, (74) invitation, (75) I will not practice, (76) drinking intoxicants, (77) disrespect, (78) eavesdropping, (79) philosophical [discussion], and (80) dwelling in a forest. Eighth section.

81. Whatever monk, being provided with a meal, should visit[123] amongst families, before a meal or after a meal, having not invited a qualified monk, except at the right time, that is a pācattika. Under those circumstances, this is the right time: the time of the giving of robes. This is the right time in this matter.

82. Whatever monk should enter the harem of a consecrated kṣatriya king who has obtained power and position in the empire when the king has not come forth, when the harem has not come forth, or when the jewels have not come forth, or should he even cross the threshold, that is a pācattika.

83. Whatever monk should have a needle case made that is made of ivory, made of bone, made of horn, made of gold, made of silver, or made of jewels, that is a pācattika involving breaking.

84. When a monk is having a couch or chair made, the legs should be made measuring eight fingers of the Sugata [measure high], except for the notched part. Should he have it made in excess of that, there is a pācattika involving cutting [down].

85. Whatever monk should sit down or lie down[124] on a chair or couch covered with cotton, that is a pācattika involving tearing [off].

86. When a monk is having a rug for sitting on made, it should be made according to measure. This is the measure here: in length, two spans of the Sugata-span; in width, one and one half; the border a span. Should he have it made in excess of that, there is a pācattika involving cutting [down].

87. When a monk is having an itch bandage[125] made, it should be made according to measure. This is the measure here: in length, four spans of the Sugata-span; in width, two spans. Should he have it made in excess of that, there is a pācattika involving cutting [down].

88. When a monk is having a varṣāśāṭikā robe made, it should be made according to measure. This is the measure here: in length, six spans of the Sugata-span; in width, two and one half. Should he have it made in excess of that, there is a pācattika involving cutting [down].

89. Whatever monk should have a robe made the measure of the Sugata's robe, the measure of the Sugata's robe for the Sugata, the Blessed One, the Tathāgata, the Arhant, the Fully Enlightened One is: in length, nine spans of the Sugata-span; in width, six; this is the measure of the Sugata's robe for the Sugata, the Blessed One, the Tathāgata, the Arhant, the Fully En-

81. Whatever monk, having been invited into a family for a meal, should visit amongst families before a meal or after a meal, when the family [which invited him] is unawares, except when there is a reason, that is a pāyantika.
82. Whatever monk should cross the threshold or vicinity of the threshold of a consecrated kṣatriya king when night has not ended and the sun has not risen, and when the jewels or what are considered to be jewels have not been removed, except when there is a reason, that is a pāyantika.
83. Whatever monk, when the half-monthly Prātimokṣa Sūtra is being recited, should say: "Just now, O Venerable Ones, do I understand this dharma which is included in the Sūtra, occurs in the Sūtra, and comes up in the recitation"; and if the monks should know, with regard to the Venerable One, that the Venerable One has previously sat in the Poṣadha ceremony two or three times, not to say oftener, there is no freedom for the ignorant monk. Then [that monk] who has fallen into offense should be dealt with according to Dharma, and further remorse should be imposed [on him], saying, "For you, O Venerable One, this which has been obtained improperly and not properly is unobtained and unacquired. You, when the half-monthly Prātimokṣa Sūtra is being recited, do not listen respectfully, do not pay respect, do not make supplication, do not meditate with a one-pointed mind, do not listen with an attentive ear, and do not listen with the conviction of the entire mind. Therefore, O Venerable One, because of remorse, there is a pāyantika."
84. Whatever monk should have a needle case made that is made of bone or made of horn, that is a pāyantika involving breaking.
85. When a monk is having a couch or chair made for the saṃgha, the legs should be made measuring eight fingers of the Sugata [measure high], except for the notched part below. Should he have it made in excess of that, there is a pāyantika involving cutting [down].
86. Whatever monk should cover or have a couch or chair covered with cotton, that is a pāyantika involving tearing [off].
87. When a monk is having a rug for sitting on made, it should be made according to measure. This is the measure here: in length, two spans of the Sugata-span; in width, one and one half; a span all round for a border. Should he have it made in excess of that, there is a pāyantika involving breaking.
88. When a monk is having an itch bandage made, it should be made according to measure. This is the measure here: in length, four spans of the Sugata-span; in width, two [spans]. Should he have it made in excess of that, there is a pāyantika involving cutting [down].
89. When a monk is having a varṣāśāṭikā robe made, it should be made

lightened One. Should he have it made in excess of that, there is a pācattika involving cutting [down].

90. Whatever monk, ill-tempered, corrupt, and angry because of malice, should accuse a monk of a groundless saṃghātiśeṣa dharma, that is a pācattika.

91. Whatever monk should knowingly confiscate for some person or other, wealth belonging to the saṃgha, accumulated in the saṃgha, that is a pācattika.

92. Whatever monk, when the half-monthly Prātimokṣa Sūtra is being recited, should say: "Just today do I understand, only now do I understand that this dharma is included in the Sūtra, occurs in the Sūtra, and comes up in the half-monthly Prātimokṣa Sūtra recitation"; if those [other] monks should know that that monk has previously entered and also previously sat down two or three times, not to say oftener,[126] there is now no freedom [from offense] because of ignorance for that monk. Then that monk who has fallen into offense should be dealt with quickly according to Dharma and according to Vinaya, and further confusion should be produced for him, saying, "This acquisition was improperly obtained by you, O Venerable One. You, when the half-monthly Prātimokṣa Sūtra is being recited, not having regard for it, not meditating on it, not paying heed to it with your entire mind, not cutting through it, listen to Dharma with an uninclined ear." This [putting] of confusion is a pācattika for that monk.

Summary: (81) with a meal, (82) [threshold] of a king, (83) needle case, (84) couch, (85) cotton, (86) rug for sitting, (87) itch bandage, (88) varṣāśāṭikā robe, (89) robe of the Sugata, (90) false accusation, (91) confiscation, and (92) ignorance. Ninth section.

Summary of the Sections: (1) lie, (2) seed, (3) unauthorized, (4) up to one day, (5) shivering, (6) with living creatures, (7) intentionally, (8) less than twenty, and (9) with a meal. The nine [sections] have been recited.

O Venerable Ones, the ninety-two pācattika dharmas have been recited. Therefore, I ask the Venerable Ones—Are you completely pure in this matter? A second time I ask the Venerable Ones—Are you completely pure in this matter? Also a third time I ask the Venerable Ones—Are you completely pure in this matter? Since there is silence, the Venerable Ones are completely pure in this matter. Thus do I understand.

according to measure. This is the measure here: in length, six spans of the Sugata-span; in width, two and one half [spans]. Should he have it made in excess of that, there is a pāyantika involving cutting [down].
90. Whatever monk should have a robe made the measure of the Sugata's robe or in excess of the Sugata's robe, that is a pāyantika. This is the measure of the Sugata's robe: in length, nine spans; in width, sixth spans. This is the measure of the Sugata's robe.

O Venerable Ones, the ninety pāyantika dharmas have been recited by me. Therefore, I ask the Venerable Ones—Are you completely pure in this matter? Since there is silence, the Venerable Ones are completely pure in this matter. Thus do I understand.[46]*

The Four Pratideśanīya Dharmas

Now, O Venerable Ones, the four pratideśanīya dharmas come up in the half-monthly Prātimokṣa Sūtra recitation.

1. Whatever monk who is not ill, dwelling on a bed and seat in the forest, being previously unawares,[127] and having accepted, with his own hand, hard food or soft food that has not been received [as a gift],[128] outside or within the dwelling place, should chew or consume it, that should be confessed by the monk who has eaten, saying: "Having fallen, O Venerable Ones, into a blameworthy pratideśanīya[129] dharma which is unsuitable for me, I confess that dharma." This is a pratideśanīya dharma.

2. Whatever monk who is not ill, having accepted, with his own hand, hard food or soft food from an unrelated nun who has entered amongst the houses, should chew or consume it, that should be confessed by the monk who has eaten, saying: "Having fallen, O Venerable One, into a blameworthy pratideśanīya dharma which is unsuitable for me, I confess that dharma." This is a pratideśanīya dharma.

3. Now monks eat by reason of being invited amongst the houses. If a nun is standing there like an instructor, saying: "Give boiled rice here; give sauce here; give condiment here"; that nun should be spoken to thus by all those monks: "You should wait, Sister, until the monks eat"; and if even one monk should not say: "You should wait, Sister, until the monks eat"; it should be confessed by those monks who have eaten, saying: "Having fallen, O Venerable One, into a blameworthy pratideśanīya dharma which is unsuitable for me, I confess that dharma." This is a pratideśanīya dharma.

4. If a monk, approaching families which are considered to be undergoing training, having been previously uninvited, and having accepted, with his own hand, hard food or soft food, should chew or consume it, that should be confessed by the monk who has eaten, saying: "Having fallen, O Venerable One, into a blameworthy pratideśanīya dharma which is unsuitable for me, I confess that dharma." This is a pratideśanīya dharma.

Summary: (1) forest, (2) among the houses, (3) monks who are invited, and (4) [families] considered under training. The four have been recited.

O Venerable Ones, the four pratideśanīya dharmas have been recited. Therefore, I ask the Venerable Ones—Are you completely pure in this matter? A second time I ask the Venerable Ones—Are you completely pure in this matter? Also a third time I ask the Venerable Ones—Are you completely pure in this matter? Since there is silence, the Venerable Ones are completely pure in this matter. Thus do I understand.

The Four Pratideśanīya Dharmas

Now, O Venerable Ones, the four pratideśanīya dharmas come up in the half-monthly Prātimokṣa Sūtra recitation.

1. Whatever monk, having accepted hard food or soft food, with his own hand, in the presence of an unrelated nun who has wandered amongst the houses for alms food, should chew or consume it, that should be confessed in the presence of the monks by that monk, going outside the ārāma, saying: "Having fallen into an unwholesome position, O Venerable Ones, I am blameworthy. Therefore, I confess that pratideśanīya dharma." This is a pratideśanīya dharma.

2. Many monks eat, having been invited amongst families. If a nun should stand there indicating, "Give soft food here; give boiled rice; give sauce"; that nun should be spoken to thus by the monks: "You should wait for a moment, Sister, until the monks eat." If even one monk should not speak to remove that nun, that should be confessed in the presence of the monks by all those monks, going outside the ārāma, saying: "Having fallen into an unwholesome position, O Venerable Ones, we are blameworthy. Therefore, we confess that pratideśanīya dharma." This is a pratideśanīya dharma.

3. There are families which have been considered by formal declaration to be undergoing training.[47]* Whatever monk, having been previously uninvited and having accepted hard food and soft food amongst such families which have been considered by formal declaration of the saṃgha to be undergoing training, should chew or consume it, that should be confessed in the presence of the monks by that monk, going outside the ārāma, saying: "Having fallen into an unwholesome position, I confess that pratideśanīya dharma." This is a pratideśanīya dharma.

4. There are forest dwellings which are considered by the saṃgha to be doubtful, dangerous, and fearful. Whatever monk, in such forest dwellings which are considered by the saṃgha to be doubtful, dangerous, and fearful, being previously unawares, should chew or consume hard food and soft food in the forest outside of the ārāma, that should be confessed in the presence of the monks by that monk, saying: "Having fallen into an unwholesome position, O Venerable Ones, I am blameworthy. Therefore, I confess that pratideśanīya dharma." This is a pratideśanīya dharma.

O Venerable Ones, the four pratideśanīya dharmas have been recited by me. Therefore, I ask the Venerable Ones—Are you completely pure in this matter? A second and also a third time I ask—Are you completely pure in this matter? Since there is silence, the Venerable Ones are completely pure in this matter. Thus do I understand.

The Sixty-Seven Śaikṣa Dharmas

Now, O Venerable Ones, the more than fifty[130] śaikṣa dharmas come up in the half-monthly Prātimokṣa Sūtra recitation.
1. "I will dress with the inner robe wrapped around," is a precept which should be observed.
2. "I will put on the robe wrapped around," is a precept which should be observed.
3. "I will go amongst the houses well restrained," is a precept which should be observed.
4. "I will not go amongst the houses with uplifted eyes,"[131] is a precept which should be observed.
5. "I will go amongst the houses with little noise," is a precept which should be observed.
6. "I will not go amongst the houses with loud laughter,"[132] is a precept which should be observed.
7. "I will not go amongst the houses with the head covered,"[133] is a precept which should be observed.
8. "I will not go amongst the houses with lifted up [robes]," is a precept which should be observed.
9. "I will not go amongst the houses in a squatting position,"[134] is a precept which should be observed.
10. "I will not go amongst the houses with the arms akimbo,"[135] is a precept which should be observed.
11. "I will not go amongst the houses with the body shaking," is a precept which should be observed.
12. "I will not go amongst the houses with the head shaking," is a precept which should be observed.
13. "I will not go amongst the houses shaking the arms," is a precept which should be observed.

Summary: (1) inner robe, (2) putting on [the robe], (3) well restrained, (4) eyes, (5) noise, (6) not laughing loudly, (7) not having the head covered, (8) not lifting up, (9) not squatting, (10) not [with] arms akimbo, (11) not [shaking] the body, (12) not [shaking] the head, and (13) not [shaking] the arms. First section.

14. "I will sit down amongst the houses well restrained," is a precept which should be observed.
15. "I will not sit down amongst the houses with uplifted eyes," is a precept which should be observed.
16. "I will sit down amongst the houses with little noise," is a precept which should be observed.

The Many Śaikṣa Dharmas

Now, O Venerable Ones, the many śaikṣa dharmas come up in the half-monthly Prātimokṣa Sūtra recitation.

1. "We will put on the inner robe wrapped around," is a precept which should be observed.
2. "We will not put on the inner robe raised too high," is a precept which should be observed.
3. "We will not put on the inner robe too low," is a precept which should be observed.
4. "We will not put on the inner robe like the trunk of an elephant," is a precept which should be observed.
5. "We will not put on the inner robe like a palm leaf,"[48*] is a precept which should be observed.
6. "We will not put on the inner robe like a ball of grain," is a precept which should be observed.
7. "We will not put on the inner robe like the head of a serpent," is a precept which should be observed.
8. "We will put on the robe wrapped around," is a precept which should be observed.
9. "We will not put on the robe raised too high," is a precept which should be observed.
10. "We will not put on the robe too low," is a precept which should be observed.
11. "We will go amongst the houses well restrained," is a precept which should be observed.
12. "We will go amongst the houses [with the body] well covered," is a precept which should be observed.
13. "We will go amongst the houses with little noise," is a precept which should be observed.
14. "We will go amongst the houses without uplifted eyes," is a precept which should be observed.
15. "We will go amongst the houses looking at the ground," is a precept which should be observed.
16. "We will not go amongst the houses with the head covered," is a precept which should be observed.
17. "We will not go amongst the houses with lifted up [robes]," is a precept which should be observed.
18. "We will not go amongst the houses in the utsaktikā posture," is a precept which should be observed.

17. "I will not sit down amongst the houses with loud laughter," is a precept which should be observed.
18. "I will not sit down amongst the houses with the head covered," is a precept which should be observed.
19. "I will not sit down amongst the houses with lifted up [robes]," is a precept which should be observed.
20. "I will not sit down amongst the houses in the utsaktikā posture,"[136] is a precept which should be observed.
21. "I will not sit down amongst the houses in the paryastikā posture,"[137] is a precept which should be observed.
22. "I will not sit down amongst the houses with the arms akimbo," is a precept which should be observed.
23. "Having sat down amongst the houses, I will not do evil with the feet or do evil with the hands," is a precept which should be observed.

Summary: (14) well restrained, (15) eyes, (16) noise, (17) not laughing loudly, (18) not having the head covered, (19) not lifting up, (20) not [employing] the utsaktikā posture, (21) not [employing] the paryastikā posture, (22) not [with] arms akimbo, and (23) not doing evil with the hands or feet. Second section.

24. "I will accept alms food respectfully,"[138] is a precept which should be observed.
25. "I will eat alms food with an equal amount of sauce," is a precept which should be observed.
26. "I will not eat alms food making a sauce," is a precept which should be observed.
27. "I will not eat alms food [while] making confused [speech]"[139] is a precept which should be observed.
28. "I will not eat alms food making the cheeks stuffed," is a precept which should be observed.
29. "I will not eat alms food putting out the tongue," is a precept which should be observed.
30. "I will not eat alms food in overly large mouthfuls," is a precept which should be observed.
31. "I will not open the mouth when the mouthful has not arrived," is a precept which should be observed.
32. "I will not eat alms food throwing mouthfuls," is a precept which should be observed.
33. "I will not eat alms food dividing mouthfuls," is a precept which should be observed.

19. "We will not go amongst the houses in the vyastikā posture,"[49]* is a precept which should be observed.
20. "We will not go amongst the houses in the paryastikā posture," is a precept which should be observed.
21. "We will not go amongst the houses jumping,"[50]* is a precept which should be observed.
22. "We will not go amongst the houses with the hands touching the feet,"[51]* is a precept which should be observed.
23. "We will not go amongst the houses in a squatting posture," is a precept which should be observed.
24. "We will not go amongst the houses kneeling down,"[52]* is a precept which should be observed.
25. "We will not go amongst the houses with arms akimbo," is a precept which should be observed.
26. "We will not go amongst the houses shaking the body," is a precept which should be observed.
27. "We will not go amongst the houses shaking the arms," is a precept which should be observed.
28. "We will not go amongst the houses shaking the head," is a precept which should be observed.
29. "We will not go amongst the houses with shoulders together,"[53]* is a precept which should be observed.
30. "We will not go amongst the houses joining the hands," is a precept which should be observed.
31. "We will not sit down on a seat amidst the houses without being authorized," is a precept which should be observed.
32. "We will not sit down on a seat amidst the houses without examining the seat," is a precept which should be observed.
33. "We will not sit down on a seat amidst the houses putting down [the weight of] the whole body,"[54]* is a precept which should be observed.
34. "We will not sit down on a seat amidst the houses placing one foot on the other," is a precept which should be observed.
35. "We will not sit down on a seat amidst the houses placing one aṇkle on the other," is a precept which should be observed.
36. "We will not sit down on a seat amidst the houses placing one thigh on the other," is a precept which should be observed.
37. "We will not sit down on a seat amidst the houses pulling up the feet," is a precept which should be observed.
38. "We will not sit down on a seat amidst the houses stretching out the

34. "I will not speak words with a mouthful in the mouth," is a precept which should be observed.

Summary: (24) respectfully, (25) equal amount of sauce, (26) no sauce, (27) not making confused [speech], (28) not stuffing the cheeks, (29) not [putting out] the tongue, (30) not too large [mouthfuls], (31) unarrived [mouthful], (32) not throwing mouthfuls, (33) not dividing mouthfuls, and (34) not speaking with a mouthful in the mouth. Third section.

35. "I will not eat alms food licking the bowl," is a precept which should be observed.

36. "I will not eat alms food licking the hands," is a precept which should be observed.

37. "I will not eat alms food licking the fingers," is a precept which should be observed.

38. "I will not eat alms food making the cucu sound," is a precept which should be observed.

39. "I will not eat alms food making the surusuru sound," is a precept which should be observed.

40. "I will not eat alms food making the śuluśulu sound," is a precept which should be observed.

41. "I will not eat alms food shaking the hands," is a precept which should be observed.

42. "I will not eat alms food scattering lumps of boiled rice," is a precept which should be observed.

43. "I will not, taking up a desire which is blameworthy,[140] think excessively about the bowl of another," is a precept which should be observed.

44. "I will not look at alms food thinking about the bowl," is a precept which should be observed.

45. "Not being ill, I will not eat alms food, obtained for myself, by begging or having boiled rice, sauce, or condiment begged for among families," is a precept which should be observed.

46. "I will not, taking up a desire for returning for more, knowingly cover up with rice the undesirable [food] which has been given," is a precept which should be observed.[141]

47. "I will not pour water with lumps of boiled rice [in it] on the ground," is a precept which should be observed.

48. "I will not accept a water pot with water containing lumps of boiled rice," is a precept which should be observed.

Summary: (35–37) three [types] of licking, (38) cucu, (39) surusuru, (40) śuluśulu, (41) not [shaking] the hands, (42) not [scattering] lumps of boiled

feet," is a precept which should be observed.
39. "We will not sit down on a seat amidst the houses exposing the genitals,"[55*] is a precept which should be observed.
40. "We will accept alms food respectfully," is a precept which should be observed.
41. "We will accept alms food [only] full to the brim [of the bowl],"[56*] is a precept which should be observed.
42. "We will accept alms food with an equal amount of sauce," is a precept which should be observed.
43. "We will accept alms food uninterruptedly,"[57*] is a precept which should be observed.
44. "We will not present the bowl when hard food and soft food has not come," is a precept which should be observed.
45. "We will not cover up sauce with boiled rice," is a precept which should be observed.
46. "Taking up the desire for more, [we will not cover up] boiled rice with sauce," is a precept which should be observed.
47. "We will not hold out a bowl with reference to hard food and soft food," is a precept which should be observed.
48. "We will eat alms food respectfully," is a precept which should be observed.
49. "We will not eat alms food finely broken up," is a precept which should be observed.
50. "We will not eat alms food in overly large mouthfuls," is a precept which should be observed.
51. "We will separate the morsels into [little] balls," is a precept which should be observed.
52. "We will not open the mouth when the morsel has not arrived," is a precept which should be observed.
53. "We will not utter inarticulate speech with a morsel in the mouth," is a precept which should be observed.
54. "We will not eat alms food making the cuccat sound," is a precept which should be observed.
55. "We will not eat alms food making the śuśaśut sound," is a precept which should be observed.
56. "We will not eat alms food making the thutyut sound," is a precept which should be observed.
57. "We will not eat alms food making the phuphphuph sound," is a precept which should be observed.

rice, (43) not blameworthy, (44) thinking about the alms bowl, (45) begging, (46) covers, (47) water in the alms bowl, and (48) [water pot] with lumps of boiled rice. Fourth section.

49. "Standing, I will not teach Dharma to one sitting who is not ill," is a precept which should be observed.

50. "Sitting, I will not teach Dharma to someone lying down who is not ill," is a precept which should be observed.

51. "Seated on a low seat, I will not teach Dharma to one seated on a high seat who is not ill," is a precept which should be observed.

52. "I will not teach Dharma to one wearing sandals[142] who is not ill," is a precept which should be observed.

53. "I will not teach Dharma to one wearing shoes who is not ill," is a precept which should be observed.

54. "I will not teach Dharma to one having his head covered who is not ill," is a precept which should be observed.

55. "I will not teach Dharma to one having his head veiled who is not ill," is a precept which should be observed.

56. "In the utsaktikā posture, I will not teach Dharma to one seated who is not ill," is a precept which should be observed.

57. "In the paryastikā posture, I will not teach Dharma to one seated who is not ill," is a precept which should be observed.

Summary: (49) not standing, (50) not sitting, (51) high seat, (52) sandals, (53) shoes, (54) [head] covered, (55) head [veiled], (56) not in the utsaktikā posture, and (57) not in the paryastikā posture. Fifth section.

58. "I will not teach Dharma to one having a knife in his hand who is not ill," is a precept which should be observed.

59. "I will not teach Dharma to one having a weapon in his hand who is not ill," is a precept which should be observed.

60. "I will not teach Dharma to one having a stick in his hand who is not ill," is a precept which should be observed.

61. "I will not teach Dharma to one having a parasol in his hand who is not ill," is a precept which should be observed.

62. "Going at the side of the road,[143] I will not teach Dharma to one going on the road who is not ill," is a precept which should be observed.

63. "Going behind, I will not teach Dharma to one going in front who is not ill," is a precept which should be observed.

64. "Going on foot, I will not teach Dharma to one going by vehicle who is not ill," is a precept which should be observed.

65. "I, not being ill, will not make excrement, urine, phlegm, or snot in green grass," is a precept which should be observed.

58. "We will not eat alms food sticking out the tongue," is a precept which should be observed.
59. "We will not eat alms food separating boiled rice," is a precept which should be observed.
60. "We will not eat alms food when an interruption is made,"[58*] is a precept which should be observed.
61. "We will not eat alms food stuffing[59*] the cheeks," is a precept which should be observed.
62. "We will not eat alms food making a smacking noise with the tongue,"[60*] is a precept which should be observed.
63. "We will not eat alms food dividing mouthfuls," is a precept which should be observed.
64. "We will not eat alms food licking the hands," is a precept which should be observed.
65. "We will not eat alms food licking the bowl," is a precept which should be observed.
66. "We will not eat alms food shaking the hands,"[61*] is a precept which should be observed.
67. "We will not eat alms food shaking the bowl," is a precept which should be observed.
68. "We will not eat alms food separating the unformed [food] into a stūpa [shape]," is a precept which should be observed.
69. "We will not, in seeking to annoy, look into the bowl of a nearby monk," is a precept which should be observed.
70. "We will not accept a water pot with living creatures [in it]," is a precept which should be observed.
71. "We will not sprinkle a nearby monk with water containing flesh," is a precept which should be observed.
72. "We will not throw away water containing flesh amongst the houses," is a precept which should be observed.
73. "We will not throw away remains of food with the bowl," is a precept which should be observed.
74. "We will not place the bowl on a place on the ground that is uncovered," is a precept which should be observed.
75. "We will not place the bowl on a slope, cliff, or mountain," is a precept which should be observed.
76. "We shall not wash the bowl while standing," is a precept which should be observed.
77. "We will not wash the bowl on a slope, cliff, or mountain," is a precept which should be observed.

66. "I, not being ill, will not make excrement, urine, phlegm, or snot in the water," is a precept which should be observed.
67. "Standing, not being ill, I will not make excrement or urine," is a precept which should be observed.

Summary: (58–59) not a knife or weapon, (60) stick, (61) parasol, (62) side of the road, (63) behind, (64) vehicle, (65) grass, (66) water, and (67) standing. Sixth section.

78. "We will not take water in the bowl from the current of a flowing river," is a precept which should be observed.
79. "Standing, we will not teach Dharma to one sitting who is not ill," is a precept which should be observed.
80. "Sitting, we will not teach Dharma to one who is lying down who is not ill," is a precept which should be observed.
81. "Seated on a low seat, we will not teach Dharma to one seated on a high seat who is not ill," is a precept which should be observed.
82. "Going behind, we will not teach Dharma to one going in front who is not ill," is a precept which should be observed.
83. "Going at the side of the road, we will not teach Dharma to one going on the road who is not ill," is a precept which should be observed.
84. "We will not teach Dharma to one having his head covered who is not ill," is a precept which should be observed.
85. "We will not teach Dharma to one having lifted up [robes] who is not ill," is a precept which should be observed.
86. "We will not teach Dharma to one in the utsaktikā posture who is not ill," is a precept which should be observed.
87. "We will not teach Dharma to one in the vyastikā posture who is not ill," is a precept which should be observed.
88. "We will not teach Dharma to one in the paryastikā posture who is not ill," is a precept which should be observed.
89. "We will not teach Dharma to one having braided hair[62]* who is not ill," is a precept which should be observed.
90. "We will not teach Dharma to one having a cap on the head[63]* who is not ill," is a precept which should be observed.
91. "We will not teach Dharma to one having a crown on the head who is not ill," is a precept which should be observed.
92. "We will not teach Dharma to one having a garland on the head who is not ill," is a precept which should be observed.
93. "We will not teach Dharma to one having the head veiled who is not ill," is a precept which should be observed.
94. "We will not teach Dharma to one mounted on an elephant who is not ill," is a precept which should be observed.
95. "We will not teach Dharma to one mounted on a horse who is not ill," is a precept which should be observed.
96. "We will not teach Dharma to one mounted on a palanquin who is not ill," is a precept which should be observed.
97. "We will not teach Dharma to one mounted on a vehicle who is not ill," is a precept which should be observed.

O Venerable Ones, the more than fifty śaikṣa dharmas have been recited. Therefore, I ask the Venerable Ones—Are you completely pure in this matter? A second time I ask the Venerable Ones—Are you completely pure in this matter? Also a third time I ask the Venerable Ones—Are you completely pure in this matter? Since there is silence, the Venerable Ones are completely pure in this matter. Thus do I understand.

The Seven Adhikaraṇa-Śamatha Dharmas[144]

Now, O Venerable Ones, the seven adhikaraṇa-śamatha dharmas come up in the half-monthly Prātimokṣa Sūtra recitation.

1. That appeasement which has arisen for the settling, for the stilling of legal questions which have arisen, namely: settlement in the presence of.[145]
2. Settlement based on recollection.[146]

3. Settlement for one no longer insane.[147]

98. "We will not teach Dharma to one wearing shoes who is not ill," is a precept which should be observed.
99. "We will not teach Dharma to one having a stick in his hand who is not ill," is a precept which should be observed.
100. "We will not teach Dharma to one having a parasol in his hand who is not ill," is a precept which should be observed.
101. "We will not teach Dharma to one having a knife in his hand who is not ill," is a precept which should be observed.
102. "We will not teach Dharma to one having a sword in his hand who is not ill," is a precept which should be observed.
103. "We will not teach Dharma to one having a weapon in his hand who is not ill," is a precept which should be observed.
104. "We will not teach Dharma to one having a coat of mail[64]* who is not ill," is a precept which should be observed.
105. "Not being ill, we will not make excrement or urine [while] standing," is a precept which should be observed.
106. "Not being ill, we will not throw excrement, urine, phlegm, snot, or other evacuated substances in the water," is a precept which should be observed.
107. "Not being ill, we will not throw excrement, urine, phlegm, snot, or other evacuated substances on a spot on the ground [covered] with grass," is a precept which should be observed.
108. "We will not climb on a tree higher than a man unless there is a disaster," is a precept which should be observed.

O Venerable Ones, the many śaikṣa dharmas have been recited by me. Therefore, I ask the Venerable Ones—Are you completely pure in this matter? A second and also a third time I ask—Are you completely pure in this matter? Since there is silence, the Venerable Ones are completely pure in this matter. Thus do I understand.

The Seven Adhikaraṇa-Śamatha Dharmas

Now, O Venerable Ones, the seven adhikaraṇa-śamatha dharmas come up in the half-monthly Prātimokṣa Sūtra recitation.
1. To a case worthy of settlement in the presence of, we shall impart settlement in the presence of.

2. To a case worthy of settlement based on recollection of, we shall impart settlement based on recollection of.

4. Settlement which effects confession.[148]

5. Settlement investigating the special nature [of the accused monk].[149]

6. Settlement decided by majority vote.[150]

7. Settlement which covers over, as with grass.[151] [These are] the seven.

O Venerable Ones, the seven adhikaraṇa-śamatha dharmas have been recited. Therefore, I ask the Venerable Ones—Are you completely pure in this matter? A second time I ask the Venerable Ones—Are you completely pure in this matter? Also a third time I ask the Venerable Ones—Are you completely pure in this matter? Since there is silence, the Venerable Ones are completely pure in this matter. Thus do I understand.

Now, O Venerable Ones, the two dharmas, Dharma and Anudharma, come up in the half-monthly Prātimokṣa Sūtra recitation.

> Here, both Vinayas are called Dharma;
> That which is the right conduct is called Anudharma.

O Venerable Ones, the two dharmas, Dharma and Anudharma, have been recited. Therefore, I ask the Venerable Ones—Are you completely pure in this matter? A second time I ask the Venerable Ones—Are you completely pure in this matter? Also a third time I ask the Venerable Ones—Are you completely pure in this matter? Since there is silence, the Venerable Ones are completely pure in this matter. Thus do I understand.

O Venerable Ones, the introductory verses of the Prātimokṣa have been recited; the introduction has been recited; the four pārājika dharmas have been recited; the thirteen saṃghātiśeṣa dharmas have been recited; the two aniyata dharmas have been recited; the thirty niḥsargika-pācattika dharmas have been recited; the ninety-two pācattika dharmas have been recited; the four pratideśanīya dharmas have been recited; the more than fifty śaikṣa dharmas have been recited; the seven adhikaraṇa-śamatha dharmas have been recited; the two dharmas, Dharma and Anudharma have been recited. All this Dharma and Vinaya, and also some other Anudharma (i.e., right conduct) of Dharma is included in the Sūtras and recorded in the Prātimokṣa Sūtra of the Blessed One, the Tathāgata, the Arhant, the Fully Enlightened One. Therefore, this discipline should be observed by all together, harmo-

3. To a case worthy of settlement for one no longer insane, we shall impart settlement for one no longer insane.
4. To a case worthy of settlement by majority vote, we shall impart settlement by majority vote.
5. To a case worthy of settlement investigating the special nature [of the accused monk], we shall impart settlement investigating the special nature [of the accused monk].
6. To a case worthy of settlement which covers over, as with grass, we shall impart settlement which covers over, as with grass.
7. To a case worthy of settlement which effects confession, we shall impart settlement which effects confession.

We should cause legal questions which have arisen to be settled, stilled, according to the Dharma, Vinaya, and Teaching of the Teacher, by imparting these seven adhikaraṇa-śamatha dharmas.

O Venerable Ones, the seven adhikaraṇa-śamatha dharmas have been recited by me. Therefore, I ask the Venerable Ones—Are you completely pure in this matter? A second and also a third time I ask—Are you completely pure in this matter? Since there is silence, the Venerable Ones are completely pure in this matter. Thus do I understand.

nious, rejoicing, without dispute, illuminating the Teaching of the Teacher, dwelling comfortably and happily under one rule, like water and milk, not dissipating what has been accumulated.

1. Enduring patience is the highest austerity,
   nirvāṇa is the highest, say the Buddhas;
   for he who injures others is not a monk,
   he who violates others is not a śramaṇa.[152]

This Prātimokṣa was eloquently spoken in summary by the Blessed One Vipaśyin, the Tathāgata, the Arhant, the Fully Enlightened One, Perfectly Enlightened for a long time, amidst a vast Bhikṣu-saṃgha.

2. Not speaking against others, not harming others,
   and restraint according to the Prātimokṣa;
   moderation in eating, secluded dwelling,
   and the practice of adhicitta; this is the
   Teaching of the Buddhas.[153]

This Prātimokṣa was eloquently spoken in summary by the Blessed One Śikhin, the Tathāgata, the Arhant, the Fully Enlightened One, Perfectly Enlightened for a long time, amidst a vast Bhikṣu-saṃgha.

3. For the wise one, trained in the steps of sagehood,
   there is no delight in superior intellect;
   for the tranquil protector, always mindful, there
   are no sorrows.[154]

This Prātimokṣa was eloquently spoken in summary by the Blessed One Viśvabhū, the Tathāgata, the Arhant, the Fully Enlightened One, Perfectly Enlightened for a long time, amidst a vast Bhikṣu-saṃgha.

4. Not to do any evil, to attain good,
   to purify one's own mind; this is the
   Teaching of the Buddhas.[155]

This Prātimokṣa was eloquently spoken in summary by the Blessed One Krakucchanda, the Tathāgata, the Arhant, the Fully Enlightened One, Perfectly Enlightened for a long time, amidst a vast Bhikṣu-saṃgha.

5. As a bee, not harming the scent or color of a
   flower, flies away, taking [only] the nectar;
   so should a sage enter a village.
6. [One should not contemplate] the faults of others,
   or what is done and not done by others;
   but one should contemplate things done and not done
   concerning himself.[156]

1. Enduring patience is the highest austerity,
nirvāṇa is the highest, say the Buddhas;
for he who harms others is not a monk,
he who violates others is not a śramaṇa.[65]*
2. Just as one endowed with sight, in exerting effort,
[should avoid] misconduct;
so the wise man should avoid the evils
in the world of men.[66]*
3. Not censuring [others], not harming others,
and restraint according to the Prātimokṣa;
moderation in eating, secluded dwelling,
and union with adhicitta; this is the
Teaching of the Buddhas.[67]*
4. As a bee, not agitating the scent or color of a
flower, flies away, taking [only] the nectar;
so should a sage enter a village.[68]*
5. [One should not contemplate] the faults of others,
or what is done and not done by others;
but one should contemplate the same difficulties
concerning himself.[69]*
6. For the wise one, trained in the steps of sagehood,
there is no delight in superior intellect;
for the tranquil protector, always mindful, there
are no sorrows.[70]*
7. Merit increases for one who gives,
enmity does not accumulate for one who is well restrained;
the virtuous one renounces evil,
and because of putting an end to the kleśas, attains bliss.[71]*
8. Not to do any evil, to attain good,
to completely subdue one's own mind; this is the
Teaching of the Buddhas.[72]*
9. Restraint of the body is good, restraint of speech is good,
and restraint in all regards is good;
the monk who is restrained in all regards
is released from all suffering.[73]*

This Prātimokṣa was eloquently spoken in summary by the Blessed One Kanakamuni, the Tathāgata, the Arhant, the Fully Enlightened One, Perfectly Enlightened for a long time, amidst a vast Bhikṣu-saṃgha.

7. There is no meditation for one without wisdom,
 and there is no wisdom for one without meditation;
 he, for whom there is meditation and wisdom
 is indeed close to nirvāṇa.[157]
 Therefore, this is the beginning for a wise monk:
 restraint of the senses, appeasement,
 and restraint according to the Prātimokṣa.[158]
8. One should constantly fulfill the virtuous, pure life,
 free from sleepiness.
 One should be versed in good manners, and be a practicer
 of goodwill;
 then with much joy, the monk [will be] close to nirvāṇa.[159]

This Prātimokṣa was eloquently spoken in summary by the Blessed One Kāśyapa, the Tathāgata, the Arhant, the Fully Enlightened One, Perfectly Enlightened for a long time, amidst a vast Bhikṣu-saṃgha.

9. Restraint of the eyes is good, restraint of the ears is good,
 restraint of the nose is good, restraint of the mind is good;
 the monk who is restrained in all regards
 is released from all suffering.[160]

This Prātimokṣa was eloquently spoken in summary by the Blessed One Śākyamuni, the Tathāgata, the Arhant, the Fully Enlightened One, Perfectly Enlightened for a long time, amidst a vast Bhikṣu-saṃgha.

These Prātimokṣas of the eminent, Fully Enlightened Ones . . .[161] (1) Vipaśyin: not employing sin, (2) Śikhin: proclaims adhicitta, (3) Viśvabhū: . . .[162] (4) Krakucchanda: not to do evil, (5) Kanakamuni: faults, (6) Kāśyapa: proclaims meditations, and (7) Śākyamuni: restraint. These are the seven ten-powered ones.[163]

. . . .

This was written by Śrīvijayabhadra, a monk of Śākya.[164]

10. He who guards his speech, is well restrained in his mind,
and does not perform evil with his body;
being purified regarding the paths of action in these three,
shall attain the road proclaimed by the ṛṣis.[74]*

11 and 12. This Prātimokṣa was recited in detail by these seven celebrated, self-possessed Buddhas who were the chief protectors and guardians of the world: Vipaśyin, Śikhin, Viśvabhū, Krakucchanda, Kanakamuni, Kāśyapa, and immediately following, Śākyamuni Gautama, the God of Gods, the charioteer who subdued men.

13. The Buddhas and Śrāvakas of the Buddhas are respectful
toward it [i.e., the Prātimokṣa];
being respectful toward it, one obtains the unconditioned path.

14. Go forth, cling to, employ the Teaching of the Buddhas;
destroy the army of the Lord of Death,
like an elephant [destroys] a house of reeds.[75]*

15. One who will diligently engage in this Dharma and Vinaya,
having abandoned birth and saṃsāra,
shall put an end to suffering.[76]*

16. This Prātimokṣa has been recited, and Poṣadha made by the saṃgha,
for the increase of the Teaching,
and for the sake of mutual protection of śīla.

17. For the sake of those for whom the Sūtra has been recited,
and for the sake of those for whom Poṣadha has been made,
you should guard śīla, as a yak protects its first-born.

18. Whatever merit has been gained from the full exposition of
the Prātimokṣa,
by that may this entire world obtain the position
of the Chief of Sages.

The Prātimokṣa is concluded.

Notes

1 Pachow's translation, "the protector whom the world follows," is untenable, for tāyinām is clearly genitive plural (see Franklin Edgerton, *Buddhist Hybrid Sanskrit Grammar and Dictionary*, 2 vols. (New Haven, Conn.: Yale University Press, 1953), Vol. II, pp. 251–252). See W. Pachow, trans., "Translation of the Introductory Section of the Text [Mahāsāṃghika Prātimokṣa Sūtra]," *Journal of the Gaṅgānāth Jhā Research Institute*, XI-XII, 1–4 (November-February-May-August, 1953–1955), 243.

1* Using the Tibetan text, which reads thams-cad-mkhyen-pa, Dr. Banerjee suggests sarvajñeya for sarvaṅkaṣa, providing a meaningful alternative to a thoroughly unusual and perhaps untenable compound. See Ankal Chandra Banerjee, ed., *Pratimokṣa-Sūtram* [*Mūlasarvāstivāda*] (Calcutta: Calcutta Oriental Press Ltd., 1954), p. 4, n. 2.

2 My translation of this verse is wholly tentative, since the verse is beset with problems. No solution is readily available for translating buddho yodaṃ. Dr. Pachow's translation also affords no help, since he ignores yodaṃ, interprets dauḥśīlavadyam as slanderous (see Edgerton, *Buddhist Hybrid Sanskrit Dictionary*, p. 469, for vadya), and takes viśuddhaśīlā, bhavatha, and apramattāḥ as singulars. See Pachow, "Translation of the Introductory Section of the Text," p. 243.

2* I have translated verses one and two of the Mūlasarvāstivādin text together, as seems appropriate for a proper understanding of the content. For a similar approach, see Satis Chandra Vidyabhusana, ed. and trans., "So-sor-thar-pa; or, a Code of Buddhist Monastic Laws: Being the Tibetan version of the Prātimokṣa of the Mūla-sarvāstivāda School," *Journal of the Asiatic Society of Bengal*, New Series, IX, 3–4 (1915), 37.

3 There is nothing here to support the contention that Pachow, "Translation of the Introductory Section of the Text," p. 243, makes regarding pure śīla existing *after* the end of the universe.

3* Both Banerjee, *Prātimokṣa-Sūtram* [*Mūlasarvāstivāda*], p. 4, n. 11, and Vidyabhusana, "So-sor-thar-pa," p. 37, point out that this verse corresponds to the Mahāparinibbāna Sutta, Chapter VI, paragraph 1.

4 Pachow, "Translation of the Introductory Section of the Text," p. 244, does not translate Tedhātuke, and it is not clear what he has in mind. One would suppose the kāma, rūpa, and arūpa dhātus are indicated. See also Thomas W. Rhys Davids and William Stede, eds., *The Pali Text Society's Pali-English Dictionary*, reprint (London: Luzac & Company, for P.T.S., 1966), p. 306 (te-).

4* This verse corresponds to Dhammapada, verse 194 [Buddhavagga, verse 16]. See Nārada Thera, ed. and trans., *Dhammapada* (Colombo: Vajirārāma, 1963), pp. 170–171. Banerjee, *Prātimokṣa-Sūtram* [*Mūlasarvāstivāda*], p. 5, n. 1, and Vidyabhusana, "So-sor-thar-pa," p. 38, n. 1, also make the appropriate reference.

5 Can yoyaṃ, as indicated in the text, be yogaṃ? Discipline seems to be the topic of the verse.

5* This verse corresponds to Dhammapada, verse 206 [Sukhavagga, verse 10]. See Nārada, *Dhammapada*, p. 179. It is quite possible that saṃvāso and satā are corruptions for the Pāli sannivāso and sadā, respectively, which would alter the translation considerably. We might amend the translation of the first half of the verse to:

> Happy is the sight of the noble ones,
> Association with them is always happy.

Banerjee, *Prātimokṣa-Sūtram* [*Mūlasarvāstivāda*], p. 5, n. 3, and Vidyabhusana, "So-sor-thar-pa," p. 38, n. 2, also cite the verse.

6 Gaṇottamo, which I have translated as Saṃgha, rather than "highest group" (which does not convey the import of the term), completes the Three Jewels.

6* I have followed I.B. Horner's notion in translating pariśuddhi as complete purity (although she renders it "entire purity"). For a succinct and discerning statement on this topic, see I.B. Horner, trans., *The Book of the Discipline*, 6 vols. (London: Luzac & Company, for P.T.S., 1938–1966), Vol. IV, pp. vi and xv. Concerning the declaration of pariśuddhi and giving of consent [chanda], Horner (on p. xv) remarks:

> If a monk, owing to illness, could not attend the recital of the Pātimokkha, he had to send his "entire purity", parisuddhi, by another. This monk conveyed it on behalf of the one who was ill and declared it (dātuṃ) to the Order; but many occasions are posited when the entire purity comes not to be conveyed on account of a variety of things that might happen to the conveyer both while on his way from the invalid to the meeting-place and after his arrival there but before he had given the entire purity. This, and the conveyance and giving, or declaration of the consent (chandaṃ dātuṃ) on behalf of a monk who is ill for the carrying out of a formal act of the Order, serve to show how extremely important it was held to be—a point stressed over and over again—that an Order should be "complete" whenever its business was being discharged.

For the Pāli canonical reference on this point, see Hermann Oldenberg, ed., *The Vinaya Piṭakaṃ*, 5 vols.; reprint (London: Luzac & Company, for P.T.S., 1964), Vol. I, pp. 120–122, or Horner, *The Book of the Discipline*, Vol. IV, pp. 158–162 [Mahāvagga II.22.1–II.23.3]. For the Mūlasarvāstivādin version see Nalinaksha Dutt, ed., assisted by Vidyavaridhi Shiv Nath Sharma, *The Gilgit Manuscripts* [Vol. III, Parts 1–4 (Vinaya-vastu); Calcutta: Calcutta Oriental Press Ltd., 1940–1950], Vol. III, 4, pp. 98–101. The whole of the Mahāsāṃghika Vinaya [Mo-ho-seng-k'i-liu] was translated into Chinese in AD 416 by Buddhabhadra and Fa-hien, and the appropriate section, Poṣadhavastu [Po-sa-fa], appears in *Taishō* 1425, pp. 446c7–450c2 [see Erich Frauwallner, *The Earliest Vinaya and the Beginnings of Buddhist Literature*, Serie *Orientale Roma*, Vol. VIII (Rome:

Instituto per il Medio ed Estremo Oriente, 1956), p. 200, for more information on this point].

7 My translation is somewhat tentative here. For Prātimokṣa recital by the nuns, consult Cullavagga X.6.1–X.8. See Oldenberg, *The Vinaya Piṭakaṃ*, Vol. II, pp. 259–261, and Horner, *The Book of the Discipline*, Vol. V, pp. 359–363. The Mūlasarvāstivādin section on nuns appears in the Kṣudrakavastu [Tsa shih], *Taishō* 1451, pp. 350b7–373c28. The Mahāsāṃghika version, Tsa sung po ch'ü fa, occurs at *Taishō* 1425, pp. 471a25–476b11.

7* The distinction between a human and one that has human form seems to be only in this text. Interestingly enough, the Mūlasarvāstivādin text adds the word saṃcintya [intentionally], seemingly exempting the bhikṣu from involuntary manslaughter, an offense which the Mahāsāṃghika bhikṣu could evidently be held culpable of.

8 Pachow, "Translation of the Introductory Section of the Text," p. 246, reads murderer.

8* sparśavihāratāṃ. See Edgerton, *Buddhist Hybrid Sanskrit Dictionary*, p. 612.

9 See Edgerton, *Buddhist Hybrid Sanskrit Dictionary*, p. 573 (samudita). Pachow, "Translation of the Introductory Section of the Text," p. 246, reads fortune teller.

9* This rule offers an interesting variance between the two texts. The Mahāsāṃghika text notes that the vihāra is "intended for himself" [atmoddeśikaṃ], thus it seems to be an individual effort by and for the monk. In the Mūlasarvāstivādin text, atmoddeśikaṃ has been replaced by saṃghoddeśakaṃ [intended for the saṃgha]. Why? Three conclusions seem possible: (1) it may be a result of an error or oversight on the part of the text's compiler; (2) the fact of the large vihāra being intended for the saṃgha carries no great significance at all; or (3) we have discovered an instructive detail, revealing information about the maturation of early Buddhist monasticism. The first conclusion is unlikely, since it is preserved in this form in the Tibetan text. On this point, see Satis Chandra Vidyabhusana, "So-sor-thar-pa," p. 42. The second conclusion is unacceptable for several reasons. First, we find numerous examples of vihāras (i.e., ārāmas) being donated to the saṃgha or individuals by various kings and lay disciples, but it is only in the developed Skandhaka text, illustrated by Frauwallner (*The Earliest Vinaya*, p. 123) to be relatively later than the date which we have set for the root Prātimokṣa, that we find any mention of a superintendent of buildings, which the monk in the rule in question certainly seems to be. Second, the word vihāra is generally agreed to have represented, in earliest times, the dwelling of a single monk, only later being adopted as the title for monastic dwellings in general. Third, the interest in monastic life is dismissed by Frauwallner (*The Earliest Vinaya*, p. 121) as having "gained greater importance only in the course of time." Thus we are led to tentatively accept the third conclusion and can make several statements in the way of summary. In the early tradition kuṭi [hut] and vihāra are almost synonymous, whereas later there exists a clear line of differentiation between the two terms. If we can accept that the period in which monastic officers come to be designated is somewhat later than that of the formation of the root Prātimokṣa text (and I do), the presence of such a monk in the Mūlasarvāstivādin text, virtually acting in the role of building superintendent, indicates that their Prātimokṣa became finalized at a later date than those in which no monastic officers are hinted at. Finally, if we consider this in the light of the enormous emphasis of the Mūlasarvāstivādins on boundary delineation [sīmā], we must ascribe the prevalence of this school to a time period when there was great interest in the Buddhist monastic institution and its preservation, previously noted by Frauwallner to be late. We should also note that in the Mahāsāṃghika text we are told that the monks should be brought to mark out the site [vastudeśanāya]. The Mūlasarvāstivādin text remarks that the monks should be brought to view the site [vastudarśanāya]. Perhaps I am overstating the difference between these two terms (and it might be only a phonological variance), but it seems to me that the Mahāsāṃghika bhikṣus entered into the selection in a more real, intimate sense than those of the Mūlasarvāstivādin school. The Mūlasarvāstivādin text gives the impression of action after the fact.

10 See Edgerton, *Buddhist Hybrid Sanskrit Dictionary*, p. 447 (yāvataka).

10* Śāsanaṃ [Teaching] is missing in the manuscript.

11 Although the text, as well as Pachow, "Translation of the Introductory Section of the Text," p. 246, is somewhat unwieldy here, the issue (masked in both) pertains to the assurance that the proper sīmā [boundary] regulations had been observed. Unless the sīmā had been appropriately delineated, it was impossible to carry out a valid Poṣadha ceremony. The Pāli Vinaya is explicit on this point, as Mahāvagga II.6.1–II.13.2 indicates. Note especially Mahāvagga II.13.1–2, where the notorious group of six (always troublesome) monks combine boundary with boundary. See Horner, *The Book of the Discipline*, Vol. IV, pp. 137–146, and Oldenberg, *The Vinaya Piṭakaṃ*, Vol. I, pp. 106–111. The importance of sīmā, however, was by no means distinct to the Pāli Vinaya. Ten pages of the Poṣadhavastu of the Mūlasarvāstivādin Vinaya, for example, are devoted to precisely these types of topics. See N. Dutt, *The Gilgit Manuscripts*, Vol. III, 4, pp. 84–94. This portion is lacking in the Mahāsāṃghika version. Our manuscript seems to indicate that the saṃgha in *this particular place* had secured the area which had been accepted by its monks. As in other portions of the text, it is best not to place too much weight on the dimensions enumerated.

11* The text reads evaṃ cetsa bhikṣurbhikṣubhirucyamānastathaiva vastu samādāya [pragṛhya tiṣṭhet] śuddhastu pratiniḥsṛjedityevaṃ kuśalaṃ. This reading, however, negates the entire value of the rule. It seems almost likely that it is a mistake in the manuscript, since it appears in the correct form later in the same rule. Therefore I have corrected it in the translation.

12 It is not my intention to review the whole upadhi [Pāli: upādi] debate which raged on in the second half of the nineteenth century. Guy Welbon, in *The Buddhist Nirvāṇa and Its Western Interpreters* (Chicago: The University of

Chicago Press, 1968), presents an admirable summary of the controversy. Especially stirring are the sections on James D'Alwis (pp. 131–146), Robert Caesar Childers (pp. 146–153), and Hermann Oldenberg (pp. 194–220). For an interesting article on the technical terms, see Arthur Oncken Lovejoy, "The Buddhistic Technical Terms Upādāna and Upādisesa," *Journal of the American Oriental Society*, XIX (1898), 126–136.

12* Read avinayaṃ instead of vinayaṃ. Since the monks are being implored not to follow the schismatic monk, it must be his negative aspects that are being listed.

13 No matter how they are arranged, the list contains only eight members.

13* The text has switched from the plural to the singular.

14 Judging by the rather strange translation equivalents that have been utilized in the past (e.g., cankers), I prefer to leave āśrava, a common but incorrect rendering of āsrava, untranslated.

14* For a discussion of the āvarhaṇa ceremony, see Edgerton, *Buddhist Hybrid Sanskrit Dictionary*, p. 107.

15 Using Edgerton's entry for bhujiṣya, I have translated bhujanyaṃ adverbially here. See Edgerton, *Buddhist Hybrid Sanskrit Dictionary*, p. 110. This rendering is pure speculation, dictated by no other apparent alternatives.

15* It appears that in the Mūlasarvāstivādin version (and the Sarvāstivādin version) it is not necessary for the trustworthy upāsikā to see the monk in order to accuse him of an offense. The Mahāsāṃghika and Pāli versions include the act of seeing as necessary in order to accuse the monk. The divergence may be a simple omission. However, it may, on the other hand, be quite instructive. By not including seeing in the rule, it opens the possibility of hearsay evidence being introduced against a monk, and since the hearsay evidence would be coming from an upāsikā, this is even more extraordinary. Perhaps at the time when the Pāli and Mahāsāṃghika versions were compiled, women were still regarded with utmost caution, and anything short of eyewitness testimony on their part was rejected, while by the time of the Mūlasarvāstivādin and Sarvāstivādin versions (which would under this supposition be somewhat later), women in the order were not held so strictly suspect.

16 Paśya vo siyāpattiḥ (in the text) makes no sense, but the Pāli has: yassa sīya āpatti so āvikareyya. See J. F. Dickson, ed. and trans., "The Pātimokkha, being the Buddhist Office of the Confession of Priests. The Pali Text, with a Translation and Notes," *Journal of the Royal Asiatic Society*, New Series, VIII (1875), 72.

16* A statement of what (wicked) act it is possible to commit under the conditions outlined in the text does not appear in the manuscript.

17 This is the usual translation equivalent for antarāyika dharma. For example, see Edgerton, *Buddhist Hybrid Sanskrit Dictionary*, p. 39 (antarāyika).

17* I am following Edgerton, *Buddhist Hybrid Sanskrit Dictionary*, p. 308 (niṣṭhita), and Huber's French translation in Finot, "Le Prātimokṣasūtra des Sarvāstivādins," p. 490.

18 Although we are tempted to avoid a discussion of the introductory (and concluding) portion of the texts as being later additions, an emphatic impression arises from it, namely, that whereas the Mūlasarvāstivādin version appears uniformly well developed and late, the Mahāsāṃghika version shows signs of a high antiquity. In the versified portion of the introduction to the Mahāsāṃghika text, the term Prātimokṣa occurs but three times, and only one of these makes any reference to a sūtra of that name. In the first case we read:

tam prātimokṣaṃ bhavaduḥkhamokṣaṃ śrutvānudhīrāḥ
sugatasya bhāṣitāṃ /
ṣaḍinriyaṃ samavarasamvṛtatvātkaronti jātīmaraṇasya
antaṃ //

The verse cited does not reveal a description of the Prātimokṣa spoken by Buddha (and it certainly does not state that it was a sūtra), but it does, however, claim that the Prātimokṣa could provide "release from the pains of becoming." Further, by restraint of the sense organs, the self-possessed "put an end to birth and death." Clearly, no doctrinal texts of any Buddhist school support the notion that nirvāṇa can be attained merely by strict observance of sīla. Nevertheless, if Prātimokṣa in this verse refers to that ancient use of the term, indicating an expression of faith in the Buddha and his Teaching, the verse takes on a new meaning: Faith and its practical application can put an end to duḥkha. Doctrinally, at least, this is sound, for we know that one stage on the way to arhantship is called śraddhānusārin or "follower in faith." For a discussion of this and similar terms, see Nalinaksha Dutt, *Early Monastic Buddhism* (Calcutta: Calcutta Oriental Book Agency, 1960), pp. 254–257. In the fourth prefatory verse we read: śīlena yuktasya hi prātimokṣaṃ. Certainly it would be absurd to take Prātimokṣa as a sūtra here. In stating "there is Prātimokṣa for one intent on śīla," the above premise is confirmed. Śīla results in faith, not nirvāṇa. It is only in the tenth introductory verse that Prātimokṣa as a sūtra is mentioned. It states there:

yāvatsūtraprātimokṣe so gaṇamadhya na bheṣyati /
tāvatsthāsyati saddharmo sāmagrī ca gaṇottame //

This, however, is contradicted shortly thereafter:

abhimukhaṃ kṣamati jarāmaraṇaṃ kṣīyati jīvate
priyaṃ hāyati saddharmā astameti.

Let us review: in the tenth introductory verse we are told that the True Dharma will stand as long as the Prātimokṣa Sūtra is preserved; later we are informed that the True Dharma is already ceasing. Can we believe that the Prātimokṣa Sūtra has already fallen into disuse? Stranger still, how can we explain this second statement in the introduction to a Prātimokṣa text? Plainly, we have uncovered a layer of stratification, the latter statement included perhaps as an inducement to reestablish pure observance. If we were asked to cite the one watchword of the entire versified section of the Mahāsāṃghika Prātimokṣa

Sūtra introduction, it would not be Vinaya, but rather śīla, a term appearing no less than sixteen times. Now śīla is a difficult word to define, but of one thing we are certain: whereas Vinaya in general indicates those moral precepts that are externally enforced and controlled, śīla is an internally administered moral guideline, wholly dependent on the individual. It is in this context that we read: aneka buddhānumataṃ viśuddhaṃ śīlaṃ. . . āhariṣyāmi. . . . The statement is critical for it reveals that pure śīla, and not Prātimokṣa Sūtras, has been praised by many Buddhas. Apart from the moral domain, we can also glean some precious bits of doctrinal information. The following terms are mentioned: triratna (Prefatory Verse 3), akuśalamūla (Introductory Verse 1), amaravitarka (Introductory Verse 2), three dhātus (Introductory Verse 4), pañcāpatti (Introductory Verse 7), and upadhi (Introduction).

The Mūlasarvāstivādin Prātimokṣa Sūtra presents an entirely different picture in its introductory section. In the versified portion, śīla is mentioned only once (Introductory Verse 5). Prātimokṣa, on the other hand, is now referred to as the essence of Vinaya. Further, it is declared to be "hard to obtain in ten millions of ages; even going beyond, to grasp and to bear [it] is much more difficult to obtain," seemingly indicating a more developed state than the primitive text. Prātimokṣa is now exalted, being regarded as the "compendium of True Dharma written by the King of the True Dharma," and as a "great treaty." Almost uniformly, the introductory verses extol its observance. Whereas the Mahāsāṃghika text simply stressed the general need for śīla, the Mūlasarvāstivādin text supplies, with apparently obvious motives, a formal (and expected) introduction to the recitation at hand by presenting a series of laudatory verses. Now the monks are likened to a guild of merchants, perhaps indicating a further development in general saṃgha life. Sticking only to the business at hand, in the verse section little reference is made to doctrinal issues: saṃsāra is mentioned once (Introductory Verse 6), prajñā once (Introductory Verse 12), and kleśa twice (Introductory Verses 17 and 18). However, the prose section does note that the bodhipakṣika dharmas, summarizing Buddha's teachings, can be obtained by diligence.

18* The problem of sīmā was discussed earlier. Dr. Nalinaksha Dutt, in a most interesting article, "The Second Buddhist Council," *Indian Historical Quarterly*, XXXV, 1 (March 1959), 54, also mentions this peculiar emphasis on sīmā by the Mūlasarvāstivādins.

19 The text seems overly explicit, using two equivalents of sexual intercourse: maithuna and grāmya dharma. The Sarvāstivādin text simply has [mai]thunạm dharmaṃ. See Louis Finot, ed., "Le Prātimokṣasūtra des Sarvāstivādins." Texte Sanskrit par L. Finot, avec la version chinoise de Kumārajīva traduité en français par Edouard Huber, *Journal Asiatique*, Série XI, II (Novembre-Décembre, 1913), 476. The Pāli also has simply methunaṃ dhammaṃ. See Dickson, "The Pātimokkha, being the Buddhist Office of the Confession of Priests," p. 73.

19* I have taken antikāt as "nearby" primarily on the basis of the santikāt appearing in the Sarvāstivādin text. See Finot, "Le Prātimokṣasūtra des Sarvāstivādins," p. 491. The Mahāsāṃghika text has no similar word while the Pāli has hatthato [from the hand of], neither affording any help. See Dickson, "The Pātimokkha, being the Buddhist Office of the Confession of Priests," p. 78.

20 pūre bhuktaṃ. I equate this to paścād bhuktaṃ, which occurs in the following rule. For the meaning, see Edgerton, *Buddhist Hybrid Sanskrit Dictionary*, p. 338 (paścādbhakta).

20* I am hard pressed to explain the gerund labdhvā, which does not seem to fit here. The Sarvāstivādin text has cīvaraṃ tu vayaṃ labdhvā kālena kalpikaṃ svahastaṃ pratigṛhya kṣipram eva kṛtvā [ācchāda] yāmaḥ. See Finot, "Le Prātimokṣasūtra des Sarvāstivādins," p. 494.

21 The phrase Dharma and Anudharma is puzzling. The manuscript tries to append a ninth class of rules, Dharma and Anudharma, after the adhikaraṇa-śamatha dharmas, but its appearance is quite artificial. It is explained there, however, that Dharma refers to both Vinayas, and Anudharma to the conduct established. See W. Pachow and Ramakanta Mishra, "The Prātimokṣa Sūtra of the Mahāsāṃghikas," *Journal of the Gaṅgānāth Jhā Research Institute*, IX, 2–4 (February-May-August, 1952), 260. In the Bhikṣuṇī Vinaya of the Mahāsāṃghika-Lokottaravādin sect we also find the same appendage. Gustav Roth points this out clearly in "Bhikṣuṇīvinaya and Bhikṣu-Prakīrṇaka and Notes on the Language," *Journal of the Bihar Research Society*, LII, 1–4 (January-December, 1966), 32, but he does not note it as especially unusual. It should also be noted that the Pārājika Dharma section is quite similar in both texts. There are, however, two features of the Mahāsāṃghika version which remain distinct. First, each rule concludes with the following:

> ayaṃ bhikṣuḥ pārājiko bhavatyasaṃvāsyo na labhate
> bhikṣuhi sārddhasaṃvāsaṃ.

In the Mūlasarvāstivādin text we read:

> ayamapi bhikṣuḥ pārājiko bhavatyasaṃvāsyaḥ.

It is only in the conclusion to the entire Mūlasarvāstivādin section that we find the phrase na labhate bhikṣubhiḥ sārdaṃ saṃvāsaṃ bhogaṃ vā. It is interesting to note that in addition to generalizing the statement at the end of the section, bhogaṃ has been added. Second, after each pārājika, the Mahāsāṃghika text adds a paragraph explaining the proposition of the rule. This narration includes the date, place, and reference for its promulgation. The appearance of this intrusion early in the text gives one the impression that they are going to be provided with a condensed Sūtravibhaṅga throughout, but these rule commentaries cease after this section and are included in no other. This brief commentary is totally lacking in the Mūlasarvāstivādin text (and all other Prātimokṣa Sūtras as well).

21* The text has the strange form dhyāyat, perhaps being from $\sqrt{}$dhī or $\sqrt{}$dhyai.

22 In this second rule the Mahāsāṃghika text indicates that the guilty bhikṣu seems only to be censured by kings [rājāno], whereas the Mūlasarvāstivādin text notes king [rājā] or king's minister [rājamātra], perhaps indicating an extension of those persons to which a monk may be held reprehensible (in addition, of course, to the saṃgha).

22* The Mūlasarvāstivādin text presents only niṣīdanaṃ. This, in itself, carries the intention adequately, but one would expect niṣīdanasaṃstaraṃ, as in the Sarvāstivādin text (Finot, "Le Prātimokṣasūtra des Sarvāstivādins," p. 497), or one of the similar forms found in the Pāli and Mahāsāṃghika versions.

23 manuṣyavigrahaṃ.

23* The form presented here, udgrāhanasat, puzzles me. The Pāli, as well as the other Sanskrit versions, simply present a causative form of ud √grah.

24 kālaṃ kuryāt. For this common idiom, see Monier Monier-Williams, *A Sanskrit-English Dictionary*, reprint of new edition in collaboration with E. Leumann, C. Cappeller, and others (Oxford: The Clarendon Press, 1964), p. 301.

24* The text should read abhiṣaktaḥ instead of abhiṣiktaḥ. See Finot, "Le Prātimokṣasūtra des Sarvāstivādins," p. 500, and Edgerton, *Buddhist Hybrid Sanskrit Dictionary*, p. 56.

25 Viśeṣādhiśeṣādhigama puzzles me. I have tried to distinguish between viśeṣa and adhiśeṣa. See Edgerton, *Buddhist Hybrid Sanskrit Dictionary*, p. 501 (viśeṣādhigama).

25* The Mūlasarvāstivādin text, taccīvaraṃ tacca śeṣamupaniḥsṛṣṭavyaṃ, is unclear. The Sarvāstivādin text (Finot, "Le Prātimokṣasūtra des Sarvāstivādins," p. 500) has sa vastuśeṣo niḥsṛ[ṣ]ta[v]yo.

26 For another reading, consult W. Pachow, *A Comparative Study of the Prātimokṣa*, Sino-Indian Studies, Vol. IV, Part 2, 1951–1955, p. 97 (note on the fourth Mahāsāṃghika pārājika dharma, designated as Msg. 4). I cannot help but think that Dr. Pachow's translation is awkward and unwieldy.

26* My translation of the second portion of this rule is quite tentative.

27 Alternate translation: with regard to a self-conceited monk.

27* See Edgerton, *Buddhist Hybrid Sanskrit Dictionary*, pp. 72 and 201 (avadhyāna and kṣepana, respectively).

28 The summaries of the rules in each section are often impossible to translate meaningfully.

28* The Mūlasarvāstivādin text has ājñā, order(s). Finot, "Le Prātimokṣasūtra des Sarvāstivādins," p. 505, records anyāvāda. Dickson, "The Pātimokkha, being the Buddhist Office of the Confession of Priests," p. 83, has aññavādake, and Pachow and Mishra, "The Prātimokṣa Sūtra of the Mahāsāṃghikas," p. 22, reads anyavāda.

29 saṃcetanikā ye śukrasya viśṛṣṭīya. There is no doubt that this reading, as it appears, is plural. See Edgerton, *Buddhist Hybrid Sanskrit Grammar*, pp. 67 (pars. 9.91–9.92) and 81 (par. 10.175). Perhaps one may read saṃcetanikā

ye-saṃcetanikāye, and after amending viśṛṣṭīye to visṛṣṭīye, read this portion of the rule as a genitive absolute.

29* See Edgerton, *Buddhist Hybrid Sanskrit Dictionary*, p. 74 (avalokayati).

30 The text reads śaparāsopiṇaṃ, which leaves me at a loss. The other versions afford no help at all. Perhaps we can amend to saparāsapiṇḍaṃ.

30* The Mūlasarvāstivādin text has ityetaṃ pratyayaṃ kṛtvā, differing from the Pāli and other Sanskrit texts. See, for example, Finot, "Le Prātimokṣasūtra des Sarvāstivādins," p. 506 (idam eva pratyayaṃ kṛtvānanyathāt).

31 The Mahāsāṃghika text, bhikṣuṇī kāyāmapi, is preposterous. Dickson, "The Pātimokkha, being the Buddhist Office of the Confession of Priests," p. 74, has taṃkhaṇikāya, and Finot, "Le Prātimokṣasūtra des Sarvāstivādins," p. 480, has tatkṣaṇaṃ. The meaning here: "for a moment."

31* For upari vihāyasi kṛtāyāṃ kuṭikāyām, see Edgerton, *Buddhist Hybrid Sanskrit Dictionary*, p. 513 (vaihāyasam).

32 appeva nāma. See Rhys Davids and Stede, *The Pali Text Society's Pali-English Dictionary*, p. 350.

32* In the Pāli and Mahāsāṃghika texts, the use of harita [grass] is not clear. In the Mūlasarvāstivādin text, however, harita is unmistakably connected with the means for covering (the vihāra), chedanaparyāyāḥ.

33 I have read pratiṣṭhihati as "stands fast" rather than "confess" as Horner does (using the commentary). See Horner, *The Book of the Discipline*, Vol. I, p. 281 (and n. 1). I must admit that Horner has support; for example, Thomas Rhys Davids and Hermann Oldenberg, trans., *Vinaya Texts*, 3 vols.; reprint (Delhi: Motilal Banarsidass, 1965), Vol. I, p. 10. In rules ten, eleven, twelve, and thirteen of this section, we shall see that if a monk abandons his wrong course, it is stated to be good, whereas if he should not abandon it, he is guilty of a saṃghātiśeṣa. One might expect that if the monk here confessed his fault, it would say ityetaṃ kuśalaṃ [this is good], but the text states that he has committed a saṃghātiśeṣa. However, the point of this rule is not confession, since confession is at the heart of the Prātimokṣa system, so that it must be assumed that sooner or later a concealed offense would be confessed. There are numerous references to offenses which are concealed for some time (see Cullavagga III; Horner, *The Book of the Discipline*, Vol. V, pp. 56–95, and Oldenberg, *The Vinaya Piṭakaṃ*, Vol. II, pp. 38–72), and the parivāsa period was designed for just that purpose. The critical issue here is that by standing fast in his malice, the monk may not recognize the gravity of his fault, or he may simply be obstinate. In either case, the mānatva probation is both necessary and desirable. My comments apply also to pratiṣṭhā, as found in the Mūlasarvāstivādin text.

33* I have interpreted arthaṃ loosely, to coincide with the offering.

34 See Edgerton, *Buddhist Hybrid Sanskrit Dictionary*, p. 560 (samagra).

34* The Mūlasarvāstivādin text has āsvādanaprekṣī. Edgerton, *Buddhist Hybrid Sanskrit Dictionary*, p. 112, enters (under āsvādanīya) meanings of "enjoyable" and "pleasant" and cites its use as a substantive in the sense of condiments. The meaning does not fit the case. However, the Pāli, Sarvāstivādin, Mahāsāṃghika, and, most critically, the other Mūlasarvāstivādin text [L. Chandra, ed., "Unpublished Gilgit Fragment of the Prātimokṣa-Sūtra," *Wiener Zeitschrift für die Kunde Süd- und Ostasiens*, IV (1960), 3], all have āsādana. Edgerton does cite this word (p. 111) and the meaning is appropriate.

35 Evaṃ asya vacanīyo is idiomatic: "Should be spoken to thus."

35* Perhaps udyūṣikāṃ, in the text, equals udyūthikāṃ. See Edgerton, *Buddhist Hybrid Sanskrit Dictionary*, p. 131.

36 For an understanding of ekuddeśo [under one rule], see Horner, *The Book of the Discipline*, Vol. I, p. 300, n.1.

36* pratyanubhavet. See Edgerton, *Buddhist Hybrid Sanskrit Dictionary*, p. 374, for the meaning.

37 dūrvvacakajātīyo. The Pāli has dubbacajātiko. See Dickson, "The Pātimokkha, being the Buddhist Office of the Confession of Priests," p. 76. For the meaning of the word, see Horner, *The Book of the Discipline*, Vol. I, p. 310, n. 1, and Edgerton, *Buddhist Hybrid Sanskrit Dictionary*, p. 272 (durvacasya). Buddhaghosa's commentary on the Pātimokkha defines dubbacajātiko as dubbacasabhāvo. See Buddhaghosa, *Kaṅkhāvitaraṇī*, edited by Dorothy Maskell (London: Luzac & Company for P.T.S., 1956), p. 47.

37* dhvajāgraṃ. See Edgerton, *Buddhist Hybrid Sanskrit Dictionary*, p. 288, for the meaning.

38 I have included community here although it does not appear in the text. This portion of the rule would be meaningless without something to increase or grow. The Pāli text has parisā. See Dickson, "The Pātimokkha, being the Buddhist Confession of Priests," p. 76. The Sarvāstivādin text, although fragmentary, does have the word pariṣad included in the rule. See Finot, "Le Prātimokṣasūtra des Sarvāstivādins," p. 486.

38* Dr. Banerjee has reconstructed bhikṣoḥ prahāramupa [darśayet antatastakaśaktika] mapi. Chandra, "Unpublished Gilgit Fragment of the Prātimokṣa-Sūtra," p. 4, has bhikṣoḥ prahāram udgūrayed antatas talaśaktikā. Although upadarśayet [promise, predict] is not totally inappropriate, udgūrayed is the better choice. According to Edgerton, *Buddhist Hybrid Sanskrit Dictionary*, pp. 37–38, antatas may be taken as "even so much as," and with the instrumental form of talaśaktikā, the rule becomes intelligible.

39 The text reads abhivastuṃ, which I presume to be vastuṃ.

39* For the meaning of sparśa in this sense, see Edgerton, *Buddhist Hybrid Sanskrit Dictionary*, p. 612 (sparśa-vihāratā). Chandra, "Unpublished Gilgit Fragment of the Prātimokṣa-Sūtra," p. 5, reads differently for the first part of the quote: gaccha tvam āyuṣman na ce[t] tvayā sārdhaṃ sparśo bhavati kathyāṃ vā niṣadyāyāṃ vā. The Mūlasarvāstivādin text is interesting in that it remarks that if the companion is dismissed after receiving alms (i.e., the first monk upheld his promise to provide alms, at least), the persuading monk is guilty of an offense. The Mahāsāṃghika text is clear: The monk who did the persuading is guilty, irrespective of any consideration of alms. The Mūlasarvāstivādin account is tantamount to stating that if no alms are provided, the persuading monk is free to dismiss his cohort, a most unusual and somewhat incongruous situation.

40 Numbers eight and nine seem to be missing in the text, but the phrase dūtena saṃghasya is included, which appears to be part of the summaries of these two rules.

40* I have translated kṣepadharmamāpadyeta rather loosely, following Horner, *The Book of the Discipline*, Vol. III, p. 59 (and n. 2). I suppose a literal reading would be "should fall into the dharma against accusation (or abuse)."

41 tatra—at once. For a similar usage see Horner, *The Book of the Discipline*, Vol. I, p. 328.

41* For the complete form of this phrase, see Edgerton, *Buddhist Hybrid Sanskrit Dictionary*, p. 443 (yathāvāditathākāri).

42 The text has parivuttha, which is the Pāli form for paryuṣita. For a comment on this Sanskrit form see Edgerton, *Buddhist Hybrid Sanskrit Dictionary*, p. 336.

42* pratodanāt. See Edgerton, *Buddhist Hybrid Sanskrit Dictionary*, p. 374.

43 For more information on disciplinary actions refer to Cullavagga III (Oldenberg, *The Vinaya Piṭakaṃ*, Vol. II. pp. 38–72, and Horner, *The Book of the Discipline*, Vol. V, pp. 56–95). Also see S. Dutt, *Early Buddhist Monachism* (Bombay: Asia Publishing House, 1960), pp. 136–138. For a bit more rigorous reading, refer to Herbert Härtel, ed. and trans., *Karmavācanā*, *Sanskrittexte aus den Turfanfunden*, Vol. III (Berlin: Deutsche Akademie der Wissenschaften zu Berlin. Institut für Orientforschung, 1956), and also Heinz Bechert's fine article, "Asokas 'Schismedikt' und der Begriff Sanghabheda," *Wiener Zeitschrift für die Kunde Süd- und Ostasiens*, V (1961), 21 ff.

43* hāsyaprekṣyam. See Edgerton, *Buddhist Hybrid Sanskrit Dictionary*, p. 394 (prekṣya).

44 niṣadyāṃ kalpeya. For this idiomatic expression, see Edgerton, *Buddhist Hybrid Sanskrit Dictionary*, p. 307 (niṣadyā).

44* pariṣkāraṃ. See Edgerton, *Buddhist Hybrid Sanskrit Dictionary*, p. 331.

45 ekoya-. The Pāli version records eko ekāya. See Dickson, "The Pātimokkha, being the Buddhist Office of the Confession of Priests," p. 77. The Sarvāstivādin version has ekaike[na]. See Finot, "Le Prātimokṣasūtra des Sarvāstivādins," p. 488. In the text at hand, eko ekāya occurs in rule two of this section.

45* For this meaning of vikalpya, see Edgerton, *Buddhist Hybrid Sanskrit Dictionary*, p. 480 (vikalpayati). Chandra, "Unpublished Gilgit Fragment of the Prātimokṣa-Sūtra," p. 7, has dattvā.

46 The seat is convenient for engaging in sexual intercourse. See, for example, Horner, *The Book of the Discipline*, Vol. I, p. 333 (the Padabhājaniya commentary on the rule), or Finot, "Le Prātimokṣasūtra des Sarvāstivādins," p. 488 (Edouard

Huber's translation of the Chinese version of the Sarvāstivādin rule).

46* Dr. Banerjee has not reconstructed the second and third interrogations concerning complete purity.

47 śraddheyavacasā. Literally, the entire phrase (including upāsikā) means: an upāsikā with words that should be trusted. Buddhaghosa, *Kaṅkhāvitaraṇī*, p. 52, comments: "Saddheyyavacasā" ti saddhātabbavacanā ariyasāvikā ti attho. Also see Horner, *The Book of the Discipline*, Vol. I, pp. 332, n. 1, and 333, nn. 1 and 2.

47* śikṣāmsaṃvṛtisaṃmatāni. See Edgerton, *Buddhist Hybrid Sanskrit Dictionary*, p. 541 (saṃvṛti).

48 There seems to be much concern regarding the proper translation of the first portion of this rule and the following two rules. For a careful discussion of the subject, see Horner, *The Book of the Discipline*, Vol. II, pp. 4 (and nn. 5 and 6), 5 (and nn. 1–3), and 6 (and nn. 1–5). Horner reviews the suggestions of Huber, Gogerly, Dickson, Rhys Davids and Oldenberg, and Law and provides her own evaluations. I should also note a further citation in Edgerton, *Buddhist Hybrid Sanskrit Dictionary*, pp. 130–131, and a full length study of the subject: Kun Chang, *A Comparative Study of the Kaṭhinavastu* ('S-Gravenhage: Mouton & Co., 1957). Our version is slightly different, beginning with kṛtacīvarehi rather than niṣṭhitacīvareṇa as the Sarvāstivādin and Mūlasarvāstivādin texts do, or niṭṭhitacīvarasmiṃ as the Pāli does. However, the Padabhājaniya commentary describes kata (i.e., kṛta) as one of the five means for having the robe material settled [see Horner, *The Book of the Discipline*, Vol. II, p. 6 (and n.1)], and the Mahāvagga uses the term katacīvara (see Oldenberg, *The Vinaya Piṭakaṃ*, Vol. I, p. 256). Our version simply generalizes, using the plural rather than the singular (as in the other versions). Finally, it should be noted that the Pāli version varies with all the Sanskrit versions in that the first word of the rule is in the locative, making it relatively easy to construe all the locatives in an absolute relationship and take bhikkhunā as an instrumental in genitive usage. Each Sanskrit text begins with an instrumental, thus necessitating an instrumental relationship with the corresponding form of bhikṣu.

48* Chandra, "Unpublished Gilgit Fragment of the Prātimokṣa-Sūtra," p. 11, has tālavṛndakaṃ [fan].

49 The text presents the Pāli form (corrected to saṃmutīyo). Edgerton, *Buddhist Hybrid Sanskrit Dictionary*, p. 541, discusses this word under saṃvṛti, noting the association with saṃmata, and we do find saṃmatyā in Finot, "Le Prātimokṣasūtra des Sarvāstivādins," p. 490. The Mūlasarvāstivādin text has saṃvṛtyā. See Banerjee, *Prātimokṣa-Sūtram* [*Mūlasarvāstivāda*], p. 15 (and n. 3).

49* Chandra, "Unpublished Gilgit Fragment of the Prātimokṣa-Sūtra," p. 11, concurs, and the phrase seems to mean, according to Edgerton, "a posture with the hands joined at the back of the neck" (*Buddhist Hybrid Sanskrit Dictionary*, p. 516).

50 For anyātikāye, see Edgerton, *Buddhist Hybrid Sanskrit Dictionary*, p. 42 (anyātaka). The other versions seem to employ various forms of a √jñā.

50* Chandra, "Unpublished Gilgit Fragment of the Prātimokṣa-Sūtra," p. 10, has -ullaṃghikayā. For the meaning, see Edgerton, *Buddhist Hybrid Sanskrit Dictionary*, p. 148.

51 The other Sanskrit versions present only the bare pravārayed. Our text seems to be following the Pāli idiom: abhihaṭṭhuṃ pavāreyya (see Horner, *The Book of the Discipline*, Vol. II, p. 51, n. 1, and Rhys Davids and Stede, *The Pali Text Society's Pali-English Dictionary*, p. 72), but furnishes abhibhāṣto rather than the appropriate form.

51* See Edgerton, *Buddhist Hybrid Sanskrit Dictionary*, p. 120 (uṭṭaṅkikā). Chandra, "Unpublished Gilgit Fragment of the Prātimokṣa-Sūtra," p. 11, has -ujjhaṃghikayā [with loud laughter].

52 The plural is used for the dual. It appears that the only way to take anyatareṣāṃ is "different," i.e., unrelated, since the other texts include some form emphasizing that the people involved are not related to the monk.

52* This reading is not at all certain. The only corresponding form is rendered by Vidyabhusana, "So-sor-thar-pa," p. 64, as "without leaning to my side."

53 See Edgerton, *Buddhist Hybrid Sanskrit Dictionary*, p. 480 (vikalpa).

53* Neither Banerjee's text (nāṃsophatikayā) nor Chandra's (nāṃsotḍhaukikayā) makes much sense. Edgerton, *Buddhist Hybrid Sanskrit Dictionary*, p. 606, does enter the term soḍhaukikā, which seems appropriate, as Pachow, *A Comparative Study of the Prātimokṣa*, Vol. V, 1, p. 18, rule 49, equates it to the Sarvāstivādin cāṃsapracālaka (see Finot, "Le Prātimokṣasūtra des Sarvāstivādins," p. 531, rules 49 and 50).

54 ca ubhau pi sahitau ekena. I have no suggestions here other than following Horner's note (*The Book of the Discipline*, Vol. II, p. 59, n. 1), based on the Padabhājaniya commentary. If two (or more) robe prices are combined to buy one superior robe [rather than two (or more) ordinary robes], the importance of kalyāṇakāmatāmupādāya is emphasized. The Mahāsāṃghika text uses the plural (whereas the Pāli and other Sanskrit texts make the giving of the robe a singular act on the part of one person), which tends to somewhat cloud the distinction between this and the following rule.

54* See Edgerton, *Buddhist Hybrid Sanskrit Dictionary*, p. 566 (samavadhāya).

55 kālena samayena (idiomatic).

55* Chandra, "Unpublished Gilgit Fragment of the Prātimokṣa-Sūtra," p. 11, reads viḍaṃgikayā. For the meaning, see Edgerton, *Buddhist Hybrid Sanskrit Dictionary*, pp. 486–487 (viḍaṅgikā).

56 The Pāli has veyyāvaccakaro ti (see Dickson, "The Pātimokkha, being the Buddhist Office of the Confession of Priests," p. 79). On the basis of a form (vaiyāpṛtyaṃkaronti) appearing later in the text, I have chosen in this case not to follow the example of the Pāli. Also see Edgerton, *Buddhist Hybrid Sanskrit Dictionary*, p. 571 (vaiyāpatya).

56* See Edgerton, *Buddhist Hybrid Sanskrit Dictionary*, p. 561.

57 For a definition of ārāmika, see Edgerton, *Buddhist Hybrid Sanskrit Dictionary*, p. 104.

57* sāvādānaṃ. See Edgerton, *Buddhist Hybrid Sanskrit Dictionary*, p. 594.

58 Bhikṣuṇā tūṣṇīṃ bhūtena uddeśe sthātavyaṃ has been translated rather freely here.

58* This translation is tentative. Vidyabhusana, "So-sor-thar-pa," p. 65, has: I shall not prefer one kind of taste to another.

59 Pratirūpo, literally an image or likeness.

59* apahārakaṃ. See Edgerton, *Buddhist Hybrid Sanskrit Dictionary*, p. 46.

60 The Mahāsāṃghika text is extremely corrupt here. I have pieced together a translation from the Pāli and the Mūlasarvāstivādin versions (see Dickson, "The Pātimokkha, being the Buddhist Office of the Confession of Priests," p. 80, and Banerjee, *Prātimokṣa-Sūtram* [*Mūlasarvāstivāda*], p. 17).
Pāli: yañjant' āyasmanto sakaṃ mā vo sakaṃ vinassāti
Mūlasarvāstivādin: prajānatvāyuṣmantaḥ svamarthaṃ mā vorthaḥ praṇaśyatv-ity.
The Sarvāstivādin text is fragmentary.

60* jihvāsphoṭakaṃ. See Edgerton, *Buddhist Hybrid Sanskrit Dictionary*, p. 614 (sphoṭakam).

61 The Mahāsāṃghika text uses the Pāli form of rug, santhata, rather than the Sanskrit form, saṃstara.

61* saṃdhūnakaṃ. See Edgerton, *Buddhist Hybrid Sanskrit Dictionary*, p. 558 (saṃdhunakam).

62 Each text seems to present its own form for this expression:
Mahāsāṃghika: kāṇakānāmeḍakalomānāṃ (Pachow and Mishra, "The Prātimokṣa Sūtra of the Mahāsāṃghikas," p. 17).
Pāli: kāḷakānaṃ eḷakalomānaṃ (Dickson, "The Pātimokkha, being the Buddhist Office of the Confession of Priests," p. 80).
Sarvāstivādin: kāḍānām e[ḍa]kalomnāṃ (Finot, "Le Prātimokṣasūtra des Sarvāstivādins," p. 496).
Mūlasarvāstivādin: kālakānāmeḍakaromnāṃ (Banerjee, *Prātimokṣa-Sūtram* [*Mūlasarvāstivāda*], p. 17).

62* I am following Vidyabhusana, "So-sor-thar-pa," p. 66, but also see Edgerton, *Buddhist Hybrid Sanskrit Dictionary*, p. 149 (uṣṇīṣa).

63 See Horner, *The Book of the Discipline*, Vol. II, p. 76, n. 4, and Edgerton, *Buddhist Hybrid Sanskrit Dictionary*, p. 215 (gocarika).

63* kholāśirase. See Edgerton, *Buddhist Hybrid Sanskrit Dictionary*, p. 207.

64 pratyottareṇa. See Edgerton, *Buddhist Hybrid Sanskrit Dictionary*, p. 379. The Mahāsāṃghika text contradicts the other Sanskrit texts, as well as the Pāli, indicating that the new rug is being made after the required six years have elapsed. The Sarvāstivādin (Finot, "Le Prātimokṣasūtra des Sarvāstivādins,"

p. 496) and Mūlasarvāstivādin (Banerjee, *Prātimokṣa-Sūtram* [*Mūlasarvāstivāda*], p. 18) versions have arvāk. The Pāli (Dickson, "The Pātimokkha, being the Buddhist Office of the Confession of Priests," p. 80) has orena ca channaṃ vassānaṃ (within six years). It may be, in fact, that Edgerton misunderstood. A rug is supposed to last for six years. After that it is perfectly lawful for a monk to obtain a new rug (following the necessary regulations, of course). See Horner, *The Book of the Discipline*, Vol. II, pp. 81–82, for the Padabhājaniya's explanation. The answer may lie in the fact that the Mahāsāṃghika text notes that if the monk has the new rug made out of a desire for something excellent, whether or not the old rug is discarded, this too is an offense. Evidently desire was to be suppressed at all costs. The rug itself seems not to be the issue at all (provided it was used for six years). Rather, the motive precipitating the commission of the new rug comes to the forefront. Clearly, need is acceptable, but desire is not.

64* I am following Vidyabhusana, "So-sor-thar-pa," p. 67.

65 For a discussion of santhataṃ and niṣīdanaṃ, see Horner, *The Book of the Discipline*, Vol. II, p. 87, n. 2, in which Horner reviews the suggestions of Rhys Davids and Oldenberg, Huber, and Vidyabhusana, as well as citing further Pāli textual references. Pages 87–89 of her translation contain the Padabhājaniya commentary on this rule. Edgerton, *Buddhist Hybrid Sanskrit Dictionary*, p. 308 (niṣīdana) also gives two references.

65* Both Banerjee, *Prātimokṣa-Sūtram* [*Mūlasarvāstivāda*], p. 37, n. 2, and Vidyabhusana, "So-sor-thar-pa," p. 69, n. 1, point out that this verse corresponds to Dhammapada 184. See Nārada, *Dhammapada*, pp. 165–166 (Buddhavagga, verse 6).

66 For the idiomatic phrase adhvānamārga pratipanna, see Edgerton, *Buddhist Hybrid Sanskrit Dictionary*, p. 19 (adhvamārga).

66* Finot's note ("Le Prātimokṣasūtra des Sarvāstivādins," p. 540, n. 2) identifies this verse as corresponding to Udānam V, 3, and Udānavarga XXVIII, 13. See, for example, Paul Steinthal, ed., *Udāna*, reprint (London: Oxford University Press for P.T.S., 1948), p. 50.

67 sāmam. This is a Pāli form. See Rhys Davids and Stede, *The Pali Text Society's Pali-English Dictionary*, p. 704. The corresponding Sanskrit form, svayaṃ, is found in the other Sanskrit texts. See, for example, Finot, "Le Prātimokṣasūtra des Sarvāstivādins," p. 497.

67* Both Banerjee, *Prātimokṣa-Sūtram* [*Mūlasarvāstivāda*], p. 37, n. 4, and Vidyabhusana, "So-sor-thar-pa," p. 69, n. 2, point out that this verse corresponds to Dhammapada 185. See Nārada, *Dhammapada*, pp. 165–166 (Buddhavagga, verse 7).

68 The Mahāsāṃghika text simply has imātāmupādāya. I have extended my translation on the basis of the Sarvāstivādin (Finot, "Le Prātimokṣasūtra des Sarvāstivādins," pp. 498–499) and Mūlasarvāstivādin (Banerjee, *Prātimokṣa-Sūtram* [*Mūlasarvāstivāda*], p. 189 and n. 5) versions: kalyāṇakāmatāṃ upādāya,

although the Mūlasarvāstivādin text has been reconstructed, in part, from the Tibetan.

68* Both Banerjee, *Prātimokṣa-Sūtram* [*Mūlasarvāstivāda*], p. 37, n. 1, and Vidyabhusana, "So-sor-thar-pa," p. 69, n. 3, point out that this verse corresponds to Dhammapada 49. See Nārada, *Dhammapada*, p. 53 (Pupphavagga, verse 6).

69 pratipeṣaṇīyāni. The Pāli and Sanskrit texts afford no help here. However, Edgerton, *Buddhist Hybrid Sanskrit Dictionary*, p. 365, enters paripuṣṭa [nourished]. Perhaps the form in the Mahāsāṃghika text is related.

69* Both Banerjee, *Prātimokṣa-Sūtram* [*Mūlasarvāstivāda*], p. 37, n. 2, and Vidyabhusana, "So-sor-thar-pa," p. 69, n. 4, point out that this verse corresponds to Dhammapada 50. See Nārada, *Dhammapada*, p. 54 (Pupphavagga, verse 7).

70 ācchāndeya vā ācchāndāpeya vā. The Mahāsāṃghika text seems to get the roots √chad and √chid mixed up. The Pāli and other Sanskrit texts all use a form of ā √chid in the rule.

70* This verse corresponds to Udānavarga IV, 7. See Finot, "Le Prātimokṣasūtra des Sarvāstivādins," p. 542, n. 1.

71 A varṣāśāṭikā cīvara is a robe for the rainy season. See Edgerton, *Buddhist Hybrid Sanskrit Dictionary*, p. 472.

71* Vidyabhusana, "So-sor-thar-pa," p. 69, n. 5, points out that this verse corresponds to Mahāparinibbāna Sutta, Chapter IV. See T. W. Rhys Davids and J. Estlin Carpenter, eds., *The Dīgha Nikāya*, 3 vols.; reprint (London: Luzac & Company for P.T.S., 1966), Vol. II, p. 136.

72 Muṣitavyam [should be taken away] makes no sense. Perhaps the compiler became confused, intending to use √vas [to wear, put on], but citing an incorrect form, with the m being a saṃdhi consonant. The Pāli has katvā nivāsetabbaṃ. See Dickson, "The Pātimokkha, being the Buddhist Office of the Confession of Priests," p. 81 (rule 24).

72* Both Banerjee, *Prātimokṣa-Sūtram* [*Mūlasarvāstivāda*], p. 37, n. 3, and Vidyabhusana, "So-sor-thar-pa," p. 69, n. 6, point out that this verse corresponds to Dhammapada 183. See Nārada, *Dhammapada*, p. 165 (Buddhavagga, verse 5).

73 I have not been able to find any references for dhunāyeya, the word appearing in the manuscript. I can only speculate that it carries the same meaning as vāyayet (from √vā, to weave).

73* Both Banerjee, *Prātimokṣa-Sūtram* [*Mūlasarvāstivāda*], p. 37, n. 4, and Vidyabhusana, "So-sor-thar-pa," p. 69, n. 7, point out that this verse corresponds to Dhammapada 361. See Nārada, *Dhammapada*, pp. 274–275 (Bhikkhuvagga, verse 2).

74 Suvuttaṃ is not found in the other Sanskrit texts, but is probably following the Pāli suvītam [well-woven]. See Dickson, "The Pātimokkha, being the Buddhist Office of the Confession of Priests," p. 82, and Rhys Davids and Stede, *The Pali Text Society's Pali-English Dictionary*, p. 643 (vīta). Another possibility is that it may be from suvuttaṃ, but the meaning of well-shaven does not fit.

74* Finot's note ("Le Prātimokṣasūtra des Sarvāstivādins," p. 543, n. 2) identifies this verse as corresponding to Udānavarga VII, 12.

75 The Pāli form, sutaccitaṃ [well-formed], is used rather than sutakṣitaṃ, the Sanskrit form.

75* Banerjee, *Prātimokṣa-Sūtram* [*Mūlasarvāstivāda*], p. 37, n. 5, points out that this verse corresponds to Saṃyutta Nikāya, I, p. 157. See M. Léon Feer, ed., *The Saṃyutta-Nikāya of the Sutta-Piṭaka*, 5 vols.; reprint (London: Luzac & Company for P.T.S., 1960), Vol. I, p. 157 (verse 23).

76 The phrase piṇḍapātramvā piṇḍapātrāhimvā puzzles me. At first glance, one is tempted to take piṇḍapātram as the alms bowl itself, and piṇḍapātrāhim as the contents of the alms bowl, thus accounting for the case difference between these two words. However, it would be senseless to give an alms bowl to a weaver. In the Sarvāstivādin (Finot, "Le Prātimokṣasūtra des Sarvāstivādins," p. 500) and the Mūlasarvāstivādin (Banerjee, *Prātimokṣa-Sūtram* [*Mūlasarvāstivāda*], p. 19) versions (rule 24 in each case) in addition to piṇḍapātaṃ we find piṇḍapātamātram, piṇḍapātasaṃvaraṃ, and piṇḍapātasaṃbalaṃ. Perhaps one of these compounds is intended here, and for lack of a better solution I have translated accordingly. In any case, the whole premise of the rule stands contradicted. The offense, according to the Mahāsāṃghika text, lies not in giving orders concerning the robe but rather in not paying for it.

76* Banerjee, *Prātimokṣa-Sūtram* [*Mūlasarvāstivāda*], p. 38, n. 1, points out that this verse corresponds to Saṃyutta Nikāya, I, p. 157. This verse forms the second half of the verse cited in note 75* above.

77 The Mahāsāṃghika text has dīghīsamuteye. The other Sanskrit texts provide no help, but the Pāli has bhikkhusammutiyā (Dickson, "The Pātimokkha, being the Buddhist Office of the Confession of Priests," p. 82). I presume our compiler intended dīrghasammutīye.

78 omṛṣyavāde. The other Sanskrit texts afford no help, but the Pāli has omasavāde (Dickson, "The Pātimokkha, being the Buddhist Office of the Confession of Priests," p. 82).

79 For ukhoṭeya, see Edgerton, *Buddhist Hybrid Sanskrit Dictionary*, p. 121 (utkhoṭayati). Also see Finot, "Le Prātimokṣasūtra des Sarvāstivādins," p. 503.

80 Vācāhi may also be taken as "sentences." See Horner, *The Book of the Discipline*, Vol. II, p. 206, rule 7.

81 The Mahāsāṃghika text, dviśeṣādhigamam, makes little sense. I have read this term as viśeṣādhigamam with the d being a saṃdhi consonant.

82 Where the Mahāsāṃghika text has bhūmi tasmiṃ, the Pāli has bhūtasmiṃ. See Dickson, "The Pātimokkha, being the Buddhist Office of the Confession of Priests," p. 83. Also see Horner, *The Book of the Discipline*, Vol. II, p. 211 (and n. 2), rule 8. Horner notes that if the claims are not true, the monk is guilty of a pārājika dharma.

83 prakāśanāsammuttīye. The other Sanskrit texts read: except with permission of

the saṃgha. See, for example, Finot, "Le Prātimokṣasūtra des Sarvāstivādins," p. 504. The Pāli reads: except with permission of the monks. See Dickson, "The Pātimokkha, being the Buddhist Office of the Confession of Priests," p. 83 (rule 9).

84 The text, pūrvve samanujo bhūtvā, should be amended to pūrvve samanujñako bhūtvā. See, for example, Finot, "Le Prātimokṣasūtra des Sarvāstivādins," p. 504. For the meaning of this phrase, see Edgerton, *Buddhist Hybrid Sanskrit Dictionary*, p. 561 (samanujñaka).

85 anyavādavihiṃsanake. I am following Edgerton, *Buddhist Hybrid Sanskrit Dictionary*, p. 42 (anyavāda), and equate vihiṃsanake with viheṭhana (which is found in the Sarvāstivādin and Mūlasarvāstivādin texts).

86 The text, odhyāyanakṣīyanake, should read avadhyāyanakṣīyanake. For avadhyāyana, see Edgerton, *Buddhist Hybrid Sanskrit Dictionary*, p. 72 (avadhyāna). For kṣīyanake, refer to the same source, p. 200 (kṣīyati). Avadhyāyana seems to be following the Sanskrit versions, whereas kṣīyanake follows the Pāli.

87 Viśikaraṃ (in the text) must equal vṛṣikaraṃ. See Banerjee, *Prātimokṣa-Sūtram* [*Mūlasarvāstivāda*], p. 21, and Edgerton, *Buddhist Hybrid Sanskrit Dictionary*, p. 507 (vṛṣikā).

88 Caturagrakaṃ (in the text) probably equals caturaśrakaṃ. See Banerjee, *Prātimokṣa-Sūtram* [*Mūlasarvāstivāda*], p. 21, and Edgerton, *Buddhist Hybrid Sanskrit Dictionary*, p. 223 (caturasraka).

89 Kuccaṃ probably equals kocavaṃ. See Edgerton, *Buddhist Hybrid Sanskrit Dictionary*, p. 193.

90 Bimbohanam is a Pāli form. See Rhys Davids and Stede, *The Pali Text Society's Pali-English Dictionary*, p. 487 (bimba), but also Edgerton, *Buddhist Hybrid Sanskrit Dictionary*, p. 400 (bimbopadhāna).

91 The other texts, Pāli and Sanskrit, afford no help here. The Mahāsāṃghika text seems to be presenting two gerunds with the second being causative (prajñāyeyatvā vā/prajñāyāyatvā vā . . .), but the forms are quite corrupt, and the distinction is not clear. The form seems less confused in the following rule. For the meaning of prajñapayati, see Edgerton, *Buddhist Hybrid Sanskrit Dictionary*, p. 358.

92 The Mahāsāṃghika text is unclear, using abhiniṣīdeya and abhiniṣadyeya. The Pāli has abhinipajjeyya for the second form (Dickson, "The Pātimokkha, being the Buddhist Office of the Confession of Priests," p. 83), while the other Sanskrit versons have a form of abhi-ni √pad.

93 The Sarvāstivādin (Finot, "Le Prātimokṣasūtra des Sarvāstivādins," p. 506) and Mūlasarvāstivādin (Banerjee, *Prātimokṣa-Sūtram* [*Mūlasarvāstivāda*], p. 21) texts have āhāryapādake. The Mahāsāṃghika text, probably closer to the Pāli āhaccapādakaṃ (Dickson, "The Pātimokkha, being the Buddhist Office of the Confession of Priests," p. 83), constructs āhatya pādake. For the meaning, see Edgerton, *Buddhist Hybrid Sanskrit Dictionary*, p. 112 (āhāryapādaka).

94 For the meaning of mṛttikāṃ, see Edgerton, *Buddhist Hybrid Sanskrit Dictionary*, p. 438 (mṛttikama).

95 Alpaharite, but see Horner, *The Book of the Discipline*, Vol. II, p. 258 (and n. 4).

96 For ālokasandhi and parikarma, see Edgerton, *Buddhist Hybrid Sanskrit Dictionary*, pp. 106 and 320, respectively.

97 The text should read yāvadvārakoṣārgalapratiṣṭhān. See, for example, Finot, "Le Prātimokṣasūtra des Sarvāstivādins," p. 506. Dvārakoṣa is defined in Edgerton, *Buddhist Hybrid Sanskrit Dictionary*, p. 273.

98 The text should read chadanaparyāyā. I have taken paryāya as "way" or "means." Horner [*The Book of the Discipline*, Vol. II, p. 258 (and n. 1)] has taken it as enclosure. Buddhaghosa, *Kaṅkhāvitaraṇī*, p. 95, has: Tattha "dvatticchadanassa pariyāyan" ti chadanassa dvattiparyāyaṃ paryāyaṃ vuccati parikkhepo.

99 For alternate readings of this ambiguous rule, see Horner, *The Book of the Discipline*, Vol. II, pp. 257–260, Rhys Davids and Oldenberg, *Vinaya Texts*, Vol. I, p. 35, and Finot, "Le Prātimokṣasūtra des Sarvāstivādins," p. 506 (Huber's French translation). For detailed discussion of lodgings in general, refer to the sixth chapter of the Cullavagga (senāsanakkhandhaka) in Oldenberg, *The Vinaya Piṭakaṃ*, Vol. II, pp. 146–179 (translation in Horner, *The Book of the Discipline*, Vol. V, pp. 204–252), and also to Dutt, *The Gilgit Manuscripts*, Vol. III, 3, pp. 119–144 (śayanāsanavastu).

100 For anūhate aruṇe, see Edgerton, *Buddhist Hybrid Sanskrit Dictionary*, p. 150 (ūhate).

101 I am following Horner, *The Book of the Discipline*, Vol. II, p. 277, for the meaning of upāśrayaṃ.

102 Horner, *The Book of the Discipline*, Vol. II, p. 297, translates: "unless there is a prior arrangement with the householder"; Huber (Finot, "Le Prātimokṣasūtra des Sarvāstivādins," p. 508) has: "escepté si le laïque [donateur] en avait auparavant conçu l'idée."

103 Paraṃparabhojane. For a brief discussion of this term, see Horner, *The Book of the Discipline*, Vol. II, p. 317, n. 3, in which Horner reviews the opinions of Rhys Davids and Oldenberg, Gogerly, Dickson, Huber, and Buddhaghosa. This rule, coupled with rule 40 (corresponding to Mūlasarvāstivādin rules 31 and 36, respectively) uncovers an interesting detail. We can construct the following chart:

School-Rule	*Acceptable Times*
Mahāsāṃghika Rule 32	Illness, giving of robes
Mūlasarvāstivādin Rule 31	Illness, giving of robes, going on a journey, *work*
Mahāsāṃghika Rule 40	Illness, giving of robes, going on a journey, being boarded on a boat, great time, meal time of the śramaṇas

Mūlasarvāstivādin Rule 36	Illness, going on a journey, being boarded on a boat, great meeting, meal time of the śramaṇas, *work*

Aside from minor differences in these lists, one observation does stand out: Work is mentioned in both rules in the Mūlasarvāstivādin version but not in either of the Mahāsāṃghika rules. Mahāsāṃghika Rule 50 reveals that monks could bathe more frequently than twice per month during times of work, and consequently it does appear that by the time these texts were finalized, monks did indeed perform work.

104 āsādanaprekṣo. See Edgerton, *Buddhist Hybrid Sanskrit Dictionary*, p. 111.

105 udakadantapoṇe. This phrase is a Pāli idiom. See Rhys Davids and Stede, *The Pali Text Society's Pali-English Dictionary*, p. 149. The Mahāsāṃghika text distorts the phrase a bit, reading anyatrodika dantapoṇe.

106 manthehi. For the meaning of mantha, I am following Horner, *The Book of the Discipline*, Vol. II, p. 323.

107 The Mahāsāṃghika text has vahirdvānīharitavyam. In addition to reading vahir for bahir and nī $\sqrt{}$hṛ for nir $\sqrt{}$hṛ, the number of bowls seems to have switched to two (rather than three). The phrase, as noted, appears in this form throughout the rule.

108 praṇītasammatāni bhojanāni. See Edgerton, *Buddhist Hybrid Sanskrit Dictionary*, p. 360 (praṇīta).

109 Mahāsamayo, in the text, has been rendered in various ways. Horner (*The Book of the Discipline*, Vol. II, p. 311, rule 32) translates: "when there is a great scarcity." Huber (Finot, "Le Prātimokṣasūtra des Sarvāstivādins," p. 510, rule 36) has: "en temps de fête." Pachow (*A Comparative Study of the Prātimokṣa*, Vol. IV, 3–4, p. 160, rule 36) reads: "when there is a great assembly."

110 Sakalikāṃ, in the text, most probably equals saṃkalikāṃ. See Edgerton, *Buddhist Hybrid Sanskrit Dictionary*, pp. 172 and 545, respectively, for the two meanings.

111 The Mahāsāṃghika text, asatā buddhyāhī tena, is extremely problematic. The corresponding passage in rule 47 reads asatādudgṛhītena. I have taken the d (in this second reading) as a saṃdhi consonant, and read udgṛhītena as "understanding" [Edgerton, *Buddhist Hybrid Sanskrit Dictionary*, p. 129 (udgṛhṇāti)]. Since there is no certainty regarding which of these forms (if either) is correct, my translation is wholly speculative. The other texts are entirely different, thus affording no clues.

112 The text should read yathāvādiṃ tathākāritāṃ. For the meaning of this phrase, see Edgerton, *Buddhist Hybrid Sanskrit Dictionary*, p. 443.

113 śramaṇuddeśa. See Edgerton, *Buddhist Hybrid Sanskrit Dictionary*, p. 534.

114 Perhaps upalāyeya, in the text, equals upalāḍayet, as in the Sarvāstivādin text (Finot, "Le Prātimokṣasūtra des Sarvāstivādins," p. 516, rule 57).

115 The Mahāsāṃghika text presents anupakhajja, corresponding precisely with the Pāli (Dickson, "The Pātimokkha, being the Buddhist Office of the Confession of Priests," p. 86, rule 43). The Sanskrit texts have anupraskadya and anupraskandya. See Finot, "Le Prātimokṣasūtra des Sarvāstivādins," p. 511, rule 42, and Banerjee, *Prātimokṣa-Sūtram* [*Mūlasarvāstivāda*], p. 23, rule 42, respectively. Also see Edgerton, *Buddhist Hybrid Sanskrit Dictionary*, p. 31 (anupraskandati).

116 The Mahāsāṃghika text has āyūhikam. I can only suggest the possibilities here. It may be from ā √yudh, but perhaps it represents āvyūhikam [on this account, see Edgerton, *Buddhist Hybrid Sanskrit Dictionary*, pp. 109 (āvyūhati) and 102 (āyūha and āyūhati)]. The Mūlasarvāstivādin text (Banerjee, *Prātimokṣa-Sūtram* [*Mūlasarvāstivāda*], p. 24, rule 47) has udyūṣikāṃ, and the Sarvāstivādin text (Finot, "Le Prātimokṣasūtra des Sarvāstivādins," p. 512, rule 47) has udyūthikāṃ.

117 The suggestions in note 116 above (correspondingly altered) apply equally to niyūhikam, although it is found neither in the Pāli nor other Sanskrit texts.

118 For talaśaktikām, see Edgerton, *Buddhist Hybrid Sanskrit Dictionary*, p. 250, and also Rhys Davids and Stede, *The Pali Text Society's Pali-English Dictionary*, p. 132.

119 For a thorough discussion of ordination, including qualifications, disqualifications, and procedures (according to the Pāli tradition), see G. De, *Democracy in Early Buddhist Saṃgha* (Calcutta: Calcutta University Press, 1955), pp. 11–56 (Part I: Chapters 1–5). Refer also to Frauwallner, *The Earliest Vinaya*, pp. 70–78, in which a careful summary of the entire Pravrajyāvastu is presented.

120 The Mahāsāṃghika text is much more elaborate (and confused) than the Pāli, Sarvāstivādin, and Mūlasarvāstivādin texts. For an alternate reading, see Pachow, *A Comparative Study of the Prātimokṣa*, Vol. IV, 3–4, pp. 182–184, rule 75.

121 viniścayakathāhi. For the meaning of this phrase, see Edgerton, *Buddhist Hybrid Sanskrit Dictionary*, p. 490 (viniścaya), and Horner, *The Book of the Discipline*, Vol. III, p. 61 (and n. 2).

122 The text should read ātyayike karaṇīye. For the meaning, see Edgerton, *Buddhist Hybrid Sanskrit Dictionary*, p. 93.

123 cāritramāpadyeya. See Edgerton, *Buddhist Hybrid Sanskrit Dictionary*, p. 229.

124 The Mahāsāṃghika text has abhipadyeya. The Pāli and other Sanskrit texts afford no help, but I suspect abhinipadyeya was intended. See rule 18 of the Pācattika portion of the text and note 92 above.

125 The text should read kaṇḍupraticchādanaṃ. See Dickson, "The Pātimokkha, being the Buddhist Office of the Confession of Priests," p. 90, rule 89. For the meaning, see Edgerton, *Buddhist Hybrid Sanskrit Dictionary*, p. 362 (pratichādana). Horner (*The Book of the Discipline*, Vol. III, p. 97) reads "itch cloth."

126 For punarvvādo bahuśo, I am following Horner, *The Book of the Discipline*, Vol. III, p. 44 (and n. 2).

127 apratisaṃveditaṃ. See Edgerton, *Buddhist Hybrid Sanskrit Dictionary*, p. 48 (apratisaṃvidita).

128 apratigṛhītam. See Edgerton, *Buddhist Hybrid Sanskrit Dictionary*, p. 362 (pratigrāhita).

129 The Mahāsāṃghika text, when referring to the title of this class of offenses, consistently uses the form pratideśanika. I simply point out its first appearance in this form here.

130 It is strange that the text does not use the number for sixty-seven, or have saṃbahulāḥ as the Mūlasarvāstivādin (Chandra, "Unpublished Gilgit Fragment of the Prātimokṣa-Sūtra," p. 11), for example, does. I am also intrigued by the fact that the Mahāsāṃghika text uniformly employs the future first singular form of the verbs associated with each śaikṣa dharma, whereas the Mūlasarvāstivādin version always presents the future first plural. The emphasis is certainly different: personal or individual in the Mahāsāṃghika text and collective in the Mūlasarvāstivādin text. The depersonalization of the Mūlasarvāstivādin text seems to indicate another attempt at generalization, setting forth saṃgha standards rather than individual maxims. One should notice that the technical terms in this section are quite difficult. Edgerton does take notice of these in his *Buddhist Hybrid Sanskrit Dictionary*, reviewing the suggestions of several other scholars, but his uncertainty is not very well concealed (particularly with regard to those terms elucidating the various postures that are to be avoided), and I am not at all certain that we understand all these terms.

131 See Edgerton, *Buddhist Hybrid Sanskrit Dictionary*, p. 122 (utkṣipati).

132 ujhaggīkāya. See Edgerton, *Buddhist Hybrid Sanskrit Dictionary*, pp. 118 (uccagghana) and 119 (ujjaṅkikā).

133 The text should read udguṇṭhikāya. See, for example, Banerjee, *Prātimokṣa-Sūtram [Mūlasarvāstivāda]*, p. 32, rule 16. For the meaning, see Edgerton, *Buddhist Hybrid Sanskrit Dictionary*, p. 129.

134 The text should read utkuṭukāya. See, for example, Banerjee, *Prātimokṣa-Sūtram [Mūlasarvāstivāda]*, p. 32, rule 23. For the meaning, see Edgerton, *Buddhist Hybrid Sanskrit Dictionary*, p. 121.

135 The text should read skaṃbhākṛto. See, for example, Banerjee, *Prātimokṣa-Sūtram [Mūlasarvāstivāda]*, p. 32, rule 25. For the meaning, see Edgerton, *Buddhist Hybrid Sanskrit Dictionary*, p. 608.

136 The text should read utsaktikāya. See, for example, Banerjee, *Prātimokṣa-Sūtram [Mūlásarvāstivāda]*, p. 32, rule 18. For the meaning, see Edgerton, *Buddhist Hybrid Sanskrit Dictionary*, p. 126.

137 The text, pallatthikāya, corresponds exactly with the Pāli form (Dickson, "The Pātimokkha, being the Buddhist Office of the Confession of Priests," p. 93, rule 26). The Sanskrit form seems to be paryastikā. See, for example, Finot, "Le Prātimokṣasūtra des Sarvāstivādins," p. 530, rule 40. For the meaning, see Edgerton, *Buddhist Hybrid Sanskrit Dictionary*, p. 337.

138 satkṛtya. See Edgerton, *Buddhist Hybrid Sanskrit Dictionary*, p. 553.

139 See Edgerton, *Buddhist Hybrid Sanskrit Dictionary*, p. 69 (avakīrṇa).

140 odhyāyana. See Edgerton, *Buddhist Hybrid Sanskrit Dictionary*, p. 72 (avadhyāna).

141 The Mahāsāṃghika text is quite problematic. I have read it as: na dinnādinnaṃ aniṣṭhaṃ jānan odanena pracchādayiṣyāmi bhūyo āgamanakāmatāmupādāyeti śikṣā karaṇīyā. The Pāli (Dickson, "The Pātimokkha, being the Buddhist Office of the Confession of Priests," p. 93, rule 36) has: na sūpaṃ vā byañjanaṃ vā-odanena paṭicchādessāmīti bhīyyokamyataṃ upādāya sikkhā karaṇīyā. The Sarvāstivādin (Finot, "Le Prātimokṣasūtra des Sarvāstivādins," p. 534, rule 83) has: [naudanena sū]paṃ praticchādayiṣyāmo bhūyaskāmatām upādāya iti śikṣā karaṇīyā. The Mūlasarvāstivādin (Banerjee, *Prātimokṣa-Sūtram [Mūlasarvāstivāda]*, p. 33, rules 45 and 46) has: nodanena sūpikaṃ praticchādayiṣyāmo iti śikṣā karaṇīyā (45); sūpikena vā odanaṃ bhūyaskāmatāmupādāya iti śikṣā karaṇīyā (46).

142 The text should read upāhanārūḍhasya. See, for example, Dickson, "The Pātimokkha, being the Buddhist Office of the Confession of Priests," p. 94, rule 62. For the meaning, see Edgerton, *Buddhist Hybrid Sanskrit Dictionary*, p. 147.

143 I am following Horner, *The Book of the Discipline*, Vol. III, p. 150, rule 72, for the meaning of utpathena.

144 For a discussion of the adhikaraṇa-śamatha dharmas, see S. Dutt, *Early Buddhist Monachism*, pp. 113–145 ("The Internal Polity of a Buddhist Sangha"), and Frauwallner, *The Earliest Vinaya*, pp. 113–116, in which the Śamathavastu of the various sects are closely reviewed.

145 See Edgerton, *Buddhist Hybrid Sanskrit Dictionary*, p. 581.

146 See Edgerton, *Buddhist Hybrid Sanskrit Dictionary*, p. 614, and Horner, *The Book of the Discipline*, Vol. III, p. 153 (and n. 3).

147 See Edgerton, *Buddhist Hybrid Sanskrit Dictionary*, p. 63.

148 See Edgerton, *Buddhist Hybrid Sanskrit Dictionary*, p. 363, Horner, *The Book of the Discipline*, Vol. III, p. 153 (and n. 5), and Huber's French translation (Finot, "Le Prātimokṣasūtra des Sarvāstivādins"), p. 538, rule 4.

149 The text should read tasyapāpeyasiko. See Edgerton, *Buddhist Hybrid Sanskrit Dictionary*, p. 248 (tatsvabhāvaiṣīya), Horner, *The Book of the Discipline*, Vol. III, p. 154 (and n. 1), and Huber's French translation (Finot, "Le Prātimokṣasūtra des Sarvāstivādins"), p. 538, rule 6.

150 The text should read yobhūyasiko. See Edgerton, *Buddhist Hybrid Sanskrit Dictionary*, p. 444 (yadbhūyasikīya), Horner, *The Book of the Discipline*, Vol. III, p. 153 (and n. 6), and Huber's French translation (Finot, "Le Prātimokṣasūtra des Sarvāstivādins"), p. 538, rule 5.

151 See Edgerton, *Buddhist Hybrid Sanskrit Dictionary*, p. 256.

152 Pachow and Mishra, "The Prātimokṣa Sūtra of the Mahāsāṃghikas," p. 42,

n. 1, point out that this verse corresponds to Dhammapada 184. See Nārada, *Dhammapada*, pp. 165–166 (Buddhavagga, verse 6). The concluding verses to the text are less revealing than the introductory. Almost all of the verses recorded in either text find their counterpart in either the Dhammapada or Udānavarga. In the Mahāsāṃghika text each verse is followed by a stock statement:

> This Prātimokṣa was eloquently spoken in summary by the Blessed One (Name), the Tathāgata, the Arhant, the Fully Enlightened One, Perfectly Enlightened for a long time, amidst a vast Bhikṣu-saṃgha.

In each case the words "This Prātimokṣa" clearly refer to the verse just presented. The Mūlasarvāstivādin text, on the other hand, presents the verses only, with a general statement as a conclusion to the section:

> This Prātimokṣa was recited in detail by these seven celebrated, self-possessed Buddhas who were the chief protectors and guardians of the world: Vipaśyin, Śikhin, Viśvabhū, Krakucchanda, Kanakamuni, Kāśyapa, and, immediately following, Śākyamuni Gautama, the God of Gods, the charioteer who subdued men.

The key here is that the use of the term Prātimokṣa reveals that the whole text is intended. Each verse is not considered a Prātimokṣa, as in the Mahāsāṃghika text. Following the verses in the Mahāsāṃghika text the manuscript breaks down. Nevertheless, some interesting information can be ascertained. First, the text is identified as being of the Lokottaravādin branch of the Mahāsāṃghika school:

> prātimokṣasūtraṃ āryamahāsāṃghikānāṃ lokottaravādināṃ mādhyāddeśikānāṃ pāṭhi. . . .

Second, the verse which supposedly converted Śāriputra to Gautama's Dharma (and also released him from duḥkha) is presented:

> ye dharmahetuprabhavātaṃ pi tathāgato avadatteṣāñca yo nirodhaṃ evaṃ vādi mahāśravaṇaḥ.

Finally, in the Mahāsāṃghika text, the word mahāyāna mysteriously occurs. The Mūlasarvāstivādin text does not conclude with the general statement concerning the seven Buddhas mentioned above. Rather it presents six additional verses, again extolling the virtues of the Prātimokṣa and its recitation. Two of these verses have been traced to the Saṃyutta Nikāya (see notes 75* and 76* above).

153 Pachow and Mishra, "The Prātimokṣa Sūtra of the Mahāsāṃghikas," p. 42, n. 2, point out that this verse corresponds to Dhammapada 185. See Nārada, *Dhammapada*, pp. 165–166 (Buddhavagga, verse 7).

154 Pachow and Mishra, "The Prātimokṣa Sūtra of the Mahāsāṃghikas," p. 43, n. 1, point out that this verse corresponds to Udānavarga IV, and cite the Sanskrit.

155 Pachow and Mishra, "The Prātimokṣa Sūtra of the Mahāsāṃghikas," p. 43,

n. 2, point out that this verse corresponds to Dhammapada 183. See Nārada, *Dhammapada*, p. 165 (Buddhavagga, verse 5).

156 Pachow and Mishra, "The Prātimokṣa Sūtra of the Mahāsāṃghikas," pp. 43–44, n. 3, point out that verses 5 and 6 correspond to Dhammapada 49–50. See Nārada, *Dhammapada*, pp. 53–54 (Pupphavagga, verses 6 and 7).

157 Pachow and Mishra, "The Prātimokṣa Sūtra of the Mahāsāṃghikas," p. 44, n. 1, point out that this verse corresponds to Dhammapada 372. See Nārada, *Dhammapada*, pp. 279 and 281 (Bhikkhuvagga, verse 13).

158 This portion of verse 7 corresponds to the first half of Dhammapada 375. See Nārada, *Dhammapada*, pp. 280 and 282 (Bhikkhuvagga, verse 16).

159 The first portion of verse 8 corresponds to the second half of Dhammapada 375. See the reference in footnote 158 above. The second portion of the verse corresponds to Dhammapada 376. See Nārada, *Dhammapada*, pp. 280 and 282 (Bhikkhuvagga, verse 17).

160 This verse corresponds to Dhammapada 360–361. See Nārada, *Dhammapada*, pp. 274–275 (Bhikkhuvagga, verses 1–2).

161 There is a break in the manuscript.

162 After Śikhin, the text becomes confused. The only way to make the summary correspond to the text is to ignore Viśvabhū. Perhaps the text intended this, since there is a stop directly following the name Viśvabhū. In the first two cases we read the summary after the name of the Buddha intended, whereas from Krakucchanda on we read the summary preceding the name.

163 Here is where the manuscript breaks down completely. It is clear, however, that the Prātimokṣa is completed.

164 Pachow and Mishra, "The Prātimokṣa Sūtra of the Mahāsāṃghikas," p. 45, n. 2, note that this line was written by another hand.

Appendix

Concordance Table: Bhikṣu Prātimokṣa Sūtras Preserved in Indic Languages

The pattern for the concordance table is to list the key word(s) as presented in the *Mahāvyutpatti* (Nos. 8364–8637, pp. 531–555 in Sakaki's edition)[1] and provide the corresponding rule number in each of the versions preserved in Indic languages. These include: (1) the Mūlasarvāstivādin (MSV) version, from two Sanskrit manuscripts edited by Ankul Chandra Banerjee and Lokesh Chandra, respectively, (2) the Mahāsāṃghika-Lokottaravādin (MSG) version, from the Sanskrit manuscript edited by W. Pachow and Ramakanta Mishra, (3) the Sarvāstivādin (S) version, from the Sanskrit manuscript edited by Louis Finot, and (4) the Theravādin (T) version, from the Pāli manuscript edited by J.F. Dickson.

	MSV	MSG	S	T
Pārājika Dharmas				
Abrahmacaryaṃ	1	1	1	1
Adattādānaṃ	2	2	2	2
Badhaḥ	3	3	3	3
Uttaramanuṣyadharmapralāpaḥ	4	4	4	4
Saṃghāvaśeṣa Dharmas				
Śukravisṛṣṭiḥ	1	1	1	1
Kāyasaṃsargaḥ	2	2	2	2
Maithunābhāṣaṇaṃ	3	3	3	3
Paricaryāsaṃvarṇanaṃ	4	4	4	4
Saṃcaritraṃ	5	5	5	5
Kuṭikā	6	6	6	6

	MSV	MSG	S	T
Mahallakaḥ	7	7	7	7
Amūlakaṃ	8	8	8	8
Laiśikaṃ	9	9	9	9
Saṃghabhedaḥ	10	10	10	10
Tadanuvartakaḥ	11	11	11	11
Kuladūṣakaḥ	12	13	12	13
Daurvacasyaṃ	13	12	13	12

Aniyata Dharmas

Aniyatau	1–2	1–2	1–2	1–2

Niḥsargika-Pāyantika Dharmas

Dhāraṇaṃ	1	1	1	1
Vipravāsaḥ	2	2	2	2
Nikṣepaḥ	3	3	3	3
Dhāvanaṃ	4	5	4	4
Pratigrahaḥ	5	4	5	5
Yācñā	6	6	6	6
Sāntarottaraṃ	7	7	7	7
Caitanakāni	8	8	8	8
Pratyekaṃ	9	9	9	9
Preṣaṇaṃ	10	10	10	10
Kauśeyaṃ	11	13	11	13
Śuddhakakālakānāṃ	12	11	12	12
Dvibhagaḥ	13	12	13	13
Ṣaḍvarṣāṇi	14	14	14	14
Vitastiḥ	15	15	15	15
Adhvorṇoḍhiḥ	16	16	16	16
Ūrṇāparikarmaṇaḥ	17	17	17	17
Jātarūparajatasparśanaṃ	18	18	18	18
Rūpikavyavahāraḥ	19	20	19	19
Krayavikrayaḥ	20	19	20	20
Pātradhāraṇaṃ	21	21	21	21
Pātraparīṣṭiḥ	22	22	22	22
Vāyanaṃ	23	26	23	26
Upamānavardhanaṃ	24	27	24	27
Datvādanaṃ	25	24	25	25

	MSV	MSG	S	T
Kārttikātyayikaṃ	26	28	27	28
Saptarātravipravāsaḥ	27	29	28	29
Varṣāśāṭyakālaparīṣṭidhāraṇaṃ	28	25	26	24
Pariṇāmanaṃ	29	30	29	30
Saṃnidhikāraḥ	30	23	30	23

Pāyantika Dharmas

Mṛṣā	1	1	1	1
Ūnavādaḥ	2	2	2	2
Bhikṣupaiśunyaṃ	3	3	3	3
Khoṭanaṃ (Utkhoṭanaṃ)	4	4	4	63
Ṣaṭpañcikayā vācā dharmadeśanāyāḥ	5	5	5	7
Samapadoddeśadānaṃ	6	6	6	4
Duṣṭhulārocanaṃ	7	8	8	9
Uttaramanuṣyadharmārocanaṃ	8	7	7	8
Saṃstutiḥ	9	9	9	81
Vitaṇḍanaṃ	10	10	10	72
Bījagrāmabhūtagrāmavināśanaṃ	11	11	11	11
Avadhyānaṃ	12	13	12	13
Ājñāviheṭhanaṃ	13	12	13	12
Mañcaḥ	14	14	14	14
Saṃstaraḥ	15	15	15	15
Niṣkarṣaṇaṃ	16	16	16	17
Anupraskandyapātaḥ	17	17	17	16
Āhāryapādakārohī	18	18	18	18
Saprāṇikopabhogaḥ	19	19	19	20
Dvau vā trayo vā chadanaparyāyadātavyāḥ	20	20	20	19
Asaṃmatāvavādaḥ	21	21	21	21
Astamitāvavādaḥ	22	22	22	22
Amiṣakiñcitkāvavādaḥ	23	24	23	24
Cīvaradānaṃ	24	28	26	25
Cīvarakaraṇaṃ	25	29	27	26
Bhikṣuṇīsārthena saha gamanaṃ	26	26	24	27
Sabhikṣuṇījālayānoḍhiḥ	27	27	25	28
Rahasi niṣadyā	28	25	28	30
Rahasi sthānaṃ[2]	29	70	29	45
Bhikṣuṇīparipācitapiṇḍapātopabhogaḥ	30	30	30	29
Paraṃparabhojanaṃ	31	32	31	33

	MSV	MSG	S	T
Ekāvasathāvāsaḥ	32	31	32	31
Dvitripātrapūrātiriktagrahaṇaṃ	33	38	33	34
Akṛtaniriktakhādanaṃ	34	33	34	35
Akṛtaniriktapravāraṇaṃ	35	34	35	36
Gaṇabhojanaṃ	36	40	36	32
Akālabhojanaṃ	37	36	37	37
Saṃnihitavarjanaṃ	38	37	38	38
Apratigrāhitabhuktiḥ	39	35	39	40
Praṇītavijñāpanaṃ	40	39	40	39
Saprāṇijalopabhogaḥ	41	51	41	62
Sabhojanakulaniṣadyā	42	53	42	43
Sabhojanakulasthānaṃ[3]	43	54	43	44
Aceladānaṃ	44	52	44	41
Senādarśanaṃ	45	55	45	48
Senāvāsaḥ	46	56	46	49
Udyūthikāgamanaṃ	47	57	47	50
Prahāradānaṃ	48	58	48	74
Udguraṇaṃ	49	59	—	75
Duṣṭhulāpraticchādanaṃ	50	60	50	64
Bhaktacchedakāraṇaṃ	51	44	51	42
Agnivṛttaṃ	52	41	52	56
Chandapratyuddhāraḥ	53	43	54	79
Anupasaṃpannasahasvapnaḥ	54	42	53	5
Dṛṣṭigatānutsargaḥ	55	45	55	68
Utkṣiptānuvṛttiḥ	56	46	56	69
Nāśitasaṃgrahaḥ	57	47	57	70
Araktavastropabhogaḥ	58	48	59	58
Ratnasaṃsparśaḥ	59	49	58	84
Snānaprāyaścittikaṃ	60	50	60	57
Tiryagbadhaḥ	61	61	61	61
Kaukṛtyopasaṃhāraḥ	62	62	62	77
Aṅgulipratodanaṃ	63	67	63	52
Udakaharṣaṇaṃ	64	66	64	53
Mātṛgrāmeṇa saha svapnaḥ	65	69	65	6
Bhīṣaṇaṃ	66	65	66	55
Gopanaṃ	67	64	67	60
Apratyuddhāryaparibhogaḥ	68	63	68	59
Amūlakābhyākhyānaṃ	69	90	69	76
Apuruṣayā striyā mārgagamanaṃ	70	68	70	67
Steyasārthagamanaṃ	71	72	71	66

	MSV	MSG	S	T
Ūnaviṃśavarṣopasaṃpādanaṃ	72	71	72	65
Khananaṃ	73	73	73	10
Pravāritārthātisevā	74	74	74	47
Śikṣopasaṃhārapratikṣepaḥ	75	75	75	71
Upaśravagataṃ	76	78	76	78
Tūṣṇīṃ viprakramanaṃ	77	79	77	80
Anādaravṛttaṃ	78	77	78	54
Surāmaireyamadyapānaṃ	79	76	79	51
Akālacaryā	80	80	80	85
Kulacaryā	81	81	81	46
Rājakularātricaryā	82	82	82	83
Śikṣāpadadravyatāvyāvacāraḥ	83	92[4]	83	73
Sūcigṛhakasaṃpādanaṃ	84	83	84	86
Pādakasaṃpādanaṃ	85	84	85	87
Avanahaḥ	86	85	86	88
Niṣadanagataṃ	87	86	89	89
Kaṇḍupraticchādanagataṃ	88	87	88	90
Varṣāśāṭīgataṃ	89	88	87	91
Sugatacīvaragataṃ	90	89	90	92

Pratideśanīya Dharmas

Bhikṣuṇīpiṇḍakagrahaṇaṃ	1	2	1	1
Paṅktivaiṣamyavādānivāritabhuktiḥ	2	3	2	2
Kulaśikṣābhaṅgapravṛttiḥ	3	4	3	3
Vanavicayagataṃ	4	1	4	4

Śaikṣa Dharmas[5]

Parimaṇḍalanivāsanaṃ	1	1		1
Nātyutkṛṣṭaṃ	2		1	
Nātyavakṛṣṭaṃ	3		2	
Na hastituṇḍāvalambitaṃ	4		6	
Na tālavṛndakaṃ	5		5	
Na kulmāṣapiṇḍakaṃ	6		7	
Na nāgaśīrṣakaṃ nivāsanaṃ nivāsayiṣyāmi	7		4	
Parimaṇḍalaṃ cīvaraṃ	8	2	12	2
Nātyutkṛṣṭaṃ cīvaraṃ	9		13	

	MSV	MSG	S	T
Nātyavakṛṣṭaṃ cīvaraṃ	10		14	
Susaṃvṛtaḥ	11	3(14)	17(18)	5(6)
Supraticchannaḥ	12		19(20)	3(4)
Alpaśabdaḥ	13	5(16)	27(28)	13(14)
Anutkṣiptacakṣuṣaḥ	14	4(15)	21(22)	7(8)
Yugamātradarśinaḥ	15		15	
Nodguṇṭhikayā	16	7(18)	31(32)	23(24)
Notkṛṣṭikayā	17		37(38)	9(10)
Notsaktikayā	18	20		
Nodvyastikayā	19			
Na paryastikayā	20	21	39(40)	26
Nojjhaṅkikayā		6(17)		11(12)
Nollaṅgikayā	21			
Noṭṭaṅkikayā	22			
Notkuṭukikayā	23(24)	9		25
Na skambhākṛtaḥ	25	10(22)	35(36)	21(22)
Na kāyapracālakaṃ	26	11	53(54)	15(16)
Na bāhupracālakaṃ	27	13	47(48)	17(18)
Na śīrṣapracālakaṃ	28	12	51(52)	19(20)
Na soḍhaukikayā	29		49(50)	
Na hastasaṃlagnikayā	30		55(56)	
Nānanujñātaḥ	31			
Na pratyavekṣānaṃ	32			
Na sarvakāyaṃ samavardhāya	33			
Na pāde pādaṃ ādhāya	34		59(60)	
Na gulphe gulpham ādhāya	35			
Na sakthani sakthyādhāya	36			
Na saṃkṣipya pādau	37			
Na vikṣipya pādau	38			
Na viḍaṅgikayā	39		57(58)	
Satkṛtya piṇḍapātaṃ	40	24	62(63)	27
Na samatīrthikaṃ	41			30
Na samasūpikaṃ	42	25	65	29(34)
Sāvadānaṃ	43			33
Pātrasaṃjñinaḥ		44	86	28(32)
Nānāgate khādanīye bhojanīye pātram upanāmayiṣyāmaḥ	44			
Na odanena sūpikaṃ praticchādayiṣyāmaḥ sūpikena vā odanaṃ	45–46	46	83	36

	MSV	MSG	S	T
Satkṛtya piṇḍapātaṃ paribhokṣyāmaḥ	48			31
Nātikṣuṇakair ālopaiḥ	49			
Nātimahantaṃ	50	30	68	39
Parimaṇḍalaṃ ālopaṃ	51		69	40
Nānāgate ālope mukhadvāraṃ vivariṣyāmaḥ	52	31	70	41
Na sālopena mukhena vācaṃ pravyāhariṣyāmaḥ	53	34	71	43
Na cuccukārakaṃ	54	38		50
Na śuścukārakaṃ	55	40	73	51
Na thutthukārakaṃ	56	39		
Na phutphukārakaṃ	57			
Na jihvāniścarakaṃ piṇḍapātaṃ [pari]bhokṣyāmaḥ	58	29	76	49
Na sikthapṛthakkārakaṃ	59	42	80	48
Nāvarṇakārakaṃ	60			
Na gallāpahārakaṃ	61			
Na jihvāsphoṭakaṃ	62			
Na kavaḍacchedakaṃ	63	33	66	45
Na hastāvalehakaṃ	64	36	78	52
Na pātrāvalehakaṃ	65	35	79	53
Na hastasaṃdhunakaṃ	66	41	81	47
Na pātrasaṃdhunakaṃ	67			
Na stūpakṛtimavamṛdya piṇḍapātaṃ paribhokṣyāmaḥ	68	26[6]		
Nāvadhyānaprekṣino 'ntarikasya bhikṣoḥ pātram avalokayiṣyāmaḥ	69	43	85	38
Na sāmiṣeṇa pāṇinodakasthālakaṃ grahīṣyāmaḥ	70	48	82	55
Na sāmiṣeṇodakenāntarikaṃ bhikṣuṃ sprakṣyāmaḥ	71			
Na sāmiṣam udakam antargṛhe chorayiṣyāmaḥ santaṃ bhikṣuṃ anavalokya	72	47	88	56
Na pātreṇa vighasaṃ cchorayiṣyāmaḥ	73			
Nānāstīrṇapṛthivīpradeśe pātraṃ sthāpayiṣyāmaḥ	74			
Na taṭe na prapāte na prāgbhāre pātraṃ sthāpayiṣyāmaḥ	75			

	MSV	MSG	S	T
Notthitāḥ pātraṃ nirmādayiṣyāmaḥ	76			
Na nadyāhāryāhāriṇyām pratisrotaḥ pātreṇodakaṃ grahīṣyāmaḥ	78			
Notthito niṣaṇṇāyāglānāya dharmaṃ deśayiṣyāmaḥ	79	49	93	70
Na niṣaṇṇā nipannāyāglānāya dharmaṃ deśayiṣyāmaḥ	80	50	94	64
Na nīcatarake niṣaṇṇā uccatarake āsane niṣaṇṇāyāglānāya dharmaṃ deśayiṣyāmaḥ	81	51	92	69
Na pṛṣṭhato gacchantaḥ purato gacchate aglānāya dharmaṃ deśayiṣyāmaḥ	82	63	91	71
Notpathena gacchantaḥ pathena gacchate aglānāya dharmaṃ deśayiṣyāmaḥ	83	62	90	72
Nodguṇṭhikākṛtāyāglānāya dharmaṃ deśayiṣyāmaḥ	84	54	95	67
Notkṛṣṭikākṛtāyāglānāya dharmaṃ deśayiṣyāmaḥ	85		98	
Notsaktikākṛtāyāglānāya dharmaṃ deśayiṣyāmaḥ	86	56		
Na vyastikākṛtāyāglānāya dharmaṃ deśayiṣyāmaḥ	88	57	99	65
Na paryastikākṛtāyāglānāya dharmaṃ deśayiṣyāmaḥ	87			
Nosṇīṣaśirase dharmaṃ deśayiṣyāmaḥ	89			
Na kholāśirase dharmaṃ deśayiṣyāmaḥ	90			
Na mauliśirase dharmaṃ deśayiṣyāmaḥ	91			
Na veṣṭitaśirase dharmaṃ deśayiṣyāmaḥ	93	55	96	66
Na hastyārūḍhāya dharmaṃ deśayiṣyāmaḥ	94			
Nāśvārūḍhāya dharmaṃ deśayiṣyāmaḥ	95		89	
Na śivikārūḍhāya dharmaṃ deśayiṣyāmaḥ	96			
Na yānārūḍhāya dharmaṃ deśayiṣyāmaḥ	97	64		63

	MSV	MSG	S	T
Na pādukārūḍhāya dharmaṃ deśayiṣyāmaḥ	98	53	103	61
Na daṇḍapāṇaye dharmaṃ deśayiṣyāmaḥ	99	60	105	58
Na cchatrapāṇaye dharmaṃ deśayiṣyāmaḥ	100	61	106	57
Na śastrapāṇaye dharmaṃ deśayiṣyāmaḥ	101	58	107	59
Na khaḍgapāṇaye dharmaṃ deśayiṣyāmaḥ	102		108	
Nāyudhapāṇaye dharmaṃ deśayiṣyāmaḥ	103	59	109	60
Na saṃnaddhāya dharmaṃ deśayiṣyāmaḥ	104			
Nāglānā utthitā uccāraprasrāvaṃ kariṣyāmaḥ	105	67	112	73
Nāglānā udaka uccāraprasrāvaṃ kheṭaṃ siṅghāṇakaṃ vāntaṃ viriktaṃ dharmaṃ deśayiṣyāmaḥ	106	66	111	75
Nāglānāḥ saharitapṛthivīpradeśe uccāraprasrāvaṃ kheṭaṃ siṅghāṇakaṃ vāntaṃ viriktaṃ dharmaṃ deśayiṣyāmaḥ	107	65	110	74
Nasādhikapauruṣyaṃ vṛkṣam adhirokṣyāma anyatrāpada	108		113	

Adhikaraṇa-Śamatha Dharmas

Saṃmukhavinayaḥ	1	1	—	1
Smṛtivinayaḥ	2	2	—	2
Amūḍhavinayaḥ	3	3	5	3
Yadbhūyasikīyaḥ	4	6	—	5
Tatsvabhāvaiṣīyaḥ	5	5	—	6
Tṛṇaprastārakaḥ	6	7	—	7
Pratijñākārakaḥ	7	4	—	4

Notes

1 I have, on occasion, altered the numerical sequence of the *Mahāvyutpatti* to keep the pattern in line with the numbering of the Mūlasarvāstivādin text, because I felt that it would be advantageous to have one of the two texts translated in this study numbered consecutively, and since the Mūlasarvāstivādin text contained the greater number of rules, it was the logical choice. I could have simply presented a concordance which listed the rule numbers of the four texts referred to, thus avoiding any necessity of altering or, for that matter, using the *Mahāvyutpatti* at all, but it has long been my firm conviction that concordance tables which simply list numbers (without a key word or phrase) tell one little and require considerable leafing through the texts in question if they are to be at all useful. Ernst Waldschmidt seems to have been the first to utilize the *Mahāvyutpatti* in preparing Prātimokṣa concordance tables (in *Bruchstücke des Bhikṣuṇī-Prātimokṣa der Sarvāstivādins*), and the method was later used by Valentina Rosen in *Der Vinayavibhaṅga zum Bhikṣu Prātimokṣa der Sarvāstivādins* [*Sanskrittexte aus den Turfanfunden*, Vol. II (Berlin: Deutsche Akademie der Wissenschaften zu Berlin. Institut für Orientforschung, 1959)]. Professor Rosen's concordance refers to the Chinese translations of the Sarvāstivādin, Mūlasarvāstivādin, Mahīśāsaka, Mahāsāṃghika, and Dharmaguptaka Prātimokṣa Sūtras, as well as the Pāli, and by preparing my concordance table in accord with this method, cross-reference between the Sanskrit and Chinese texts should now be quite simple.

2 The *Mahāvyutpatti*, rahasi sthānaṃ, seems to contrast the previous rule (rahasi niṣadyā). However, the corresponding rule in the Theravādin, Sarvāstivādin, and Mahāsāṃghika texts reads precisely as the preceding rule with one exception: The monk is now enjoined not to perform this action with a woman [mātṛgrāma], whereas the previous rule was prescribed with reference to a nun [bhikṣuṇī]. The Mūlasarvāstivādin text does indeed employ an optative form of √sthā, but again it is laid down with reference to a woman rather than a nun.

3 This rule emphasizes that the monk is now, whether standing, sitting, or lying down, concealed amongst the family. The seeming contrast of the *Mahāvyutpatti* phrase with the previous rule thus disappears, especially when one considers that the essence of the previous rule is not that the monk is sitting down, but that he is intruding on the family.

4 Although Mahāsāṃghika rule 92 does find a place in the concordance, the reader should note that two Mahāsāṃghika rules (23 and 91) are excluded from this section of the *Mahāvyutpatti*, as all other versions, excepting the Theravādin, have only 90 rules in the Pāyantika section. Looking a bit farther down the list, one notes that in the Theravādin column rules 91 and 92 are present, but rules 23 and 82 are absent. It is interesting to note that the two Theravādin rules which are missing correspond to the two missing Mahāsāṃghika rules. The first rule relates to admonishing nuns, while the second refers to confiscating saṃgha property for another person.

5 Constructing a concordance table for the Śaikṣa section is considerably more difficult

than for the other sections of the texts, because this section provides significant differences both in the number of rules and their content among the various schools. Rosen's work, cited in note 1 above, does not even attempt a table. W. Pachow has some pertinent material in *A Comparative Study of the Prātimokṣa* (*Sino-Indian Studies*, Vol. IV, Part 2, pp. 69–79), but it deals mainly with the Chinese texts. Using the Mūlasarvāstivādin version as the main text, I have constructed a tentative table. However, some problems should be outlined. Three Mūlasarvāstivādin rules (47, 77, and 92) have no *Mahāvyutpatti* counterpart. Nine Mahāsāṃghika rules (8, 19, 23, 27, 28, 32, 37, 45, and 52) have no *Mahāvyutpatti* counterpart. Sixteen Sarvāstivādin rules (9–11, 16, 23–26, 29, 30, 64, 72, 74, 77, 84, and 87) are missing in Finot's edition. In addition, a great many others have been reconstructed. Another nineteen have no *Mahāvyutpatti* counterpart (3, 8, 15, 33, 34, 41–46, 61, 67, 75, 97, 100, 101, and 104). Seven Theravādin rules (35, 37, 42, 46, 54, 62, and 68) also have no counterpart. One last difficulty must be pointed out. Several pairs of rules occur in the Mahāsāṃghika, Sarvāstivādin, and Theravādin texts, the only difference being in the action verb. The *Mahāvyutpatti* makes no such distinction; and rather than omit the second of each pair, I have included each in parentheses, creating perhaps an artificial but useful distinction.

6 This may be an inappropriate placement, as I have translated the Mahāsāṃghika text as sūpa. However, I am aware of the possibility of the text of the rule being correct and the summary of the section in the Mahāsāṃghika text being faulty.

Bibliography

Books

Bagchi, S. (ed.). *Mūlasarvāstivādavinayavastu*. Volume I. Number 16 of *Buddhist Sanskrit Texts Series*. Darbhanga: The Mithila Institute of Post-Graduate Studies and Research in Sanskrit Learning, 1967.

Banerjee, Ankul Chandra (ed.). *Prātimokṣa-Sūtram* [*Mūlasarvāstivāda*]. Calcutta: Calcutta Oriental Press, 1954.

———. *Sarvāstivāda Literature*. Calcutta: D. Banerjee (Calcutta Oriental Press Private), 1957.

Bareau, André. *Les premiers conciles bouddhiques*. Paris: Presses Universitaires, 1955.

———. *Les Sectes Bouddhiques du Petit Véhicule*. Saigon: École Française d'Extrême-Orient, 1955.

———. *Recherches sur la biographie du Buddha dans les Sūtrapiṭaka et les Vinayapiṭaka anciens: de la quête du l'Éveil à la conversion de Śāriputra et de Maudgalyāyana*. Paris: École Française d'Extrême-Orient, 1963.

Beal, Samuel (trans.). *Catena of Buddhist Scriptures From the Chinese*. London: Trübner & Co., 1871.

Buddhaghosa. *Kaṅkhāvitaraṇī*. Edited by Dorothy Maskell. London: Luzac & Company, for P.T.S., 1956.

———. *Samantapāsādikā*. Edited by Junjirō Takakusu and Makoto Nagai. 7 vols. London: Luzac & Company, for P.T.S., 1924–1927.

———. *Samantapāsādikā*. Historical introduction translated as *Inception to Discipline* by N. A. Jayawickrama. London: Luzac & Company, for P.T.S., 1962.

———. *Visuddhimagga*. Edited by Henry Clarke Warren and revised by Dharmananda Kosambi. Cambridge, Mass.: Harvard University Press, 1950.

Chang, Kun (trans.). *A Comparative Study of the Kaṭhinavastu*. Volume I of *Indo-Iranian Monographs*. 'S-Gravenhage: Mouton & Co., 1957.

Childers, Robert Caesar. *A Dictionary of the Pāli Language*. 4th impression. London: Kegan Paul, Trench, Trübner & Co., 1909.

De, Gokuldas. *Democracy in Early Buddhist Saṃgha*. Calcutta: Calcutta University Press, 1955.

Dharmatrāta (compiler). *Udānavarga*. Edited by Franz Bernhard. Volume X of *Sanskrittexte aus den Turfanfunden*. Göttingen: Vandenhoeck & Ruprecht, 1965.

Dutt, Nalinaksha. *Aspects of Mahāyāna Buddhism and Its Relation to Hīnayāna*. London: Luzac & Company, 1930.

———. *Early Monastic Buddhism*. Calcutta: Calcutta Oriental Book Agency, 1960.

——— (ed.). Assisted by Vidyavaridhi Shiv Nath Sharma. *The Gilgit Manuscripts*. Volume III, Parts 1–4 (Vinayavastu). Calcutta: Calcutta Oriental Press, 1940–1950.

Dutt, Sukumar. *Buddhist Monks and Monasteries of India*. London: George Allen & Unwin, 1962.

———. *Early Buddhist Monachism*. Revised edition. Bombay: Asia Publishing House, 1960.

———. *The Buddha and Five After Centuries*. London: Luzac & Company, 1957.

Edgerton, Franklin. *Buddhist Hybrid Sanskrit Grammar and Dictionary*. 2 vols. New

Haven, Conn.: Yale University Press, 1953.

Frauwallner, Erich. *The Earliest Vinaya and the Beginnings of Buddhist Literature.* Volume VIII of *Serie Orientale Roma.* Rome: Instituto per il Medio ed Estremo Oriente, 1956.

Härtel, Herbert (ed. and trans.). *Karmavācanā.* Volume III of *Sanskrittexte aus den Turfanfunden.* Berlin: Deutsche Akademie der Wissenschaften zu Berlin. Institut für Orientforschung, 1956.

Hofinger, M. *Étude sur la concile de Vaiśālī.* Louvain: Bureaux du Muséon, 1946.

Horner, I. B. (trans.). *The Book of the Discipline.* 6 vols. London: Luzac & Company, for P.T.S., 1938–1966.

Jinananda, B. (ed.). *Upasaṃpadājñaptiḥ.* Volume VI of *Tibetan Sanskrit Works Series.* Patna: Kashi Prasad Jayaswal Research Institute, 1961.

Jones, J. J. (trans.). *The Mahāvastu. Translated from the Buddhist Sanskrit.* 3 vols. London: Luzac & Company, 1949–1956.

Lamotte, Étienne. *Histoire du Bouddhisme Indien des origines à l'ère Śaka.* Louvain: Publications Universitaires, 1958.

Lévi, Sylvain, Takakusu, Junjirō, and Demiéville, Paul (eds.). *Hōbōgirin Fascicule Annexe* [*Tables du Taishō Issaikyō*]. Tokyō: Maison Franco-Japonaise, 1931.

Lin, Li-kouang. *L'Aide Mémoire De La Vraie Loi.* Paris: Adrien-Maisonneuve, 1949.

Macdonell, Arthur Anthony. *A Practical Sanskrit Dictionary.* Reissue. Oxford: Oxford University Press, 1958.

———. *A Sanskrit Grammar for Students.* Reprint of 3rd edition. Oxford: Oxford University Press, 1962.

Malalasekera, G. P. *Dictionary of Pāli Proper Names.* 2 vols. London: John Murray, 1937–1938.

———. *The Pāli Literature of Ceylon.* Reprint. Colombo: M. D. Gunasena & Co., 1958.

Minayeff, Ivan Pavlovitch (ed. and trans.). *Prātimokṣa Sūtra.* St. Petersburg, 1869.

Misra, G. S. P. *The Age of Vinaya.* New Delhi: Munshiram Manoharlal, 1972.

Monier-Williams, Monier. *A Sanskrit-English Dictionary.* Reprint of new edition in collaboration with E. Leumann, C. Cappeller, and others. Oxford: The Clarendon Press, 1964.

Ñāṇamoli Thera (ed. and trans.). *The Pāṭimokkha.* Bangkok: The Social Science Association of Thailand, 1966.

Nanjio, Bunyio. *A Catalogue of the Chinese Translation of the Buddhist Tripiṭaka, the Sacred Canon of the Buddhists in China and Japan.* Oxford: The Clarendon Press, 1883.

Nārada Thera (ed. and trans.). *Dhammapada.* Colombo: Vajirārāma, 1963.

Oldenberg, Hermann (ed.). *The Vinaya Piṭakaṃ.* 5 vols. Reprint. London: Luzac & Company, for P.T.S., 1964.

Pachow, W. *A Comparative Study of the Prātimokṣa.* In *Sino-Indian Studies*, Volume IV, Parts 1–4 and Volume V, Part 1, 1951–1955.

Pischel, R. *Comparative Grammar of the Prākṛit Languages.* 2nd edition. Translated from the German by Subhadra Jhā. Delhi: Motilal Banarsidass, 1965.

Prebish, Charles S. A Survey of Vinaya Literature. Unpublished monograph.

Przyluski, Jean. *Le Concile de Rājagṛha.* Paris: Paul Geuthner, 1926–1928.

Renou, Louis and Filliozat, Jean. *L'Inde Classique.* Tome II. Paris: Imprimerie Nationale, 1953.

Rhys Davids, Thomas W. (trans.). *Buddhist Birth Stories*. London: G. Routledge & Sons, 1925.

Rhys Davids, Thomas W. and Oldenberg, Hermann (trans.). *Vinaya Texts*. 3 vols. Volumes XIII, XVII, and XX of *Sacred Books of the East*. Reprint. Delhi: Motilal Banarsidass, 1965.

Rhys Davids, Thomas W. and Stede, William (eds.). *The Pali Text Society's Pali-English Dictionary*. Reprint. London: Luzac & Company, for P.T.S., 1966.

Rockhill, W. Woodville (trans.). *The Life of the Buddha and the Early History of His Order*. Boston: J.R. Osgood & Co., 1885.

Rosen, Valentina (ed. and trans.). *Der Vinayavibhaṅga zum Bhikṣu Prātimokṣa der Sarvāstivādins*. Volume II of *Sanskrittexte aus den Turfanfunden*. Berlin: Deutsche Akademie der Wissenschaften zu Berlin. Institut für Orientforschung, 1959.

Sakaki, Ryōzaburō (ed.). *Mahāvyutpatti*. 2 vols. Kyōto: Shingonshū Kyōto Daigaku, 1925.

Sanghasena (ed.). *Sphuṭārthā Śrīghanācārasaṃgrahaṭīkā*. Volume XI of *Tibetan Sanskrit Works Series*. Patna: Kashi Prasad Jayaswal Research Institute, 1968.

Takakusu, Junjirō and Watanabe, Kaikyoku (eds.). *Taishō Shinshū Daizōkyō*. 100 vols. Tokyo: Daizō Shuppan Company, 1924–1934.

Thomas, Edward J. *The History of Buddhist Thought*. Reprint of 2nd edition. London: Routledge & Kegan Paul, 1963.

———. *The Life of the Buddha as Legend and History*. 3rd edition, revised. London: Routledge & Kegan Paul, 1960.

Vaidya, P. L. (ed.). *Divyāvadāna*. Number 20 of *Buddhist Sanskrit Texts Series*. Darbhanga: The Mithila Institute of Post-Graduate Studies and Research in Sanskrit Learning, 1959.

Waldschmidt, Ernst (ed. and trans.). *Bruchstücke des Bhikṣuṇī-Prātimokṣa der Sarvāstivādins*. Volume III of *Kleinere Sanskrittexte*. Leipzig: Deutsche Morgenländischen Gesellschaft in Kommission bei F. A. Brockhaus, 1926.

Whitney, William Dwight. *Sanskrit Grammar*. 10th issue of 2nd edition. Cambridge, Mass.: Harvard University Press, 1964.

———. *The Roots, Verb-Forms, and Primary Derivatives of the Sanskrit Language*. Reprint. New Haven: American Oriental Society, 1945.

Wieger, Léon. *Bouddhisme Chinois*. Volume I. Reprint. Paris: Cathasia, 1951.

Winternitz, Moriz. *A History of Indian Literature*. 2 vols. Translated into English by Mrs. S. Ketkar (Volume I) and Miss H. Kohn (Volume II), and revised by the author. Calcutta: University of Calcutta, 1927–1933.

Articles

Banerjee, Ankul Chandra (ed.). "Bhikṣukarmavākya." *Indian Historical Quarterly*, XXV, 1 (March 1949), 19–30.

Bareau, André. "La Construction et le Culte des Stūpa d'après les Vinayapiṭaka." *Bulletin De L'École Française D'Extrême-Orient*, L, 2 (1962), 229–274.

Bechert, Heinz. Review of Kun Chang: *A Comparative Study of the Kaṭhinavastu. Zeitschrift der deutschen morgenländischen Gesellschaft*, 110 (1960–1961), 203–205.

———. "Some Remarks on the Kaṭhina Rite." *Journal of the Bihar Research Society*, LII, 1–4 (January-December, 1966), 29–51.

Chandra, Lokesh (ed.). "Unpublished Gilgit Fragment of the Prātimokṣa-Sūtra." *Wiener Zeitschrift für die Kunde Süd- und Ostasiens*, IV (1960), 1–13.

Chang, Kun. Review of Pachow: *A Comparative Study of the Prātimokṣa. Journal of the American Oriental Society*, 80 (1960), 71–77.

Csoma De Körösi, Alexander. "Analysis of the Dulva [Vinaya]." *Asiatic Researches*, XX (1836).

Demiéville, Paul. "À propos du concile de Vaiśālī." *T'oung Pao*, XL (1951), 239–296.

———. "L'origine des sectes bouddhiques d'après Paramārtha." *Mélanges Chinois et Bouddhiques*, I (1931–1932), 15–64.

Dickson, J. F. (ed. and trans.). "The Pātimokkha, being the Buddhist Office of the Confession of Priests. The Pali Text, with a Translation and Notes." *Journal of the Royal Asiatic Society*, New Series, VIII (1876), 62–130.

———. "The Upasampadā-Kammavācā, being the Buddhist Manual of the Form and Manner of Ordering Priests and Deacons. The Pali Text, with a Translation and Notes." *Journal of the Royal Asiatic Society*, New Series, VII (1875), 1–16.

Dutt, Nalinaksha (ed.). "Bodhisattva Prātimokṣa Sūtra." *Indian Historical Quarterly*, VII, 2 (June 1931), 259–286.

———. "Gilgit Ms. of the Vinaya Piṭaka." *Indian Historical Quarterly*, XIV, 2 (June 1938), 408–424.

———. "The Second Buddhist Council." *Indian Historical Quarterly*, XXXV, 1 (March 1959), 45–56.

Filliozat, Jean and Kuno, Hōryū (eds.). "Fragments du Vinaya des Sarvāstivādin." *Journal Asiatique*, CCXXX (Janvier-Mars, 1938), 21–64.

Finot, Louis (ed.). "Fragments du Vinaya sanskrit." *Journal Asiatique*, Série X, XVIII (Novembre-Décembre, 1911), 619–625.

——— (ed.). "Le Prātimokṣasūtra des Sarvāstivādins." Texte Sanskrit par L. Finot, avec la version chinoise de Kumārajīva traduité en français par Edouard Huber. *Journal Asiatique*, Série XI, II (Novembre-Décembre, 1913), 465–557.

———. "Mahāparinibbāna-sutta and Cullavagga." *Indian Historical Quarterly*, VIII, 2 (June 1932), 241–246.

Franke, R. Otto. "Die Gāthās des Vinayapiṭaka und ihre Parallelen." *Wiener Zeitschrift für die Kunde des Morgenlandes*, XXIV (1910), 1–32, 225–280.

———. "The Buddhist Councils at Rājagaha and Vesālī as Alleged in Cullavagga XI., XII." *Journal of the Pali Text Society*, 1908, 1–80.

Frauwallner, Erich. "Die buddhistischen Konzile." *Zeitschrift der deutschen morgenländischen Gesellschaft*, 102 (1952), 240–261.

Horner, I. B. "The Pattern of the Nissaggiyas." *Indian Historical Quarterly*, XVI, 2 (June 1940), 268–291.

Jaworski, Jan. "La section de la Nourriture dans le Vinaya des Mahīśāsaka." *Rocznik Orientalistyczny*, VII (1931), 53–124.

———. "La section de l'Ordination dans le Vinaya des Mūlasarvāstivādin." *Compte Rendus des Séances de la Societe des Sciences et des Lettres de Varsovie*, XXIII, 1 (1931), 1–48.

———. "La section des Remedes dans le Vinaya des Mahīśāsaka et dans le Vinaya pāli." *Rocznik Orientalistyczny*, V (1927), 92–101.

Lamotte, Etienne. "Adirājya et Bhadrāśva dans le Vinaya des Mūlasarvāstivādins." *Bulletin De L'École Française D'Extrême-Orient*, XLIV, 1 (1947–1950), 152–158.

———. "La légende du Buddha." *Revue de l'Histoire des Religions*, CXXXIV (1948), 37–71.

La Vallée Poussin, Louis de. "Essai d'identification des Gāthas et des Udānas en prose de l'Udānavarga de Dharmatrāta." *Journal Asiatique*, Série X, XIX (Mars-Avril, 1912), 311–330.

———(ed.). "Nouveaux Fragments de la Collection Stein. I. Fragments de Tunhuang, 2. Fragment d'un Kammavācaṃ." *Journal of the Royal Asiatic Society*, 1913.

———(ed.). "Nouveaux Fragments de la Collection Stein. I. Fragments de Tunhuang, 3. Fragment d'un śikṣās." *Journal of the Royal Asiatic Society*, 1913.

———. "Opinions sur les relations des deux véhicules au point de vue du Vinaya." *Académie Royale de Belgique de la Classe des Lettres et des Sciences morales et politiques*, Série V, XVI, 1–2 (1930), 20–39.

———. "The Buddhist Councils." *Indian Antiquary*, XXXVII (1908), 1–18, 81–106. Also published in *Le Muséon*, VI (1905), 213–323.

La Vallée Poussin, Louis de and Ridding, C. M. (eds.) "A Fragment of the Sanskrit Vinaya. Bhikṣuṇī-karmavācanā." *Bulletin of the School of Oriental and African Studies*, I, 3 (1920), 123–143.

Lévi, Sylvain. "Note sur des manuscrits provenant de Bamiyan [Afghanistan] et de Gilgit [Cachemire]." *Journal Asiatique*, CCXX (Janvier-Mars, 1932), 1–45.

———. "Observations sur une langue précanonique du Bouddhisme." *Journal Asiatique*, Série X, XX (Novembre-Décembre, 1912), 495–514

———. "Sur la récitation primitive des textes bouddhiques." *Journal Asiatique*, Série XI, V (Janvier-Février, 1915), 401–447.

———(ed.). "Tokharian Prātimokṣa Fragment." *Journal of the Royal Asiatic Society*, 1913, 109–120.

———(ed.). "Un fragment tokharian du Vinaya des Sarvāstivādins." *Journal Asiatique*, Série X, XIX (Janvier-Février, 1912), 101–111.

Müller, Edward (ed.). "Khuddasikkhā and Mūlasikkhā." *Journal of the Pali Text Society*, 1883, 86–132.

Nagai, Makoto. "Buddhist Vinaya Discipline or Buddhist Commandments." In B. C. Law (ed.), *Buddhistic Studies*. Calcutta: Thacker & Spink, 1913.

Pachow, W. (trans.). "Translation of the Introductory Section of the Text [Mahāsāṃghika Prātimokṣa Sūtra]." *Journal of the Gaṅgānāth Jhā Research Institute*, XI–XII, 1–4 (November-February-May-August, 1953–1955), 243–248.

Pachow, W. and Mishra, Ramakanta. "The Prātimokṣa Sūtra of the Mahāsāṃghikas."

Journal of the Gaṅgānāth Jhā Research Institute, IX, 2–4 (February-May-August, 1952), 239–260.

———(eds.). "The Prātimokṣa Sūtra of the Mahāsāṃghikas." *Journal of the Gaṅgānāth Jhā Research Institute*, X, 1–4 (November-February-May-August, 1952–1953), Appendix 1–48.

Prebish, Charles S. "A Review of Scholarship on the Buddhist Councils." *The Journal of Asian Studies*, XXXIII, 2 (February 1974), 239–254.

———. "The Prātimokṣa Puzzle: Fact Versus Fantasy." *Journal of the American Oriental Society*, 94, 2 (April-June, 1974), 168–176.

———. "Theories Concerning the Skandhaka: An Appraisal." *The Journal of Asian Studies*, XXXII, 4 (August 1973), 669–678.

Przyluski, Jean. "Fables in the Vinaya-Piṭaka of the Sarvāstivādin School." *Indian Historical Quarterly*, V, 1 (March 1929), 1–5.

———. "Le nord-ouest de l'Inde dans le Vinaya des Mūlasarvāstivādins et les textes apparentés." *Journal Asiatique*, Série XI, IV (Novembre-Décembre, 1914), 493–568.

———. "Le Parinirvāṇa et les Funérailles du Buddha." *Journal Asiatique*, Série XI, XI (Mai-Juin, 1918), 485–526; Série XI, XII (Novembre-Décembre, 1918), 401–456; Série XI, XIII (Mai-Juin, 1919), 365–430; Série XI, XV (Janvier-Mars, 1920), 5–54.

Rockhill, W. Woodville (trans.). "Le Traité D'Émancipation ou Pratimoksha Sutra." Traduit du Tibétain par M. Woodville Rockhill. *Revue de l'Histoire des Religions*, IX, 1–2 (1884), 3–26, 167–201.

Roth, Gustav. "Bhikṣuṇīvinaya and Bhikṣu-Prakīrṇaka and Notes on the Language." *Journal of the Bihar Research Society*, LII, 1–4 (January-December, 1966), 29–51.

———. "Terminologisches aus dem Vinaya der Mahāsāṃghika-Lokottaravādin." *Zeitschrift der deutschen morgenländischen Gesellschaft*, 118 (1968), 334–348.

Sāṅkṛtyāyana, Rāhula. "Sanskrit Palm-Leaf Mss. in Tibet." *Journal of the Bihar and Orissa Research Society*, XXI (1935), 21–43.

Schlingloff, Dieter. "Zur Interpretation des Prātimokṣasūtra." *Zeitschrift der deutschen morgenländischen Gesellschaft*, 113 (1963), 536–551.

Takakusu, Junjirō. "Buddhaghosa's Samantapāsādikā in Chinese." *Journal of the Royal Asiatic Society*, New Series, XXIX (1897), 113–114.

———. "Pāli Elements in Chinese Buddhism. A translation of Buddhaghosa's Samantapāsādikā, a commentary, on the Vinaya, found in the Chinese Tripiṭaka." *Journal of the Royal Asiatic Society*, New Series, XXVIII (1896), 415–439.

Thomas, Edward J. "Pre-Pāli Terms in the Pātimokkha." In *Festschrift Moriz Winternitz*. Leipzig: Otto Harrassowitz, 1933.

Vidyabhusana, Satis Chandra (ed. and trans.). "So-sor-thar-pa; or, a Code of Buddhist Monastic Laws: Being the Tibetan version of the Prātimokṣa of the Mūla-sarvāstivāda School." *Journal of the Asiatic Society of Bengal*, New Series, IX, 3–4 (1915), 29–139.

Waldschmidt, Ernst. "Reste von Devadatta-Episoden aus dem Vinaya der Sarvāstivādins." *Zeitschrift der deutschen morgenländischen Gesellschaft*, 113 (1963), 552–558.